The Bonobo Way
The Evolution of Peace through Pleasure

*An Alternative Great Ape Paradigm
for Human Sexuality*

The 12 Steps to Releasing Your Inner Bonobo

Susan M. Block, Ph.D.

The Bonobo Way

Copyright © 2014 by Susan M. Block, Ph.D.

All rights reserved. No part of this publication may be reproduced, distributed or transmitted in any form or by any means, including digital, photocopying, recording, or other electronic or mechanical methods, without the prior written permission of the publisher, except in the case of brief quotations embodied in critical reviews and certain other noncommercial uses permitted by copyright law. Inquiries should be addressed to:

Gardner & Daughters, Publishers
8306 Wilshire Boulevard
Suite 1047
Beverly Hills, CA 90211
(310) 568-0066
http://drsusanblockinstitute.com
bonoboville.com

Cover design by Maximillian Lobkowicz

Ordering Information:
Quantity sales. Special discounts are available on quantity purchases by corporations, associations, libraries and others. For details, contact the publisher at the address above.

Printed in the United States

Trade Paper ISBN: 978-0-692-32376-2

Dr. Susan Block

For Pr. Chim & Pr. Max

Table of Contents

Prologue	1
PART I: Meet the Bonobos	
Chapter 1: Our Long-Lost Kissing Cousins	
Finding My Prime Mate	4
The Nature of Sex… and Love	5
Chapter 2: Meetings with Remarkable Apes	
The Chivers Effect	8
AOL Censors Bonobos	9
Noble and Kinky	10
Chapter 3: Welcome to Bonoboville	
Aristocratic Apes	12
Jamming with Kanzi	12
The Bonobo Funnies	14
Chapter 4: Bonobo Sexualis	
The Bonobo Sutra	17
Love Hormone Highs	17
Chapter 5: Erotic Politics and Bonobo Economics	
Bonobo Handshakes & Human Testimony	20
Bonobo Sex Therapy	21
Bonobo Gals Pick Up the Check	22
Chapter 6: Peace through Pleasure	
Resolving Conflict with Sex 24	
Common Chimps Sometimes Kill Each Other	25
No Bonobo Murders or Wars	25
Chapter 7: The Bonobo Mystique	
Anatomist Tiffs & African Wars	27
Sex Makes You Smarter	29
Hollywood Defames Bonobos	29

Chapter 8: Food, Sex & Culture
   Bonobos vs. Chimps:
     Organic Buffet vs. Bullet-Riddled McDonald's   32
   Baboons Go Bonobos   34

Chapter 9: Hot Bi Girls & Sweet Mama's Boys
   Bonobo Sisterhood   37
   Bonobo Boyishness & the Fountain of Youth   38
   MILFs Rule Bonoboville   40

Chapter 10: Hoka-Hoka: The Bonobo Tango
   Hoka-Hoka Lubricates Life   43
   "Bonobo-Bashing in the New Yorker"   43

Chapter 11: Sperm Wars: The Super Bowl of Sex
   Bonobos Have Balls   46
   Sperm Competition Illuminates "The Lifestyle"   47
   Make Sperm Wars, Not Real Wars!   48

Chapter 12: The Kiss
   A Thunderclap of Bonobo-Human Connection   51
   A Profound Interspecies Event (PIE)   52

Chapter 13: An Alternative Great Ape Paradigm for Humanity
   Is War Wired Into Our Genes?   55
   Are We Killer Apes?   56
   Being "Humane" Is Actually Very Bonobo   58

Chapter 14: 50 Shades of Bonobo
   My King Kong   60
   Are You In a State of Anthropodenial?   61
   Humans Swing Too   62
   Are Women More Monogamous Than Men?   64
   Polyamory & Designer Relationships   65
   Bisexuality Keeps the Peace in Bonoboville   66
   Tantra & The Tao of Bonobo   67
   Bonobo BDSM   68
   Human Perversion or Sexual Diversity?   69
   My Monogamish Boho-Bonobo Marriage   70
   Bonobos Are Single But with Lots of Company   71

Chapter 15: Release Your Inner Bonobo

    The Bonobo Liberation Challenge   74
    The Unexpected Aphrodisiac of Shame   75
    Go Bonobos!   75
    Real 40-Year Old Virgin Gets Laid & Finds Love (In That Order)   76
    Human Bonobovilles Must Be Adults Only   79
    "Bonobos Hold the Key to a World without War"   80

PART II: The 12 Steps to Releasing Your Inner Bonobo

    A Different Kind of "12-Step Program"   82

Step 1: See the Bonobos.

    Seeing Bonobos May Arouse Deep Feelings   86
    What If Watching Bonobo Sex Creeps You Out?   87
    Relax, Reboot, Press PLAY   87
    Play at Work   88

Step 2: Be a Bonobo.

    Breathe in a Rainbow   89
    Have You Forgotten How to Play?   91
    Erotic Theater of the Mind   92
    Bonobo Medibation   94
    Rape & Other Disturbing Fantasies   95
    Puritans, Like Poachers, Shoot to Kill Your Inner Bonobo   96

Step 3: Go Bonobos in Bed.

    Unleash the Erotic Animal Within   99
    Romp & Wrestle or Cuddle & Groom   100
    The Ideal is The Enemy of The Real   102
    Empathize as You Fantasize   103
    "She's Everything I Want! What's Wrong with Me?"   104

Step 4: Outercourse Is In

    Eroplay, Chero & the Art of the Tease   109
    Trust Kills Lust   110
    Can a Chimp Be a "Porn Addict"?   111
    The Power to Give Pleasure   113

Step 5: Mix Food and Sex.

    Why Are We So Emo About Eating?   115

The Oral Sex Diet	116
Don't Let the Kids Eat Up Your Holidays	117
The Bonobo Rainforest Diet	118
Bonoboville Communion	119
Prozac, Sex and Love	120

Step 6: Explore the "Opposite" Sex Within You.

The Sexes Aren't Really "Opposite"	122
Bonobo Boys Aren't Brutes & the Gals Aren't Pushovers	123

LADIES:

Sexual Tupperware & the Plastic Fantastic Female	125
Take a Bonobo Moment	127
Kegel Yoga to Holy Water	128
What Makes You Thrive?	130
Do the Hoka-Hoka	131

GENTLEMEN:

Did You Marry the Wrong Woman?	133
Does Your Soft Side Make You Hard?	134
Male Backlash & Female Whiplash	135
Mama Mia	137
Nice Guys Sometimes Win	138

Step 7: Make Peace through Pleasure.

Bonobo Alchemy: Turn Anger into Desire	140
Too Angry For Sex	141
Anger Management, Bonobo Style	143
Can Jealousy Be an Aphrodisiac?	146
The Shape of Things to Cum	148
Why Men Love "Sluts"	149
Jealousy Edgeplay	150

Step 8: Practice Ethical Hedonism.

Pleasure Is the Root of All Good	153
You Can Have Your Sex & Eat It Too	155
Were America's Founding Fathers Ethical Hedonists?	156
The Power of Negative Thinking	157
What Does "Ethical Hedonism" Mean to You?	158
Ethical BDSM	159

    Eco-Sexual Ethics   160
    The Best Laid Plans May Not Get You
        Laid the Way You Planned   161

Step 9: Be Bonobo Friendly.
    Falling in Love Makes You Go Bonobos Without Even Trying!   164
    Maximize Your Erotic Capital   165
    How About a Friendly Game of Stranger?   167
    Casual Hookups & Friends-with-Benefits   168
    Social Media "Friends"   168
    "I Was Just Being Bonobo-Friendly, Your Honor"   170

Step 10: Create Your Own Bonoboville.
    Time for a Different Party!   171
    "Saturday Night Group Therapy"   172
    No Couple is an Island   174
    Party Like a Bonobo   175
    Revolutionary Bonobovilles from Iran to LA   176
    Witness & Be Witnessed   179
    Porn Star Bonobovilles   180
    Beware of False Bonobovilles!   182
    Stealth, Science & Love Songs of Bonoboville   183
    Love the Earth You Make Love On   185

Step 11: Swing through Life.
    The World is Our Real Estate   186
    Hot Date: Bridge-Climbing with the Suicide Club   188
    Sex Heals a Billion Times More Than It Kills   190
    My NDE & the Blowjob from Hell   191
    "Do Not Put Anything in Your Vagina"   193
    Bonobo Yoga Gets You Ready to Swing   195

Step 12: Save the Bonobos, Save the World.
    "Heart of Darkness"   197
    BCI & the Bonobo Peace Forest   198
    Claudine André: Saint Joan of the Bonobos   200
    If We Lose the Bonobos, We Lose Part of Ourselves   202
    A Cause That's Right and Sexy   205
    Help the Bonobos & They Will Reciprocate   206

Epilogue: Go Forth and Go Bonobos	207
Appendix A:	
Where You Can Help	208
Appendix B:	
Where You Can See Bonobos around the World	210
Acronyms & Abbreviations	212
Bibliography	214
Acknowledgements	230
About the Author	233

The Bonobo Way

Prologue

Lana is a voluptuous brunette with a seductive smile and big, sparkling, cocoa eyes. Flirtatious and fun-loving, she has a couple of boyfriends, but enjoys her gal pals just as much, if not more. Though she loves to party and play practical jokes, she's a conscientious mom and respected leader in her community. Gentle yet assertive, she can be fierce when crossed, but she's also quick to forgive, turning hostility into harmony with remarkable empathy and a playful flair. In many ways, she's just like a lot of wonderful women we all know. But Lana is not a woman, nor even human. Lana is a bonobo.

PART I
Meet the Bonobos

Chapter 1: Our Long-Lost Kissing Cousins

"We are here to awaken from our illusions of separateness."
— Thich Nhat Hanh, Zen Peace Activist

Deep in the heart of the hot, wet African rainforest, there lives a tribe of peacemakers who share a multiplicity of pleasures and make a very special kind of love. South of the sprawling Congo River, in the midst of war-ravaged territory, some 2,000 miles from the arid Ethiopian desert where the oldest human fossils have been found, lies this lush and steamy jungle paradise, the only natural habitat of the bonobo.

If you don't know bonobos from bananas, please allow me to introduce you to the long-lost kissing cousins you never knew you had. Meet the bonobos, the rare and marvelous "make love not war" great apes who swing through the trees as well as with each other. Get ready to have your heart stolen, your fancy tickled, your spirit charged and your mind blown by this very special, newly discovered branch of your hominid family tree.

If you're already a fellow bonobo lover, welcome! You probably know that bonobos are very sexual and share close to 99% of our genes, but have you heard how they use sex to prevent murder and war? Do you know why the females are able to gently but firmly rule the roost in "Bonoboville," keeping the males gentle and firm?

You may have learned that bonobos are highly endangered, but are you aware of the ecologically innovative steps now being taken to save our randy relatives from extinction? Do you know what recent bonobo studies reveal about the nature of lust, trust, arousal, orgasm, cooperation, compassion, morality, dominance, submission, being human, and even being humane? *Just what do these great apes know about sex—and the rest of life—that we don't?* Might bonobos provide an exciting new primate paradigm that could help make the world a more peaceful, egalitarian, sustainable—and sexier—place for all of us?

Which brings me to us, and more specifically, to you. Is your "inner bonobo" yearning to swing free? Would you like to tap into the hot, natural, sexual, *bonoboësque* energy flowing through your veins right now so you can better relish the pleasures of life, cope with the pain, win friends, influence people, be all you can be, and possibly revolutionize society—or at the very least, improve your love life?

Then grab a swinging vine, release your preconceptions, and come with me...

Why me? I'm not a primatologist, anthropologist or apologist. I happen to be a sexologist—a love searcher, sex researcher and therapist with a couple of doctorates under my garter belt and a *magna cum laude* bachelor's in theater studies. You may wonder what the study of theater has to do with bonobos. All I can say is that I thought it was the sexiest major on Yale's curriculum because it was the only one that gave me credit for kissing a classmate. As an undergrad, I felt a powerful thirst for knowledge, carnal and scholastic, and theater was my drink of choice. Looking back, I see now that it set the stage for my current work in erotic theater therapy, sexual psychodrama, and bonobo liberation therapy, a.k.a. BLT (far more delicious than the sandwich and a lot less fattening).

I had considered majoring in anthropology, perhaps a more appropriate field for a future bonobo buff. But none of my old anthro professors said a word about bonobos. They taught us that humanity's closest relatives were murderous, male-dominant, warrior chimpanzees, and that our social systems most closely resembled those of the even more vicious savanna baboons. Though I enjoyed *Planet of the Apes*, anthropology was too depressing to pursue for a peace-loving, feminist, romantic hedonist like me.

Little did I realize that several decades before, Yale might have been home to America's first bonobo-in-residence, Prince Chim.[1] No one knew it at the time, because no one knew what a bonobo was back in 1924. But this ape's charisma, loving disposition and keen sensitivity relative to other "common" chimpanzees was unmistakable. Observing in *Almost Human* that he was "a prince of his kind," his human patron, Dr. Robert Yerkes, seems to have been quite taken with the charming Prince Chim.

Finding My Prime Mate

Like my prehistoric hunter-gatherer ancestors, I hit the road fairly often in my footloose youth. From Yale's Dramat to Afghanistan's Bamiyan

---

[1] According to pioneering Japanese primatologist Takayoshi Kanō's book, *The Last Ape*, "Prince Chim (was) raised at Yale University from 1923 to 1924." Other sources, including the Yerkes Laboratory, say that Yerkes didn't start his primate lab at Yale until 1925, and Prince Chim died in Cuba the year before. Whatever the truth is, he was definitely the first bonobo-in-residence in the Western Hemisphere.

Buddhas, from the tantric ashrams of Kathmandu to the libertine scenes of the *Côte D'Azur* and deep down into the dungeons of New York's aptly named meat-packing district, I searched and researched sex, love and the politics of pleasure (mostly among humans), until balmy Southern California seduced me into settling down. There, I started a private sex therapy practice that has grown into an institute, counseling men, women and gender-nonconforming individuals, married and unmarried couples, polyamorous trouples, families and communities around the world.

All of that searching and researching climaxed when I met my favorite research subject, who turned into my primary research partner and "prime mate," my charming Prince Max. Unlike so many sex researchers who fall in and out of love (with their research as well as each other), we're still researching, still married and, almost three decades later, more in love than ever thanks to a little bit of luck and the Bonobo Way.

As part of the research, and just for fun, we broadcast a live weekly show from the studio at our own little "Bonoboville," with various offshoots, including a handful of HBO specials. We call our studio the "Speakeasy" on Saturday nights because we try to "speak easy" about things that aren't so easy to speak about—like our personal sexual feelings, fears and fantasies—with professors, porn stars, authors, animal trainers, singers, swingers, masked celebrities, lapsed clergy, artists, exhibitionists, voyeurs and connoisseurs, as well as some of the more adventurous couples we counsel. We are "therapists without borders," and we do "radio without boundaries." Sometimes our shows turn into orgies that have become legendary, or as my cousin Elliot has said, "Scandalous."

What can I say, Cuz? That's how it goes with sex research sometimes. And that's how it goes with love.

The Nature of Sex... **and Love**

My first glimpse of bonobos was through a 1993 PBS mini-series entitled, *The Nature of Sex*. It was a telecommunications sexual revelation... for me, anyway. Keep in mind that this was six years before the Bloodhound Gang would sing about doing it "like they do on the Discovery Channel." Seeing close-up footage of any kind of animal sex was quite enthralling for a budding sex researcher who also happened to be a first-time wife. It was almost two years into our conjugal adventure, and I was just starting to wonder how my handsome new husband and I were supposed to keep our post-honeymoon sex life from sliding into the dark sinkhole of monogamous monotony that had swallowed up the marriages of so many of our friends, family and clients, not to mention all of our own previous relationships. How could a free spirit stay free… and married?

The Nature of Sex opened up an escape hatch above the sinkhole and into the wild. At least, that's how I felt about it, though I wasn't sure why. I know what you're thinking, but no, seeing animals have sex didn't make me want to have sex with animals! But I loved watching them "do it" like we do it and, usually after an hour or so, I was feeling pretty amorous for my own kind. Every night the series aired, rutting donkeys, whooping monkeys, trumpeting elephants and screaming peacocks bonked through my brain as Max and I made hot, newly wedded love, our bodies moving to the pounding beat of biological drums, our orgasms expanding like vibrating tentacles, fingers, feet, paws or wildly beating wings, connecting us with our fellow mammals, as well as birds, reptiles, amphibians, insects and all living, breathing, copulating life on Earth.

I loved the zebras, the cheetahs, the fruit flies, the octopi and the rest. But *The Nature of Sex* "climaxed" with a species I'd never heard of before, "bonobos," which the narrator also called by their Latin/scientific name *Pan paniscus*. I knew "Pan" as classical Greek mythology's horned and horny god of the wild, so maybe I shouldn't have been surprised. But when the bonobos started swinging onto my screen, well… what can I say? Today, I've got a whole book's worth of stuff to say, but back then, I couldn't utter a word. Imagine looking into an evolutionary funhouse mirror and seeing a side of yourself you've never seen before, shocking yet deeply familiar.

"Who are these vibrant, joyful creatures that look so much like me, only hairier?" I wondered. "And what's with all the sex?" They weren't just going at it for procreation. They were engaging in sex for recreation and interpersonal communication, very much like humans, but without the pretense, hypocrisy and shame. I got very excited, but no, I still didn't want to have sex *with* them. I wanted to have sex *like* them (at least occasionally), in that playful yet deeply meaningful way of theirs I started calling the Bonobo Way.

But would it keep our sex life out of the dreaded sinkhole? Only time would tell.

Dr. Susan Block

Chapter 2: Meetings with Remarkable Apes

"I ask you to believe nothing that you cannot verify for yourself."
— G. I. Gurdjieff, *Meetings with Remarkable Men*

When I first met Lana, she was a randy teenager, and I was a horny housewife a couple years into attempting to follow the Bonobo Way, though I still hadn't encountered a bonobo in real life. Now here I was looking at three of them actively engaged in what we might call foreplay, seemingly oblivious to me and the other gawking humans behind the shatterproof glass surrounding their verdant abode.

Not that I expected any acknowledgment, I was thrilled just to see them. *There they were!* And they were going at it just like on *The Nature of Sex*, except this wasn't some faraway rainforest on my boob tube. This was the San Diego Zoo and they were doing it right in front of me and a bunch of other people! I squinted through the big window, a portal to another world, trying to get a better view of the primal love scene before us. All I could see was a mass of wriggling fur and finger-like toes until my eyes focused in on one male and two females kissing, ear-tonguing and giving each other enthusiastic oral sex, punctuated with occasional somersaults, smacks and nibbles on fruit and leaves. Sometimes they interacted as a threesome. Other times, two would cavort together, while the third played with herself, alternating between fingering and using a red rubber ball as a kind of sex toy, rubbing and bouncing it vigorously against her large pink vulva.

I watched, transfixed. I'd participated in some threesomes myself, as well as public group sex scenes on and off the air, but this casual yet passionate pansexuality[2] in the middle of a family zoo literally bowled me over. I took a step back, stumbled, and, not being as agile as a bonobo myself, practically fell on the pavement in amazement.

Fortunately, a plaque on the wall next to the window broke my fall before I went tumbling down to the feet of my fellow zoo-goers. A quick

---

[2] Pansexuality, or "omnisexuality," indicates a sexual and/or emotional interest in all types of lovers, regardless of gender or orientation. Both terms, pansexuality and *Pan paniscus*, are rooted in the Greek god Pan who had lovers of all genders and in the ancient Greek word *pan*, which means "all."

The Bonobo Way

perusal of the names on the inscription revealed that the one jilling off with the beach ball was a 15-year-old female named Lana. As a sex therapist, I was impressed by how Lana rubbed and tapped the round, slippery, rubbery surface against her engorged pink clitoris like a woman searching for the best way to angle her favorite sex toy. A very uninhibited, pleasure-loving woman, that is.

Suddenly, Lana went from a tense squat into a big floppy-armed collapse, letting the ball roll down the ravine. Was she okay? Had she just climaxed? Within seconds, she flipped up and bounded over to the glass, near where I was still leaning against the plaque. Did she notice me? She puckered up her expressive pink lips as if to blow me a quick kiss, and then bounded back to her mates.

The Chivers Effect

I grabbed the bicep of my own prime mate, gushing about how this great ape had just blown me a kiss. Alas, it happened too fast for my "witness"[3] to witness, and his slight irritation (or was it my imagination?) made me panic: Was he annoyed? Neurotically, but not irrationally, I wondered: Could this be the beginning of the dreaded sinkhole slide? After all, the forces of evolution don't always take us to a better place, especially in the realm of romance. Was the honeymoon now—having known each other ten years (four while married)—officially over?

In about five seconds, Pr. Max's twinkle caught my eye, and I had my answer. Because even if he missed Lana's lightning-quick smooch (and even if I was making much too much of it), the scene was already working its magic like Cupid's proverbial arrow into both of our bloodstreams as the primal power of *The Nature of Sex* came flooding back through our slightly worn marriage like a monsoon through the mighty Congo. We got so excited being around these kiss-blowing, bonking bonobos that we could have done the deed right there in front of them, if not for all the humans wandering around. Instead, we hightailed over to our suite at the San Diego Doubletree where we swung through doubletrees, tripletrees and multiple rainforests of rapture, floating so high above that stinky old sinkhole that we couldn't even see it any more.

I won't speak for Max, but one source of my orgasmic delight that night may well have been what I now call the "Chivers Effect." Research

---

[3] "Witness" is a pet name that Max and I have for each other since we have been through so much together, witnessing so many big and small moments in each other's lives.

psychologist, Dr. Meredith Chivers, conducted a 2010 meta-analysis, finding, among other things, that most women (straight, gay and bi) became aroused by watching films of bonobos having sex, though very few admitted to it. It's important to note that this response is largely physiological and not subjective or even quite conscious. Still, the mysterious excitement that some women feel from watching bonobos have sex, even though we do not find the apes themselves sexually appealing, can act on as a subtle aphrodisiac.

Sapped by the "Chivers Effect," or just tapped by a day at the zoo, I nestled into the narcotic nest of my hubby's arms, blissful but curious as to how long this wild bonobo magic would last... and how far it would go.

AOL Censors Bonobos

We woke up groggy the next day and rushed downstairs to a San Diego Mensa conference where I gave a talk in which I mentioned seeing the bonobos and was surprised out of my grogginess to learn that most of these high IQ folks had never even heard of them. Then again, just a few years before, neither had I. Sensing their significance and just becoming aware of their high level of endangerment, as well as being grateful for the odd boost they were already giving my own sex life, I felt driven to spread the word. When Max and I got back to LA, we posted a few photos of Lana and her friends on a webpage to support the bonobos and share the Bonobo Way.

Five weeks later, we got our virgin taste of bonobo censorship when our very first webhost, America Online (AOL), deleted our page without warning. Talk about summary execution! AOL Supervisor Lexie Haines did send us a personal, bizarrely cheerful email stating that our page could be reinstated if we'd simply refrain from using words like "masturbation," "orgasms" and "horny." Moreover, "the photos of chimpanzees having sex should come down." No wonder most folks didn't know bonobos from bonbons. Not only were they rare, they were bowdlerized!

We wasted no time finding another less puritanical webhost for Lana and her friends, and responded to Ms. Haines' inadvertently hilarious yet ominously censorious list of no-no's in our next show entitled, "AOL and the KKK." They may have been bullish on expurgating bonobos as well as human sexuality, but AOL generously allowed the decidedly unevolved Ku Klux Klan to post a site preaching their notorious brand of bigotry in those early days of the World Wide Web. Though the then-mighty service provider's flagrant anti-sex hypocrisy was deeply disturbing, it made us all the more determined to use this newfangled media outlet called the Internet to "agitate, stimulate and educate" people about bonobos and their amazing sexuality.

Noble and Kinky

On my second trip to the zoo, Lana blew me another kiss. That made me feel special, but on visit number three, I couldn't help but notice that she and her mates were bestowing the same sweet greeting on many of my fellow tourist-voyeurs. What happened to my "special" status? I was on the verge of crushing disappointment when I remembered that the bonobos are the special ones, ambassadors from a primordial world of peace through pleasure, inviting us in one kiss at a time.

"Mommy, Daddy, what are they doing?" a little girl asked, watching the bonobos play. Her forehead and palms were pressed against the glass, as if she thought she could break on through to the other side[4] and join them if only she pushed hard enough.

"Looks like they need private time!" her father barked back, steering the girl away from the window as her mother brightly proposed, "Let's go see the hippos!"

Not everybody is quite ready for the Bonobo Way, and far be it from me to push it on anyone, especially some stressed-out parents at the zoo.

On the other hand, maybe they're more ready than they realize. Ready or not, its moment has come. The time is now for human beings to step up to the plate and protect our kissing cousins from extinction, as well as learn as much as we can from them about our noblest and kinkiest characteristics, our capacity for peace (even world peace) through pleasure, more satisfying relationships, better communication, hotter sex and deeper love.

But before we go there, let's venture back up the mighty, muddy Congo to the land of Lana's wild ancestors, where we will investigate the recent history and many mysteries of this remarkable fellow being we call "bonobo."

---

[4] With kisses to Jim Morrison and The Doors.

Chapter 3: Welcome to Bonoboville

"Wilderness is Paradise enow."
— Omar Khayyám

Bonobos may be the world's greatest cooperators, but humans still can't seem to agree on certain things about them, starting with how to say their name. There are two distinct schools of pronunciation: I say *bo-NO-bo*, you say *BON-a-bo*—let's call the whole thing off![5] Whatever the accent, the Comedy of Enunciation Errors[6] began as the name "bonobo" was picked up by a couple of German zoologists, Drs. Eduard Tratz and Heinz Heck, based upon a misspelling on a shipping crate of chimps (possibly not even bonobos!) from the Congolese town of *Bolobo*.

To make matters even murkier, for many years, people called bonobos "pygmy chimpanzees,"[7] and some still do, which drives a lot of other people bonkers since bonobos are not much smaller in girth than our other closest relative, the common chimpanzee (*Pan Troglyodyte*). When standing upright, bonobos actually tend to be taller than common chimps.

A more satisfying definition of their melodious moniker can be found in an extinct Bantu language which translates "bonobo" to "ancestor." The Bongandu people, one of several tribes that inhabit the Équateur province around the bonobo habitat at Wamba in the Democratic Republic of Congo (DRC), have long recognized these amazing apes as close relatives from our not-too-distant past. They call the bonobos "our brothers."

Though the origins of their name remain as misty as the rainforest, their closeness to us is clear. The 2012 sequencing of the bonobo genome by Germany's Max Planck Institute has shown that the Bongandu are scientifically correct: *Pan paniscus* are indeed the brothers and sisters (or at least the close cousins) of *Homo sapiens*, as they share about 98.7% of our genetic material.

Apparently, some six million years ago, our great ape or *hominid* common ancestor diverged, and humans took a separate path. Then, about

---

[5] With a bow to Louis Armstrong and Ella Fitzgerald...
[6] ...And a curtsy to Shakespeare.
[7] The "pygmy" designation might refer to the indigenous pygmy peoples of the region.

two million years ago, common chimpanzees and bonobos split from each other.[8] Since then, our species have gone on to lead extremely different lives, but our genetics remain remarkably similar. In fact, over three percent of the human genome is more closely related to either the bonobo or the chimp than the two apes are to each other.

According to many experts, including renowned primatologist Dr. Frans de Waal, this DNA blueprint indicates that both bonobos and common chimps are as close to humans as foxes are to dogs. I don't know about you, but that's closer than I feel to some of my human relatives. Though bonobos tend to be a lot hairier than us—and they don't build houses or churches or Pentagons like we do—these primates look and act remarkably human. They often even go beyond the merely "human," and enter the realm of the truly "humane."

Aristocratic Apes

Genetically speaking, bonobos and common chimps are considered equally close to humans. But, as Dr. de Waal and others have pointed out, bonobos *look* more like us than common chimps or any other animal. If "looks make the man," or the ape, take note: bonobos have smaller ears, less prominent brow ridges, pinker lips, larger eyes and wider, cuter, more engaging, "neotenous" (youthful), individualized faces than common chimps.

This eternal youthfulness, along with their more gracile physiques, longer legs and a greater tendency to walk upright than their "common" cousins, sometimes while carrying objects in their hands, has led some to call bonobos the "aristocratic ape." *Pan paniscus*' body proportions have also been compared with those of the *australopithecines*, probable ancestors of *Homo sapiens*, who lived and loved during the Plio-Pleistocene era some five million years ago.

Jamming with Kanzi

Moving from the outer contours of the body into the deep wrinkles of the brain, *Pan paniscus* demonstrates remarkable intelligence on many fronts and in human terms. The most prominent examples have been shown by Dr. Sue Savage-Rumbaugh, visionary psychologist of Iowa's

---

[8] The other great ape species, including two types of gorillas and orangutans, split off earlier in prehistory.

Bonobo Hope Sanctuary and named one of *Time* magazine's 100 most influential people in 2011. Many of her findings are based on studying Kanzi,[9] the "rock star" bonobo who beats humans at Pac-Man, cooks hot dogs and toasts marshmallows over a campfire he made himself, has chatted with Oprah and played music with fellow rock stars Peter Gabriel and Paul McCartney. Gabriel called the cross-species musical collaboration "one of my most extraordinary experiences as a musician."

People once assumed that since bonobos and other apes don't talk like we do, they don't have language, but that might be due to a prejudice toward human vocalizing among human researchers. Despite our many other similarities, human and bonobo vocal chords are extremely different, and it's very difficult for us to comprehend their high-pitched hooting and squealing. They, however, seem to have an easier time understanding us, especially if they have been reared by humans.

Not only does Kanzi comprehend human language, he's trilingual (not counting his own bonobo language). He understands around 3000 English words and communicates with humans through signing as well as pointing to geometric and pictorial symbols, or lexigrams, on a computer keyboard (he can create around 500 words with this method), using the artificial language of "Yerkish" developed for bonobos and chimps to communicate with humans and named for the Yerkes Primate Center, which moved from Yale to Emory University where Kanzi was born.

Kanzi's high-level linguistic ability demonstrates that bonobos are capable of acquiring complex language skills through social interaction involving both *Homo sapiens* and *Pan paniscus*. Not only does he use words for things like "potato" and "ball" and actions like "walk" and "cook," he presses lexigrams to convey emotions such as "happy," "sad," "careful" and "scary," using prepositions like "on" and "at" to make full sentences.

"It's unnerving talking to an animal in the expectation that they will actually answer you. In English," observes Tom Leonard in *The Daily Mail* after his meeting with this remarkable ape.

With a little help from his human friends, Kanzi also learned to make stone tools from flint to crack open food-filled logs. "The appearance of stone tool technology in the archeological record is considered to represent a major advance in the cognitive capacity of early *Homo*," Dr. Savage-Rumbaugh points out in a *Wired* interview. "This leap is traditionally

---

[9] In Swahili, "Kanzi" means "buried treasure."

assumed to propel *Homo* far beyond present-day *Pan,* and to define a kind of arbitrary 'mental boundary' between our ancestors and all living apes." Bonobos in the wild don't appear to make tools, but with just a little incentive (yummy-smelling, hard-to-reach food) and training, Kanzi learned to make wedges, choppers and drills similar to those used by our "Stone Age" hominid ancestors.

But Kanzi is very much a 21st century bonobo. A couple days after his interview with Leonard, he continued their conversation via Skype, chatting and peering into the *Daily Mail* reporter's refrigerator to see if he had anything good to eat (he didn't).

Kanzi is considered a "genius" ape, but he's not alone. Other bonobos-in-residence at the Bonobo Hope Sanctuary, such as Kanzi's half-sister, the late, great Panbanisha, her son Nyota and Kanzi's son Teco, also show high levels of intelligence compared to other primates, even humans. At just four months old, an age when most human children can't say "Papa," Teco began communicating the way his father does, using a touch screen tablet, to request a grape.

As for bonobo musicality, Kanzi may be the equivalent of a bonobo Beatle, but sister Panbanisha could have been a simian Kesha. "They are improvising together, she is not just playing along," asserted UNC Greensboro's BioMusic Program director, Dr. Patricia Gray, when viewing a recording of Panbanisha and Gabriel doing a synthesizer duet. Demonstrating that other bonobos "got rhythm" too, Dr. Gray and University of Connecticut psychologist, Dr. Edward Large, teamed up to create a "bonobo-friendly" drum that could handle 500 pounds of thumping, kicking, gnawing, rocking and rolling so the bonobos could bang out a beat. Interestingly, bonobo percussionists prefer a tempo of 280 beats per minute, the syllabic rate at which most humans speak.

The Bonobo Funnies

Many psychologists consider humor, even if it's just a chuckle, a hallmark of humanity. But bonobos also love to laugh when tickled physically or mentally. Moreover, they even crack the jokes, and the complexity of their funny bones could probably get some of them jobs at Comedy Central.

One of my show guests, "Champions of the Wild" filmmaker Christian Bruyère, related how Panbanisha put him through a comedic gauntlet before consenting to let him film her. Via computer sign language and gestures, she turned the tables on the award-winning director, directing him to dress up in a gorilla costume and pretend to scare an on-site employee. Dutifully, Bruyère donned the furry suit, then beat his gorilla chest and chased the staff member down a hill. All the while, Panbanisha enjoyed the slapstick scene from her director's chair. Only after Bruyère followed her precise, Keatonesque directions did this demanding diva consent to his original request that she be in his movie. I should be so smart in my dealings with Hollywood filmmakers.

Some primatologists place the bonobo IQ at the level of the average human seven-year-old. But their EQ or EI (Emotional Intelligence) is certainly much higher. According to landmark research conducted by Drs. Peter Salovey[10] and John D. Mayer, emotional intelligence is "the ability to monitor one's own and others' feelings and emotions, to discriminate among them and to use this information to guide one's thinking and actions." Being empathetic as well as cool under pressure when others get hot under the collar has won many a poker game, as well as other "games" of life, love and power.

In a 2011 intelligence competition run by behavioral biologist Dr. Jeroen Stevens, a female bonobo named Djanoa bested all the common chimp contestants by cooperating with her teammates while the leading chimp contenders were plagued by "alpha-male infighting." In honor of bright Djanoa and her *Pan paniscus* pals who "showed persistence and motivation," the Antwerp Zoo crowned the bonobos "the world's cleverest apes." I'm guessing the zoo wasn't counting humans when bestowing that title. Or maybe it was.

Studies are one thing, but then there's just the way bonobos make you feel. They're so "almost-human" on so many levels that science doesn't even know how to test yet. Just look into any bonobo's big brown eyes, and you may well feel like you're connecting with a living version of the Missing Link.[11]

---

[10] Dr. Salovey is now President of Yale, using his formidable EQ to lead higher academia into a more empathic future.
[11] Of course, I'm not saying bonobos *are* the "Missing Link," an unscientific, "early Darwinian" term for some sort of connection in the "Great Chain of Being" that hasn't yet been discovered in the fossil evidence. Creationists have misused the word, arguing that if the "link" is "missing," then evolution must be wrong. Scientists tend to shun the term preferring "transitional fossil."

Chapter 4: Bonobo Sexualis

"Sexual behavior is not confined to one aspect of their life that they set aside. It permeates their entire life."
— Dr. Sue Savage-Rumbaugh in *Champions of the Wild*

And of course, there's the sex. If you know anything about bonobos, you probably know they have *a lot* of sex. And they have it in a dazzling array of ways. It's even built into their sexual anatomy. Common chimps and most other mammals only have sex via rear entry, a.k.a. "doggy style," because the females' genitalia are rotated decisively toward the back. Doggy style is a great position for porn because it's so animal, but not so hot for intimacy, which thrives on eye contact. Bonobos are all about erotic intimacy, and the females' big pink vulvas are rotated forward, allowing them to have sex face-to-face. They often look deeply into each other's eyes while in the so-called "missionary" position or "female superior," not to mention while hanging from a branch with one hand and holding one's sweetheart by the rump with the other.

In fact, bonobos "do it" in as many, if not more, positions than we humans can, and they *do* do it—a lot.

Sometimes it seems like they just can't get enough. If you believe in the concept of "sex addiction" (which I don't), you might call bonobos the sex addicts of the animal world. Erotic feeling infuses almost every aspect of life in Bonoboville. Healthy bonobos partake in some kind of sex play almost every day, often several times a day.

Female bonobos are in heat far more often than their common chimp counterparts and engage in sexual play even when not in heat, almost always sporting those bulbous, fat *and* phat (at least to bonobos!), tumescent, bubblegum-pink vulvas that only bloom in other great apes during mating season. Most animals restrict their mating to a certain time when everyone can easily see and smell who's fertile. Keeping estrus a mystery all year long, as bonobos do, is a sexual pattern more like human females than that of any other mammal, leading to more frequent, less procreative erotic possibilities for all.

The Bonobo Sutra

When it comes to sex, are bonobos into quantity or quality? Both! Several studies bear this out, including those by Kanō in the wild (1973), de Waal in zoos (1995), and Hare and Woods in primate centers and sanctuaries (2010). In a veritable Bonobo Sutra of positions, *Pan paniscus* partake in various kinds of erotic activities with multiple partners, some of it seemingly "casual," but much of it extremely passionate and deeply intimate.

The list of bonobo sex activities is more impressive than the original Kama Sutra or the menu at Dennis Hof's Bunny Ranch: massage, body-licking, cunnilingus, fellatio, masturbation, tickling, genito-genital rubbing, penis-fencing, testicle play, rump-rubbing, group sex, incest, inter-generational sex, mixing food with sex ("eating while eating"), breast and nipple play, erotic grooming, foot play, ear-tonguing, anal play, genital play with inanimate objects utilized as "sex toys," extensive eye-gazing and lots of long, deep, soulful French kissing.

Bonobo eroticism doesn't discriminate between genders. All bonobos are, according to their fashion, bisexual or pansexual. Some bonobo sex is relatively private, but most is out in the open where others may watch or join in. Sex merges seamlessly with other behaviors, making wild Bonoboville resemble an old-fashioned Love-In, especially around lunchtime.

You might call bonobos "promiscuous," and technically you'd be right. But that's not to say they're reckless, random or uncaring in their sexuality. Rather, *Pan paniscus* is more in tune with the original Latin root of promiscuous, *miscere*, which simply means "to mix." Considering the variety of positions and partners they enjoy, there's no doubt that bonobos like to mix it up. This is the same sense in which Drs. Christopher Ryan and Cacilda Jethá, two of our favorite guests on the show, describe the sex lives of prehistoric humans as "promiscuous" in their landmark best-seller, *Sex at Dawn: The Prehistoric Origins of Modern Sexuality*.

Love Hormone Highs

What is bonobo promiscuity all about? It involves what Dr. Alan Dixson calls "multi-male/multi-female mating systems" that feature ongoing, erotic, caring relationships with a *mix* of individuals within a close-knit tribe, as well as select members of neighboring tribes and attractive strangers. That's also how Ryan and Jethá contend that prehistoric humans once lived and loved for a couple hundred thousand years before the advent of civilization around 12 thousand years ago, and how our bodies and minds are *still* wired to live and love. But we'll talk more about *us* later… let's get back to bonobos.

Their ability to engage in remarkably intense sexual relations with so many partners in "multi-male/multi-female mating systems" is reflected in their complex emotions. As any sexpert worth two orgasms knows, turning on your partner requires "tuning in" to your partner. And as virtually all primatologists who study them have observed, bonobos show extremely high levels of interpersonal awareness, empathy, compassion, tolerance, vulnerability, altruism, reciprocity, cooperation, musicality and sensitivity. And then there's how bonobos gaze deeply into each other's eyes, intimately tuning into each other like Tantric sex practitioners or two people very much in love.

Studies have shown that, unsurprisingly, all these erotic and affectionate activities release relatively high levels of oxytocin and vasopressin in bonobos, compared to other great apes. Oxytocin, known as the "love hormone," flows through us during birth and nursing, as well as during orgasms, cuddling, hugging and pleasant social situations. What's more, humans and bonobos seem to possess a similar section of DNA, important to the release of oxytocin, which common chimps appear to lack. Vasopressin is a mammalian hormone that often accompanies oxytocin, facilitating "pair-bonding" and other types of social closeness. Vasopressin levels also increase during erectile response in male sexual arousal. The upshot is that, biochemically speaking, one good hug, kiss, lick or stroke leads to another. Higher levels of love hormones in bonobos translate to higher levels of bonobo love.

Yet bonobo lovemaking itself, i.e., penis-in-vagina (PIV) intercourse, is often quick and seemingly nonchalant. This may look to some human observers like "casual sex." But as you learn the functions and principles of sex in Bonoboville, you'll find that "casual" doesn't describe it at all, at least not in the random sense of the word.

Indeed, it's not just *how* they have sex, but *why* they have sex that makes bonobos so interesting, important and relevant to the story of our lives.

Chapter 5: Erotic Politics and Bonobo Economics

"Bonobos lubricate the gears of social harmony with sex."
— Natalie Angier, *The New York Times*

What is the point of all this sex? Like all animals and most life forms, one vital purpose of *Pan paniscus* sex is procreation. Are adult bonobos aware that having sexual intercourse leads to the birth of baby bonobos? Probably not, though our human-bonobo communication skills aren't quite advanced enough for anyone to have that particular conversation with them... yet. What we do know is that rather than simply having sex for the sake of *pro*creation, bonobos do it for *re*creation, i.e., for fun.

Unlike most mammals, *Pan paniscus* have sex when the females aren't fertile, and PIV intercourse is just one course on the Bonobo Sutra menu of thousands of positions and types of erotic exchange, much of which some of us call foreplay. This is one reason why, despite all that sexual activity, bonobos have rather low reproductive rates. Besides, anyone who has watched bonobos in the heat of the moment knows that whether it's quick and dirty or long and languorous, they sure look like they're having some fun.

But recreation only tells part of the sexual story. There are also *re*lations, i.e., relationships. Yes, there is such a thing as bonobo love. But it's less an exclusive romantic kind of love and more a caring friends-with-benefits kind of love. If bonobos spoke English to each other, an erotic invitation might go, "Hey, Girlfriend, are you free this afternoon? Want to hang out under the umbrella tree, munch nuts and each other?" Sex is about getting "in sync" and staying "in touch," quite literally. It's an intrinsic part of bonobo friendship, between the same and opposite sex, much like doing lunch, drinks, hot yoga or a nice sweaty game of racquetball is for us.

And it's not just friendship. Sex permeates politics in Bonoboville, but without the sense of scandal that accompanies human politics. Bonobos naturally live in what primatologists call a "fission-fusion" society, meaning that the size and composition of the group tends to vary throughout the day or week. Some members of a bonobo tribe might go off as a twosome or threesome (fission) to forage and fornicate during the day, but rejoin the parent group (fusion) to nest, sleep, groom, lick, rub and cuddle at night.

Again, this could have been how our human hunter-gatherer ancestors operated in an "uncivilized" world where sensuous touch may not have been exclusive, monogamous or even very private, but a communal fission-fusion affair.

Bonobo Handshakes & Human Testimony

How are bonobo politics negotiated through sex? Often it's an "I'll scratch your genitalia if you'll scratch mine" manner of politicking. The human handshake is a common gesture of trust and friendliness, especially among politicians. The "bonobo handshake," a term made famous by research scientist Vanessa Woods (whom I had the pleasure of interviewing on my show regarding her marvelous memoir of that name), is an affable hand-to-genitals greeting. It's one of the most popular ways to say hello in fission-fusion Bonoboville, easing tensions and enhancing the socio-political status of those who engage in it most effectively. There's nothing like a friendly handshake to establish social cooperation, but the bonobo handshake takes erotic politics to a whole new level.

Or is it really so new to us? I don't know how many of our human ancestors grabbed each other's junk to say good morning, but the history behind the word "testify" gives us a clue. The root (so to speak) is the same as that of the word "testicles," from the Latin *testiculus*, the diminutive of which is *testis*, meaning "witness." So a man's package is his "little witness" or, for some, his star witness in the trial of his life.

Indeed, back in Old *Test*ament times, it seems that when our forefathers swore an oath, they didn't put their hands on the Bible. After all, these were "Bible times," and the Bible hadn't been written yet. When they testified, they put their hands on their testicles, i.e., they swore by their family jewels. The Bible coyly calls this part of the male body the "thigh," as in Genesis 24:2 when Abraham tells his servant Eliezer to "put thy hand under my thigh and I will make thee swear to the Lord of Heaven and Earth..." Whereupon Eliezer obediently cups his hand under his master's "thigh" (i.e., his patriarchal sack of tiny future Israelites), and swears his solemn oath. Don't try this in court (even if the bailiff is as hot as Alexandra Silk on Playboy TV's old *Judge Julie*), but do consider it for what it is: a Biblical bonobo handshake.

Can I get a witness?

Like human preachers eager for witnesses, bonobos adore erotic attention, and not just from their sex partners, but from their whole congregation of friends and potential lovers. The high-pitched chirping copulation call—the female bonobo equivalent of moaning, "Oh God, oh baby, oh my Goooodddd!"—lets their comrades know they're getting it on.

It's not unusual for any female primates (including humans) to call out during sex for reproductive purposes, informing other males within earshot that they're fertile, hot and ready for more. But Dr. Zanna Clay, an Emory University researcher working with the great de Waal, found that bonobo females call out *even when having sex with other females.*

According to Dr. Clay's study, which she did with Dr. Klaus Zuberbühler, low-ranking bonobo females are especially likely to vocalize during sex with high-ranking ones. When the alpha female is in the vicinity, copulation calls are loudest, showing that these vocally exhibitionistic bonobo gals aren't just doing it to reproduce, but for social and strategic political advantage, as well as the joy of sharing one's pleasure with the group.

Bonobo Sex Therapy

Another vital purpose of sex in Bonoboville is to ease stress. In this case, the invitation might go something like this: "Aw… don't be so upset. Come here and sit on my face," or "You're making me nervous, but if you would please just pet my penis, I'll calm right down." Just because bonobos live in a kind of "Garden of Earthly Delights"[12] doesn't mean they never get anxious or angry. In fact, their high levels of sensitivity and empathy might make them more susceptible to certain types of stress, as well as more likely to offer erotic favors or "bonobo sex therapy" to soothe a tense or irritated confrère. There are all kinds of social pressures and complexities in Bonoboville, and sex—for bonobos (and humans)—is a great stress-reliever. If more humans would use sex to ease stress like bonobos do, the gargantuan antidepressant industry might collapse. But alas, it's not so simple… Or is it?

The logistics often come down to cold hard cash. So let's take a look at

---

[12]Having long been visually inspired by the famous painting by Hieronymus Bosch, which strikes me as very bonoboësque, I was delighted to discover in *The Bonobo and the Atheist* that his fellow Dutchman Frans de Waal is also a Bosch fan. Apparently Bosch was "going bonobos" before any humans knew what a bonobo was.

"bonobo economics." Life in Bonoboville is a pared-down "sharing economy," operating on a reciprocal barter system in which sex and food are the main currencies. For example, one exchange might go: "I'll trade you a banana for a blowjob."[13]

Imagine how this kind of money market would shake up Wall Street! Then again, it's already there. "Massage parlors are a Wall Street tradition," writes Anka Radakovich in *The Wild Girls Club, Part 2*. Services like "High Class NY," which allegedly charged stock traders from $400 to $3,600 an hour[14] for their escorts' time, can attest to that. Now imagine all those hookers holding their clients' testicles as they testify. All rise!

Bonobo Gals Pick Up the Check

Trading food (or money) for sex is not unique to humans and bonobos. It's extremely common to many animals, even insects. Prostitution is the world's oldest profession because it's far older than humanity itself. Throughout our ecosystem, especially in the animal world, you often have to pay to play.

But it's usually the male who does the paying in most species by providing food in exchange for sex. Among bonobos, it's often the lady who picks up the check, and therein lies one of the keys to the extraordinary success of bonobo economics and the peace-through-pleasure dividend it affords.

---

[13] For those of you currently trying to visualize a bonobo blowjob (BJ), it involves a lot more licking than sucking and not much deep-throating. No facials have been reported as of press time.
[14] According to Brooklyn District Attorney Charles Hynes, who indicted the "ring" in 2011, it earned more than $7 million over three years servicing "high-end customers coming from the financial markets. People with nothing but money."

Chapter 6: Peace through Pleasure

"War is over! If you want it."
— John Lennon and Yoko Ono

The most revolutionary way bonobos use sex is for conflict resolution. It's the main reason why these apes are my heroes. The methods they use vary with the situation and personalities involved. One possible script might go something like this: fight, kick, slap, bite—"Ouch! Time out! Let's turn around and rub butts—quick, before someone *really* gets hurt! Mmm... That hits the spot. I feel much better now. How about you? Do you remember why we were so mad at each other before? Because I don't! Now how about a kiss?"

This kind of erotic conflict resolution probably won't show up on any anger management curriculum anytime soon... though maybe it should. It might sound fancifully utopian to some, and it has been unscientifically mocked by a few war-relishing commentators, including Dinesh D'Souza and P. J. O'Rourke, and it will surely be mocked again.

But there's no denying that it works. As far as we know, there is no murder or war whatsoever among bonobos. In fact, post-fighting bonobo love may just be the most effective make-up sex on the planet.

Many primatologists have observed that social interactions among bonobos are in general far less hostile than among common chimpanzees. In a 2014 study, Drs. Clay and de Waal studied 36 "semi-free" bonobos of all ages using standardized "Post-Conflict/Matched Control" methods and found that "consolation and reconciliation were both marked by significant increases in the occurrence of sexual behaviors. Reconciliation was almost exclusively characterized by sexual contacts," as well as simple affectionate behaviors such as hugging.

"This may have to do with the rubbing of sexual organs causing reductions in cortisol levels in the blood or causing increases in 'bonding' hormones such as oxytocin or vasopressin," Dr. Clay observed. Cortisol is known as the "stress hormone" so it's no stretch to see how a hug or a lick in the right place at the right moment can turn the closed fist of anger into an open hand of love.

Dr. James Rilling, director of Emory University's Laboratory for Darwinian Neuroscience, went farther, using non-invasive neuro-imaging technology to compare common chimp and bonobo brains. He found that "the neural circuitry that mediates anxiety, empathy and the inhibition of aggression in humans is better developed in bonobos than in chimpanzees." No wonder Djanoa won the gold.

Resolving Conflict with Sex

Not that bonobos are angels. They're animals, just as we are. They're hunter/gatherers like us too, so they hunt other animals and eat meat along with their fruit and veggie staples. Bonobo bashers have used the fact that bonobos can be carnivores to deny their peacefulness, but there's a big difference between hunting other species for food and using lethal aggression against members of your own species. To reiterate this important and often misunderstood point, I'm not suggesting that bonobos are always mild and gentle. Sometimes they fight, they just fight a lot less than common chimps (or humans). Like all great apes, including humans, bonobos are greatly influenced by their environment. Most of the isolated episodes of bonobo violence reported in captivity stem from zoos or sanctuaries misunderstanding various essential aspects of bonobo social structure thereby inadvertently creating an uncomfortable and confusing situation for them. Still, they never resort to killing.

Bonobos have been known to hurt their human caretakers, though most incidents appear to be accidental. One hand-biting incident occurred at the San Diego Zoo when keeper Mike Bates was trying to get Ikela, a pregnant and very uncomfortable bonobo, to open her mouth for teeth-cleaning. In the process, she snapped and inadvertently bit off the tip of his finger. Though the bite was unfortunate, what happened next was truly remarkable: another bonobo (remember Lana?) actually retrieved the fingertip and brought it back to Mike intact. Mike's fingertip was successfully reattached later at the hospital, thanks to Lana's quick thinking.

Not all bonobo attacks have such happy endings, but none have been lethal so far. In other words, bonobos may fight and bite, but somehow they avoid homicide. They are the world's master peacemakers.

"Chimpanzees tend to resolve conflict by using aggression, while bonobos are more likely to use behavioral mechanisms like sex and play to diffuse tension," observes Rilling in his comparison of bonobo and chimp neural circuitry. "The social behaviors of the two species mirror individual differences within the human population."

After I met Lana in 1996, I read everything I could find about bonobos, including Kanō and de Waal, as well as the eloquent work of a Harvard anthropology professor, Dr. Richard Wrangham, another great guest on my show,[15] whose witty, British-accented descriptions of sex and peace among the bonobos inspired me to continue on the Bonobo Way. In his book *Demonic Males: Apes and the Origins of Human Violence,* which he wrote with Dr. Dale Peterson, Dr. Wrangham describes bonobos as "chimpanzees with a threefold path to peace. They have reduced the level of violence in relations between the sexes, in relations among males, and in relations between communities."

Common Chimps Sometimes Kill Each Other

Not to condemn common chimps, who are also very close to humans. They're certainly not the unceasingly bloodthirsty "killer apes" of human fantasy any more than gorillas are King Kongs with a taste for blondes.

But lethal intergroup aggression, premeditated murder (including vicious torture worthy of Hannibal Lecter), cannibalism and territorial "wars" have been documented dozens of times among *Pan troglodyte,* from Dr. Jane Goodall's famous studies of chimps in Tanzania in the 1970s to Dr. John Mitani's 2010 research in Uganda.

Speaking of King Kong, gorillas are relatively peaceful compared to the sometimes-brutal common chimps. However, they can be killers too. Newly established silverbacks and other male gorillas often intentionally murder babies sired by competing males, as observed by Dr. Dian Fossey, herself tragically murdered—by humans—in 1985.

No Bonobo Murders or Wars

Bonobos, on the other hand, have never been observed deliberately killing other bonobos—not the young, the old, the weak or the strong. Nor have they been seen "making war" of any kind on each other, in the wild or in captivity. At least, not so far.

It's possible that the unprecedented recent encroachment of human culture will change bonobo society, much as civilization, industrialization

---

[15] A few months after I interviewed Dr. Wrangham, a *Grist Magazine* reporter told me that our show had become something of a scandal at Harvard. Must be because I went to Yale…

and corporatization have "modernized" many human cultures. As noted, evolution does not always involve things getting better, natural selection being emotionally and morally impartial. So someday we may find bonobos killing their own kind. They are also quite physically capable of killing humans thanks to their fang-like canines and upper body strength, which is about five times as great as ours.

But for now, no bonobo has ever been seen committing an act of lethal aggression against another bonobo or any other ape. Why not? Apparently, all that hot sex cools them out. Sex, tolerance, play and mutual pleasure are keys to keeping the peace in Bonoboville, reinforcing social relations based upon the give-and-take reciprocity of sensual, erotic pleasure. This is in stark contrast to the pain and fear we see common chimps (and humans) wielding to maintain order. Bonobos use positive touch to prevent and restrain negative touch. They make peace through pleasure.

And that, in a coconut shell, is why I love them.

Chapter 7: The Bonobo Mystique

"It is high time for increased public awareness of this appealing, fascinating primate, one that presents a major challenge to traditional notions of human origins."
— Dr. Frans de Waal, *Bonobo: The Forgotten Ape*

What's really going on here? How do they stay so peaceful? How does it relate to all that sex? How does it relate to us? Primatologists are just starting to address these vital questions. After all, bonobos appeared quite recently in the great ape taxonomy game. German zoologist Dr. Johann Friedrich Blumenbach identified common chimps in 1776, but bonobos weren't officially classified as a separate species until 1928.

A few years before, Yale's pioneering primatologist, Robert Yerkes, compared Prince Chim with other chimpanzees he was studying at the original Yerkes Laboratory of Primate Biology. Dr. Yerkes considered Pr.[16] Chim to be "sanguine, venturesome, trustful and energetic," as opposed to Panzee the common chimp, who was "distrustful, retiring and lethargic."[17] It has now been established from photographs that the charming Prince Chim was a bonobo.

Anatomist Tiffs & African Wars

But Yerkes doesn't get the official credit for identifying bonobos. The "discovery" took place in a colonial museum in Tervuren, Belgium. German anatomist Ernst Schwarz was examining what colleagues thought was a juvenile chimpanzee skull when he realized it was an adult skull of what he suggested was a subspecies of chimpanzee that he called (depending on which account you go by) *Pan satyrus* or *Pan satyrus paniscus*.

In true competitive anthropoid fashion, Harold Coolidge, an American anatomist, later declared he was actually the one who first made the discovery while working in that same museum. Dr. Schwarz wasn't alive

---
[16] Pr. is an abbreviation for Prince.
[17] To be fair, I should note that Panzee was much younger than Chim and suffered from tuberculosis.

to defend himself when Dr. Coolidge made his claim, but the American (who did the post-mortem on Pr. Chim) did properly classify the bonobo as *Pan paniscus*, a separate species from the common chimpanzee.

The scientific community didn't start calling them bonobos until Tratz and Heck found that misnamed crate from the town of Bolobo in 1954. It would then be almost another two decades before wild bonobos were seriously studied by groundbreaking Japanese primatologist Takayoshi Kanō in the early 1970s. Dr. Kanō ventured into the vast rainforests of what was then Zaire, now the DRC, surveying over 2000 kilometers on a bicycle, often spinning his wheels through hostile territory, until he discovered a group of wild bonobos living near a peaceful human populace in the bonobo-friendly village of Wamba. There he established the first bonobo research station, the Luo Scientific Reserve, overseeing the longest continuous field study of *Pan paniscus* in the wild.

Some of Kanō's observations of bonobos, expressed in *The Last Ape: Pygmy Chimpanzee Behavior and Ecology*, are downright lyrical: "They prove that individuals can coexist without relying on competition and dominant-subordinate rank." What an inspiration to war-weary, peace-hungry, sex-horny humanity… especially in the 1970s!

Unfortunately, Kanō's work remained obscure for years. *The Last Ape* wasn't even published until 1992. Then, in 1994, just a year after I got my first glimpse of *Pan paniscus* on that PBS special, the bonobos' potential to teach humans about peace through pleasure was put on hold with brutal force, as the Rwandan genocide broke out, its refugee crisis and brutal political conflicts spilling into the rainforest, the bonobos' only native habitat. The Second Congo War followed in 1998, making continued field research almost impossible. Most universities and foundations weren't (and still aren't) exactly lining up to fund bonobo research. Conditions in the DRC are much better now, but still unstable. If the rebels don't get you, the Ebola might.

Another reason for this reluctance, whispered and giggled about throughout the stately halls of academia, is because bonobos are just so explicitly sexual. They're the unabashed porn stars in our great ape family. On top of looking a lot like humans, their overt sexuality can be downright embarrassing, especially when trying to secure tenure.

It all contributes to humanity's general confusion about these enigmatic close cousins of ours, the bonobos, and the bonobo mystique.

Sex Makes You Smarter

It's unfortunate that so many in academics have shunned bonobo studies because of their "hyper" sexuality. It's also rather ironic given recent research indicating more sex makes mammals more intelligent.

A 2013 University of Maryland study by Drs. E.R. Glasper and E. Gould shows that having regular sex creates new neural pathways in the section of the brain that forms memories leading to improved cognition and hippocampal functioning over time. Whenever I hear "hippocampus," I imagine a college dorm for large semi-aquatic mammals, but it's really a major component of the brain in humans and other vertebrates, playing important roles in short and long-term memory as well as spatial navigation and other functions. Related research published by Konkuk University in Seoul, South Korea shows that regular sex improves sharpness and memory despite chronic stress in the environment.

Of course, these particular experiments were performed on middle-aged rats and male mice respectively, but it's easy to see why we academically-inclined great apes have something to get excited about—lots of sex probably makes you smarter!

With more evidence like this coming out, maybe the great universities of the world and their financiers will soon see fit to honor and award bonobo studies *because* of their extraordinary sexuality. Several important studies are now being done, mostly on bonobos in captivity, some of which are mentioned in this book, but much more is needed. Until then, despite their growing popularity, the bonobo mystique remains.

Hollywood Defames Bonobos

To make that mystique mistier, the titans of Hollywood have barely recognized the existence of bonobos, and what little effort they've made they've gotten wrong (and in a rather more disturbing way than Tratz and Heck mistaking bonobo for Bolobo), at least so far.

Take the iconic *Planet of the Apes* series. Imaginative and provocative as the original was, the franchise has never been strong on accuracy in its portrayal of apes. But the latest 20th Century Fox installments, *Rise* and *Dawn of the Planet of the Apes,* both otherwise-thoughtful works of dystopian fantasy cinema with cool special effects and widespread appeal, come as close to bonobo defamation as a sci-fi movie can get, calling the character of Koba, the most murderous and warmongering (not to mention the ugliest and scariest-looking) ape in this APEocalypse, a "bonobo."

This is like calling Hitler a pacifist or a shark an angelfish. The filmmakers explain that Koba is so vicious because he was "kept captive by humans and experimented on." Sounds plausible if you don't know bonobos, but as Dr. Brian Hare of Duke University's Institute for Brain Sciences[18] explains in *Live Science*, "that explanation doesn't work." He tells the touching story of Etumbe, an orphaned bonobo who had been subject to horrible torture at the hands of real hunters and human biomedical lab workers. Yet, Etumbe, who was rescued by the Lola ya Bonobo[19] sanctuary and eventually released back into the wild, never killed anyone, bonobo nor human. On the contrary, Dr. Hare describes how Etumbe initiated a heartfelt farewell, grasping both his hands and, looking into his eyes, conveying great warmth and, if I may extrapolate, a palpable sense of forgiveness toward those who subjected her to ceaseless torment for so many years.

Etumbe and her fellow bonobos embody forgiveness as well as peace through pleasure. Anyone with a passing familiarity with *Pan paniscus* (including screenwriters who bother to do a little research) realizes how preposterous it is to villainize the "make love not war" bonobo as a mass murderer. Unfortunately, most people don't know bingo about bonobos, and many get their first impressions of these peaceful primates from these summer blockbusters. Are the filmmakers exploiting the increasingly popular keyword "bonobo" with nefarious motives, or are they just, like so many in Hollywood, breathtakingly ill-informed?

Blame it on the bonobo mystique. In a survey taken by Duke's Hominoid Psychology Research Group survey, only 15 percent of those with a university level education even knew that bonobos are great apes, let alone that when it comes to the golden rule, they're the *greatest* apes.

The solution lies in research, education, conservation and getting the truth out. The truth is much sexier, cooler and more meaningful than any celluloid ape fantasy could ever be. If Hollywood did its homework before making a movie where bonobos are in charge of things, we'd be queuing up at the local multiplex to see *Planet of the Bonobos: Rise of the Orgasm*. Too bad that's not cumming soon to a theater near you. Then again, maybe it one day will be. I can't wait to hear some hot sexy actor growl, "*Damned*

---

[18] Dr. Hare also happens to be married to *Bonobo Handshake* author and researcher Vanessa Woods.
[19] Much more on Lola ya Bonobo in Step 12.

dirty bonobos!"[20]... though it'll give "dirty" a whole different meaning.

---

[20] With a pat on Charleton Heston's naked tush for that immortal line "Get your stinking paws off me, you damned dirty ape!" from the original *Planet of the Apes*.

Chapter 8: Food, Sex & Culture

"After a good dinner one can forgive anybody, even one's own relations."
— Oscar Wilde, *A Woman of No Importance*

What's lunch got to do with it?

Sharing food is as vital to the quality of life in Bonoboville as sharing the love. In fact, they often go together. In stark contrast to common chimps who tend to be rather stingy, bonobos make it a point to share munchables with family, friends *and* interesting strangers. Meals are especially scrumptious when seasoned with the sauce of sex. As *Sex at Dawn*'s Dr. Ryan says, "Nothing gets a bonobo orgy started faster than a feast."

Why are bonobos so open-handed with food (and sex) while their chimpanzee brothers and sisters are tightfisted? Most primatologists agree with a theory I first heard from Dr. Richard Wrangham back in 1996: that bonobos evolved to be such sexy beasts due to a geographical split occurring one to three million years ago, when the Congo River's sudden change in course literally changed the course of history. The tremendous watery shift divided a group of great apes that had just recently broken off from those that would evolve into humans. Since none of these apes could swim (both bonobos and chimps still can't), they've remained separated by the great river ever since.

Those that wound up to the north evolved into common chimps, and those to the south became bonobos. North and south may as well have been different planets, as two completely different types of great ape societies arose from the rift. As the eminent and witty Stanford neuroscientist/primatologist Dr. Robert Sapolsky puts it, "Chimps are from Mars. Bonobos are from Venus."

Bonobos vs. Chimps: Organic Buffet vs. Bullet-Riddled McDonald's

According to the theory, the apes to the north had a much tougher time finding food, and had to compete with gorillas for the limited edibles available. Typically knuckle-walking on the ground, oftentimes in dry savannas without the looming protection of the rainforest, they were, and still are, constantly exposed to danger. Whenever common chimps go out to "do lunch," they're also at risk of *being* lunch. Leopards, lions and other predators roam freely in chimpanzee habitats, any of which could easily ruin any ape's appetite as well as erotic mood.

Meanwhile, down south, nestled between the Congo and Kasai rivers, in the heart of the world's second largest rainforest, the bonobos evolved without the same pressures. The Congo Basin is a natural salad bar of plentiful, diverse and nutritious food. Moreover, the lucky bonobos have long enjoyed what primatologists call "relaxed feeding competition" where they never have to share scarce resources with gorillas or struggle to find their next meal. Then and now, bonobos spend most of their time high above the rainforest floor, eating well, swinging through trees and sleeping in nests between branches under an arboreal awning, a natural jungle canopy bed.

The contrast in the living conditions of the bonobo and the common chimp is like the difference between a tropical paradise featuring several all-you-can-eat organic buffets and a run-down, gang-infested neighborhood with a single bullet-riddled McDonald's. Where would *you* rather spend a romantic weekend?

An abundance of food makes for better, more leisurely sex and allows tribes to grow bigger, all while keeping everyone well fed. Bonobo groups tend to be larger and more stable than chimp troops, enabling females to bond as they forage together, consolidating their social power and keeping the males sexually happy and calm. Growing up with ample nourishment and reliable protection also means you can take a little longer to grow up. This allows your slowly developing baby brain to spend years basking in your doting mama's attention and love which, in turn, teaches you to be attentive and loving (i.e., trusting, tolerant, cooperative, compassionate, sensuous and playful) and to choose attentive and loving lovers.

Does this mean that when apes like us feel safe and have enough to eat, we're not as apt to kill each other and more inclined to make love? Yes, indeed. But the story's a little more complex than that. And it's not just because most of us would barf from a lunch of fresh termites, a bonobo delicacy.[21]

---

[21] On the other hand, termites are on the menu for some human tribes in Africa and Asia. The little critters are, in fact, quite nutritious, packing a good store of fat and protein, and have a nutty flavor when roasted.

Another element in the equation is bonobo culture, which may be at least as important to the delicate balance of their peace-through-pleasure society as their rainforest zip code. *Sex at Dawn*'s Dr. Ryan maintains the cultural factor is critical because "a few million years is plenty of time for the bonobo population to swell to maximum carrying capacity. According to the theory of natural selection, once that happened, individual bonobos would face the same ruthless Malthusian selective pressures as any other species. The struggle for survival would become paramount and they'd face the same competition for food as the chimps do, resulting, theoretically, in the same aggressive behavior."

Why didn't that happen? Ryan sees an answer in the nongenetic, non-environmental, learned *culture* of the bonobos. Some scientists and most religionists cringe at talk of any non-human culture. However, our primate relatives reveal that we aren't the only animals to teach our children how we do things—from what to eat, to how to fight, to when, where and with whom to have sex. Moreover, the fact that these things can be done quite differently in other zip codes doesn't appear to be exclusively human either.

Baboons Go Bonobos

Since we've never known bonobos to kill one another, it's tough to figure out where their seemingly "innate" ability to make peace through pleasure comes from. But perhaps we can see what the process might have been like a few hundred thousand years ago through observations of some of our more distant relatives. Illustrating primate cultural change, Dr. Sapolsky tells the enthralling tale of "Forest Troop," a clan of savannah baboons on the untamed Serengeti who dramatically transformed their culture within one generation. Interestingly enough, the catalyst to change was food. In this case, some very bad food.

A species of Old World monkey, baboons are notoriously brutal. Adult males have been observed savagely killing each other, raping the females and making war on other tribes in the wild. At the start of Sapolsky's study, Forest Troop was no different. A neighboring group's alpha males were even more violent, there being something of value (food!) to fight over. Their territory included a cornucopia of discarded junk food in a garbage dump outside a Kenyan guesthouse. Sapolsky dubbed this gang "Garbage Dump Troop," observing that the most powerful males fought off the others and feasted on all the leftover burgers, stale French fries, cookie crumbs and melted ice cream on a daily basis. When males from Forest Troop infiltrated Garbage Dump Troop's precious dump, all of the warriors in both tribes battled each other for the delectable scraps that they never shared with the females, children or more passive males. These aggressive, gluttonous, high-ranking thugs also stopped many social, sensuous, calming activities such as grooming. Who has time to groom with all that tasty trash to fight over?

Life in Baboonville got progressively bloodier and more combative, until it suddenly turned upside down. One fateful day, some tainted meat was thrown into the dump, and all the big-shot baboons that fed there contracted tuberculosis and died, leaving behind the females, youngsters and nice guys who, due to their subordinate statuses, hadn't been privileged enough to dine on the infected beef. Now suddenly, these non-violent, more socially adept and very well groomed "survivors" were in charge of things. Rates of aggression plummeted. Rates of grooming skyrocketed. Sensuous pleasure and harmony reigned. Sapolsky even observed adult males grooming each other, "a behavior nearly as unprecedented as baboons sprouting wings."

Apparently, these baboons went bonobos!

The amazing thing is that, over the years, they seem to have *stayed* bonobos, or at least bonoboësque. Some two decades after the deadly tuberculosis outbreak, Sapolsky's Forest Troop was still uncharacteristically peaceful, sensuous and affiliative, spending a lot more time grooming than fighting and making love, not war. How did they do it? Since baboon boys leave their birth troop after puberty, there were soon new, violent males from other colonies entering Forest Troop who, if baboon violence was truly inborn, should have pummeled the females and mellow males into submission. Yet Forest Troop's extraordinarily harmonious (for baboons), cuddly, nurturing, female-friendly, measurably less stressful vibe persisted as the rowdy new recruits were gently but firmly schooled by the rest of the troop into keeping the peace, bonobo-style.

Though more study is needed to determine the complex mechanisms involved in such behavioral changes, they do indicate that baboon wars and bonobo peace have, at least in part, a cultural foundation. Describing this aspect of bonobo culture as a "self-domestication" process in their 2011 paper, Drs. Wrangham, Hare and Victoria Wobber say that bonobos essentially tame each other the way humans domesticate dogs (unless you're breeding pit bulls), by deliberately "selecting" against brutes and bad attitudes. If only we humans selected our mates with the same attention to harmony. Maybe one day, we will…

After all, the Bonobo Way is not just for bonobos. If a bunch of baboons can release their "inner bonobo," maybe us grouchy, gun-toting humans can too.

Chapter 9: Hot Bi Girls & Sweet Mama's Boys

"Female power is the *sine qua non* of bonobo life, the magic key to their world."
— Dr. Richard Wrangham, *Demonic Males*

Modern feminists would do well to take a page from the bonobo playbook. Unlike common chimps and other great apes whose males tend to intimidate, batter and harass the females, bonobo society is not male-dominated. Bonobo gals are on essentially equal footing with the boys. Some primatologists, like Dr. Isabel Behncke Izquierdo (famous for her sexy science TED Talks on bonobo play) and Dr. Amy Parish of the University of Southern California, even give the ladies the edge, characterizing bonobos as "matriarchal." I call them the most feminist apes on Earth.[22]

Bonobo Sisterhood

Where do these gals (who are slightly smaller and physically weaker than the males) get their moxie? Female bonobos cultivate powerful relationships with each other, creating their own version of "solidarity" or "sisterhood," even though adult females in any one group are generally not sisters, nor closely blood-related at all.

Among bonobos as well as common chimps, girls migrate to another group once they reach childbearing age. This effectively keeps the rate of incest between bonobo fathers and brothers and their fertile daughters and sisters rather low, despite all the mixed mating. And getting out from under the overbearing thumbs of moms and siblings seems to help the young ladies develop strength and character.

They certainly are sexually precocious. In a recent study of common chimpanzees and bonobos, Dr. Verena Behringer and other scientists from the Max Planck Institute, working with the Antwerp Zoo, found that female bonobos enter puberty around three years earlier than their chimp

---

[22] Though bonobos are the most female-dominant great apes, among other "lesser" primates, such as rhesus monkeys, the females have also been found to be more aggressive than the males, sexually and otherwise.

counterparts. When it comes to sex, bonobo girls are early developers.

Itching to sow their wild oats, they also begin their migration into new groups sooner than chimpanzee girls who generally encounter hostility from the veteran females who view the new crop as competition (for food, not males). In Bonoboville, it's the opposite. The mature doyennes see the recent arrivals as potential allies, protégés and friends.

It's a process. As soon as an adolescent bonobo babe joins her new clan, she starts to literally suck up to one of the group's *grande dames*. The young arrival hangs around the sidelines looking for an older female to act as her matriarchal mentor and welcome her into the scene. The older female will show her new young friend the ropes as they groom each other, have sex and eat together (often all at the same time!). It's worth noting that bonobo female prestige tends to increase with age. There are no old, forgotten grandmas in Bonoboville. And those females who promote good relations garner the most clout.

These "hot bi girls" of the Great Ape World develop intense female alliances in which erotic activity plays an integral part. They aren't just "gay for pay." Girl-girl sex in Bonoboville is at least as passionate and important as boy-girl.

Bonobo Boyishness & the Fountain of Youth

In contrast to their wandering sisters, the bonobo boys stay home with Mom. Though bonobo mothers and sons avoid PIV intercourse, they are extremely close, emotionally intimate and physically affectionate, as well as politically entwined, throughout their lives.

Bonobo males also stay younger longer than their chimpanzee counterparts. They are particularly sweet-tempered, playful and boyish, even when no longer boys, especially compared to common chimps, who are just as good-natured as babies, but quickly mature into grumpy old apes.

What's the secret to this bonobo Fountain of Youth? One reason for the males' "paedomorphism" (the retention of typically juvenile traits in adults), lies in their relatively high thyroid levels of the "T3" (triiodothyronine) hormone. T3 is essential to many basic bodily functions in bonobos and humans and is associated with the production of neurotransmitters like serotonin and norepinephrine that regulate feelings of well-being and responses to stress. Bonobo guys hold onto a lot less stress than chimps (and many humans), diverting and converting conflict into erotic reconciliation.

In an associated Max Planck Institute study analyzing thyroid hormones in urine samples, Dr. Behringer determined that male bonobos retain elevated levels of the T3 hormone well into adulthood. In contrast, male chimp T3 levels and male human T3 levels (to a lesser degree) drop after puberty. Low T3 levels in humans are known to cause clinical depression. This late decline of thyroid hormones in male bonobos helps keep them charmingly boyish, relatively good-tempered and female-friendly, as though they are constantly imbibing from that bonobo elixir of youthfulness.

It's not just nature. Nurture also keeps them young at heart. Baby bonobo boys are pampered little princes, coddled by their doting mothers and looked after by Mama's loyal gal pals. If an older bonobo male tries to assault a baby boy, the mom brigade will usually swoop down on him, sometimes even before he lands a punch or bite. This stands in stark contrast to the hard lives of young male chimps, who are often harassed, tortured and sometimes killed by the big guys, even in full view of their mothers and sisters who are usually too timid to defend them.

This kind of deep, active, early mothering is critical to keeping the peace in Bonoboville. In a study comparing bonobos who were raised by their mothers to orphans, Drs. de Waal and Clay found that the mom-raised apes could show empathy and shower erotic attention on their adversaries immediately after a fight, while their motherless counterparts were more likely to throw long, shrieking tantrums (though none have ever turned murderous like Hollywood's fictional Koba).

As babies, both bonobo males and females need their moms, but unlike the girls, the older boys still do! While common chimp males form alliances to start wars, bonobo males seldom pal around together, preferring the company of the ladies, including their moms. They are "philopatric," derived from the Greek term for "home-loving," meaning they stay in the area they were born. Moreover, a bonobo male's rank in his tribe is based on his mother's status, even when he's all grown up.

In the past, zoos often separated bonobo sons from their mothers, wreaking havoc in their communities. A direct consequence of the separation was that powerful females would gang up on hapless, motherless males, creating a dangerous imbalance. Now, most zoos have wised up and keep the mother-son unit together, making both humans and bonobos more peaceful and much happier.

MILFs Rule Bonoboville

Does that make bonobo males the "Mama's Boys" of the Great Ape World? Perhaps, but the strong relationship between a happy bonobo boy and his hot bisexual mom is one of the cornerstones of peace in Bonoboville. Gentle but firm, the MILFs[23] of Bonoboville lay down the law, keeping the males gentle and firm.

"Essentially, it's like a debutante society," explains Dr. Hare, "where mothers have to introduce their sons into polite society and it's through your mother, as a bonobo, that you will gain access to other females." Hare's theory of bonobo self-domestication says that over the course of evolution, bonobo females "domesticated" the males by only mating with the sweet-tempered ones, the "nice guys" with high T3 levels, boyish appeal and cool moms. A bonobo male's popularity is so directly related to his mama's connections that when the mother of a high-ranking bonobo male dies, he loses some of his status, not to mention his easy "in" with her girlfriends.

So… do bonobo boys behave themselves because their moms are watching? It could explain part of the peace-through-pleasure bonobo mystique. Another part goes back to the bonobo female herself. She is groomed (literally and figuratively) by bonobo culture to be the more active and independent gender. She matures earlier than her brothers (or her chimpanzee cousins) and must leave her mother behind before she reaches adolescence to go off to a new group, take new lovers and make new girlfriends.

These strong gal pal relationships help the females stick together and keep the males agreeable, as has been observed by Dr. Frances J. White of the University of Oregon, America's foremost expert on *Pan paniscus* in the wild, having studied them in Lomako Forest in the DRC since 1983. If a bonobo male is arrogant or ignorant enough to attack a female or her infant, her girlfriends will "correct" him, sometimes painfully, but never lethally.

Common chimp females have a much rougher life, especially in the wild, as Dr. White noted in her *Pan troglodyte* studies in Uganda. When a female common chimp is battered (a frequent occurrence), attacked or even gang-raped by dominance-displaying males, her fellow females generally

---

[23] "MILF" is the abbreviation for the colloquial term "Mother I'd Like to Fuck," first documented on the Internet in the 1990s and popularized by the 1999 film *American Pie*.

look the other way, rarely lifting one hairy little finger to help her, even when she screams in pain.

If you're a bonobo female, your gal pals have your back.

Chapter 10: Hoka-Hoka: The Bonobo Tango

"Sex is emotion in motion"
— Mae West

What makes bonobo female friendships so powerful? Sex! Okay, it's slightly more complex than that (isn't it always?), but sex *is* a major ingredient. Bonobo girls strengthen their friendships by performing what primatologists call "genito-genital" or "GG" rubbing, the act of rapidly swishing, pressing and bouncing their swollen pink labia and protruding clitorises against each other. Sometimes this results in intense orgasm, though often it's just a quick swish. Some scientists call it "frotting" (from the French *frottage*), tribadism (Victorian English) or the more modern "tribbing."

The most onomatopoetic name for the action is "hoka-hoka" from the Bongandu language. Hoka-hoka sounds like a bonobo tango[24], and that's just what it looks like, only it's a rapid vulva-to-vulva dance rather than slow cheek-to-cheek. To use an altogether different dance metaphor, you might consider hoka-hoka to be a crotch-to-crotch twerking duet.

Though they sometimes do it standing up or hanging from a tree, the older female (let's call her Mary) generally lies down and spreads her legs, allowing the younger (we'll name her Mimi) to climb on top and commence swishing and rubbing, often accompanied by mutual clutching, muscular contractions and those high-pitched screams that let everybody in Bonoboville know that Mary and Mimi are getting it on.

Bonobo ladies grow closer to each other through hoka-hoka, consolidating social and political connections along with their orgasms and copulation calls. Hoka-hoka can also be a warm-up for male-female sex. This may be yet another reason why bonobo gals are far more likely to initiate erotic activity with the males than any other great ape females, including humans. They're constantly diddling each other.

Hoka-Hoka Lubricates Life

All this hoka-hoka-fueled solidarity and sexual assertiveness with the boys translates into more bonobo girl power. Not only do these dominant female apes run the show sexually, they also get first dibs on food. They can then barter their edibles for erotic favors, from fellow females or lucky males, essentially "paying" for the kind of sex they want with the partners of their choice. So if you think no self-respecting female would ever pay for sex, take a look at the bonobos. These ladies know what they want, and they don't mind paying for it.

Hoka-hoka lubricates life in Bonoboville. But it has created some interesting friction—in the form of another rather heated debate—in the human primatology world. Most scientists agree that GG-rubbing between female bonobos can be more enthusiastic than sex between males and females. But at least one prominent primatologist at the Max Planck Institute, Dr. Gottfried Hohmann, would rather not even call it "sex."

I confess there's a personal side to this story. When I first saw *The Nature of Sex* in 1993, no one in my world knew a bonobo from a Brillo pad. Thanks to the wonderful work of Drs. Kanō, de Waal, White, Savage-Rumbaugh and others, bonobos gained international recognition as the "Make Love Not War" chimpanzees within a short span of time. But with fame often comes defamation, especially when wild sex is in the mix.

"Bonobo-Bashing in the New Yorker"

And so it came to pass that veteran journalist Ian Parker attempted to deflate the bonobo's buoyant aura in the esteemed pages of *The New Yorker*. He archly derided the work of some of the bonobos' best friends in the human world and hinted ominously that his article would debunk the central ideas of the Bonobo Way. In fact, Mr. Parker's endlessly meandering critique doesn't debunk much of anything but his own presumptions.

For instance, as reported by Parker, Dr. Hohmann (also one of the

---

[24] Part of the tango's origins came from brothels in Argentina. The men, while waiting for the women to finish up with previous customers, would tango in order to "keep themselves warm." Contrary to popular belief, this tango was originally a dance between two men, making it even more fitting as a counterpart to the female-female bonobo "dance" of hoka-hoka.

scientists on the bonobo/chimp hormone studies) admits to observing hoka-hoka numerous times. "But does it have anything to do with sex?" Hohmann asks. He then, according to Parker's story, answers himself curtly: "Probably not."

Really? Since when does rubbing engorged, lubricating genitalia against each other, often while embracing, French-kissing and having what looks and sounds like a major orgasm, "not... have anything to do with sex?" Unless you are limiting your definition of "sex" only to PIV intercourse, which hardly seems right for a creature that is known for engaging in sex for recreation a lot more than procreation.

Dr. de Waal defended bonobo ladies' favorite form of sex as being "sex" in his rebuttal to Parker's story, reprinted in *The Bonobo and the Atheist*. I was tickled that he referenced my article, "Bonobo Bashing in the New Yorker," to support his point that hoka-hoka is indeed a form of sex, no matter how euphemisms may characterize it. As de Waal puts it, some primatologists and journalists "will say that bonobos are 'very affectionate,' when the apes in fact engage in behavior that would get you quickly arrested if shown in the human public sphere."

Maybe Hohmann and Parker are labeling hoka-hoka "not sex" in the same sense that former President Bill Clinton did, when he said, "I did not have sex with that woman." To be fair, Billy Jeff, always a lover of strong females and erotic play (his use of a cigar as a dildo is as resourceful as Lana's use of a ball as a vibrator), was one of our more bonoboësque Commanders-in-Chief.

Chapter 11: Sperm Wars: The Super Bowl of Sex

"Every one of us is the person we are today because one of our recent ancestors produced an ejaculate competitive enough to win a sperm war."
—Dr. Robin Baker, *Sperm Wars: Infidelity, Sexual Conflict and Other Bedroom Battles*

According to The New Yorker, Dr. Hohmann was deeply perplexed as to why the "males, the physically superior animals, do not dominate the females, the inferior animals? ... It is not only different from chimpanzees but it violates the rules of social ecology." Or does it, Dr. Hohmann? Because it certainly doesn't violate the Bonobo Way.

So why do these bigger, stronger bonobo males put up with all that freewheeling female power? Primatologists argue over this like Congress debating a health care bill. It seems pretty simple to me, but maybe that's because I'm a sex therapist: Bonobo guys know they've got a good thing going. Just give the ladies some R-E-S-P-E-C-T,[25] and get plenty of S-E-X-X-X all year round.

All that ample erotic opportunity does appear to make bonobo guys less competitive with each other. Despite the lack of social rivalry, however, fierce sexual fighting between male bonobos does exist, but on a microscopic scale akin to spermatozoid competition, a.k.a. "sperm wars."

You may have seen the term "sperm wars" or "sperm competition" in a guppy breeding manual or cuckolding[26] website, but what do they mean? Conventional wisdom used to say that semen contained only one kind of sperm with a single goal: to swim to the egg and inseminate it. Everybody thought that the ejaculatory release of spermatozoa was like the proverbial gunshot sending all the little tadpoles swimming upstream in a race to the mothership.

---

[25] With appreciation to Aretha Franklin.
[26] "Cuckold" is an old English term for a husband whose wife has sex with other men, with or without his consent. The cuckold may be humiliated by the experience, very aroused or both. In the 21st century, there has been a resurgence of interest in the cuckold's predicament, cuckold sex, cuckold fantasies, cuckold porn, hot wives, big bulls and the consensual cuckold lifestyle.

Then, in the 1970s, while looking at semen under powerful microscopes, biologists found that only 1% of a single male's sperm count contains the actual egg-inseminators. So, what are the rest of those tadpoles up to... what about the 99%?

Bonobos Have Balls

It turns out that sperm behave not so much like a bunch of individual marathon runners, but more like an army platoon or a football team. The offensive players are the tackles and fullbacks in the Big Game going on inside the female's reproductive tract. They don't ever even try to race to the egg because their job is to hunt, tackle and kill sperm using powerful spermicidal enzymes.

What sperm are they trying to kill? Not other sperm from the same male, that wouldn't be very good teamwork, would it? These "killer" tadpoles are trying to attack and destroy sperm from *another* male that might be sharing the vagina with them. There's even chemical warfare in sperm wars. The attack sperm contain "weaponized" toxic enzymes for destroying the "enemy." It's not a walk in the park, however, for the attack sperm that come up against "defensive" sperm on the other side that block and protect their respective inseminator-quarterback brothers from incoming attacks.

Various scientists have applied the "sperm competition" theory of evolutionary biology since Dr. Øjvind Winge coined the term in the 1930s while studying guppy genetics. In 1970, an evolutionary biologist, Dr. Geoffrey Alan Parker, discovered the phenomenon in yellow dung flies. Other scientists, such as Dr. Robin Baker, extended the theory beyond tiny fish and poop-loving insects to all sorts of animals, including common chimps, bonobos and humans.[27] In bonobos, where most of the females in any given tribe are having sex with most of the males, as well as with strange males from neighboring groups, the sperm wars phenomenon reaches its apex, making bonobo sperm competition the Super Bowl of Sex in the Great Ape League.

Here are some measurements to give you some perspective of the scale of the Bonobo Super Bowl: If humans had the same testicle-to-body size ratio as bonobos, the average human male's family jewels would be almost

---

[27]We'll delve deeper into how sperm competition operates within humans in "Bonobo Liberation Step 7: Making Peace through Pleasure" in the second half of this book.

four times as big as they are. *Testify to that, Mr. Bollocks!* Don't let anybody tell you that nice guys finish last, or that peace-loving bonobo dudes don't have balls.

Yet despite their big *cojones* and the sperm wars raging within the reproductive tracts of their female counterparts, the bonobo males themselves aren't very competitive at all in the world *outside* of the vaginal Super Bowl. They literally "Make Sperm Wars, Not Real Wars." They don't partake in the deadly raiding parties and other acts of ape "war" and "terrorism" that sometimes occur among male common chimps, not to mention humans.

Don't get me wrong, bonobo males do fight sometimes. But they tend to resolve the conflict before it descends into carnage by mounting each other, engaging in oral or manual sex, initiating a bonobo handshake, "turning the other cheek" for butt-to-butt contact, rubbing those big nutsacks against each other, or perhaps a strong female steps in for a conciliatory MFM threesome.

Or maybe the boys just "need a hug"—which doesn't have to lead to something more hardcore... though often enough, it does.

That "something" often turns out to be erotic "penis fencing." When I first heard the term, I imagined a "white picket fence" of dicks around a house. Then I thought of an elite corps of pointy cocks feinting and lunging at each other while shouting "*En garde!*" In reality, penis fencing is the male bonobo version of GG-rubbing during which the participants rub their erect penises against each other, sometimes to reduce violent tension. This is not to be confused with the more vicious "penis fencing" among certain hermaphroditic flatworms wherein one tries to inseminate the other by piercing the other's skin with its two-headed, dagger-shaped penis. Ouch! Bonobo penis fencing is much more pleasurable, non-penetrative and may stimulate the sperm wars effect, especially if females are watching.

Sperm Competition Illuminates "The Lifestyle"

I raised guppies as a child, but the tropical fish books my parents bought me never said anything about Dr. Øjvind Winge and sperm competition. I first learned about it lolling around a different kind of water tank—a hotel pool filled with naked humans frolicking like bonobos at a 1996 *Lifestyles* convention. In between orgies and seminars, Terry Gould, an investigative journalist who made a name for himself interviewing mobsters about organized crime, was interviewing me about ethical hedonism and the Bonobo Way for his pioneering book, *The Lifestyle.* As we talked about bonobos and watched the swingers swing, Gould filled me in on Baker's sperm wars theory.

I was fascinated, having often wondered why so many men in the swinging Lifestyle loved seeing their wives and girlfriends have sex with other men. Even Max found it titillating. So did many of my sex therapy clients, though most were too embarrassed to tell their wives. Weren't these husbands jealous? And even if they were, why did many of them want to make love to the wife immediately after she'd been with another man—even a consensual gangbang with several men? Sperm wars illuminated this mystery, and a whole lot more.

According to the theory, whenever a man gets ready to have sex with a woman, he unconsciously (or sometimes consciously) considers the odds of her being with another man. If he believes that she's his faithful wife or girlfriend, he might love and adore her, but his erection won't be at its strongest, nor will his semen volume be at its fullest. Reflexively, since his testicles "know" they don't have to fight an adversary, they don't generate the full team of several hundred million sperm, including both offense and defense with all their toxic and counter-toxic plays. Instead, the man "conserves" his semen, and might ejaculate 90 million or less. After all, he just needs a few runners to reach an egg when he has no rivals. It's like a football game with only one team on the field. The players might have fun tossing the ball around, but they're not going to play very hard as they meander, unchecked, toward an easy score.

But if the man feels he does have competition, if he sees his lady having sex at a swing club, if he enjoys a threesome with her and another man, if he thinks she's cheating on him, watches her flirt or dance with another guy or even if he just vividly imagines her engaging in "slutty" behavior, his testicles will often spring into action and produce as many as hundreds of millions of warriors, blockers and inseminators alongside the regular runner sperm. After all, there's a war on! There's a big game to be won! The result is that he has greater arousal, more ejaculate and a more intense orgasm than usual.

Make Sperm Wars, Not Real Wars!

Although sperm competition may be more prominent in Bonoboville, it can also occur within all kinds of human marriages. Whether hubby "likes" the idea of his wife having sex with another guy or not—whether he's a happy swinger, a humiliated cuckold, a curious voyeur, a knowledgeable polyamorist, a controlling pimp, an angry victim or just a confused spouse—sperm wars occur every day, everywhere.

Studies have shown that a husband's sperm count rises when his wife is away for a few days, even if he's ejaculated as much as he normally does during her absence. Not knowing exactly what the little lady is up to when she goes out "with the girls" or stays late "in a meeting" can send that urgent telegram of arousal to a man's balls to *assemble the army*, so he's hot, hard and ready to jump her bones by the time she gets home. This tends to happen whether the man is insanely jealous or filled with sweet compersion.

Often considered the opposite of jealousy, the word "compersion" is used by swingers and polyamorists to convey the empathetic, bonoboësque joy they feel for their partners' pleasure with others. The term is said to have originated within the old polyfidelitous Kerista commune of San Francisco. Compersion can be a natural reaction to circumstances or it can be learned. Typically, parents feel this kind of empathetic joy for their children's joys and accomplishments, and fans feel it when their team wins. But polyamorous couples also experience compersion when their lovers are pleasured by others. In some ways, compersion is the height of erotic love just as jealousy can be the pits. Not everyone is capable of compersion or even wants to be, but it certainly makes the sperm wars effect more enjoyable.

Now, if only we could keep the wars between sperm and stop the ones between people, we would have peace through pleasure. And it might be less outrageous than it sounds. After all, the bonobos do it.

Chapter 12: The Kiss

"Kiss me and you will see how important I am."
— Sylvia Plath

It was my fourth visit to Lana's domain. A French film crew from Mona Lisa Productions' *Humanimal: The Animal Mind* (a documentary series about the closeness of humans to other animals), came to shoot a live RadioSuzy1 broadcast as well as a private (as private as you can get with a French film crew shooting you) BLT[28] session with a young married couple.

There are many reasons a couple or individual might come to us for BLT. In this case, the wife wanted the husband to be more sensitive in bed, and the husband wished the wife would be more aggressive. The Bonobo Way was very well-suited to help both fulfill each other's desires and, after watching a film of bonobos, they had the "hottest sex ever" right here in the Institute.[29] The French, despite being French, were impressed, but wanted more. They wanted to see actual bonobos.

We took the 405 Freeway south to the Bonoboville at the San Diego Zoo on a sweltering September day. An hour after we arrived, I realized how lucky I'd been to witness bonobos having so much sex on my other visits. Like *Homo sapiens*, *Pan paniscus* aren't always ready to spring into action. That day, they looked like how I feel when I've had too much "Bonoboville Communion"[30] the night before and not enough coffee in the morning. Listless and lethargic, they lay on their backs, gazing up at the treetops.

The zookeeper explained that, earlier that morning, she'd separated the females to keep them from "bonding," so they wouldn't gang up on the males. She sounded reasonable enough, but I had a hunch that "bonding" was euphemistic zoo-talk for hoka-hoka, and that the zookeeper was doing whatever zookeepers do to keep the females from having sex with each

---

[28] Remember, that's Bonobo Liberation Therapy—hold the mayo.
[29] More juicy details about exactly how that happened in Chapter Fifteen: Release Your Inner Bonobo.
[30] Bonoboville Communion will be described in delicious detail in Step 5: Mix Food & Sex. For now, suffice it to say, it involves drinking and licking.

other. Cattle prods came to mind, though I'm sure the zoo's systems are much more compassionate. In any case, since female-female sexuality is a cornerstone of bonobo society, when these ladies couldn't "bond," the whole tribe fell into a funk.

So did the French. The only people who can make you feel guiltier than a Jewish mother with heartburn is a French film crew on a tight schedule. They looked at me expectantly. Here they were paying me in cash euros to shoot a segment that would open the door to the transformational world of bonobo sexuality for their audience of cultured and horny European animal lovers. But all the bonobos were staring up at the sky or picking their noses. What could I do?

I scanned the lounging apes and spotted my old friend Lana, who was now the tribe's alpha female. She had a tiny month-old infant nursing at her generous breast (yes, mama bonobos can be quite busty[31]). Before I could even catch her eye, she scampered up to the window, infant in tow, opened her lips and hooted at me. I wondered, "Is this her standard bonobo-human hoot, or did she recognize me?" Eight years after our first encounter, Lana's face was thicker and more weatherworn, though it still twinkled with youthful openness, displaying those endearingly "juvenile" characteristics so integral to bonobo harmony.

As Lana's big baby-brown eyes caught my blue ones, she pursed her lips into another hoot… Or was it a kiss?

A Thunderclap of Bonobo-Human Connection

"I'm so glad to see you again," I cooed back at her, and she seemed to concur. I couldn't hear her through the thick glass and I probably wouldn't have understood her even if I could. But as she hooted and I cooed, I felt the rush of our connection. We were two creatures on one wavelength. We just didn't speak quite the same language.

What we lacked linguistically, we filled in physically. Lana slapped her big gnarled left hand up on the glass, blinking at me suggestively. "What could she be suggesting?" I wondered as I laid my freshly-manicured fingertips on the other side of the partition, hooking up with her, right hand to left hand, and fingers to fingers. She swiveled her chin and laughed as if I'd just taken the bait. Then I placed my left palm upon the window. She followed with her right. Not to be outplayed, she upped the ante by leaning

---

[31] As one of my breast fetishist friends pointed out, "You can't spell 'bonobos' without 'boobs.' It would just be 'no'."

back and putting her huge leathery foot on the glass, stretching her coral-colored lips into a dramatic big O and swiveling her chin like an exotic dancer.

She seemed to be hooting, "I dare you to follow me now!" Naturally, I kicked off my flip-flops and placed my bare, pedicured tootsies up to hers, sensing her powerful toes pushing hard against the thick glass. Sitting there, ass on the ground, feet up on the window, I felt like a kid learning a new kind of mime[32] from a friend. One key juvenile characteristic of bonobos is that they never stop playing, no matter how old they are.

Then I remembered our Gallic pals who, of course, had been filming us all along with great excitement. I realized that, whether she knew it or not, Lana was helping me, one sexpert to another, by tossing some cinematic meat to the hungry cameras.

But for me, this was more than just a film shoot. It was a bonobo-human thunderclap. "We have looked to the stars searching for contact with intelligent beings," says anthropologist Itai Roffman of Haifa University's International School of Evolution. "However, they have been with us all along, and are called *Pan*."

I felt like Elliot touching fingertips with E.T., except this was with the feet of a fellow Earthling, my primate cousin, Lana.

A Profound Interspecies Event (PIE)

Then Lana reminded me she was my *kissing* cousin by pursing her flexible lips as she had before, but now showering me with peck after peck after peck, a flurry of tiny kisses against the window between us. I found myself peck-kissing her back, caught up in her seductive spell, not considering the fact I was kissing a non-human ape, albeit through crystal-clear glass.

Suddenly, Lana backed away and hooted to her girlfriends who had been calling her the whole time. Lolita slowly and curiously ventured toward the window, but Ikela leaped up like a jaguar and pounded on the glass, baring her teeth. Was she angry? Jealous?

Whatever Ikela's motivation, I was grateful for that substantial partition. Then, just as swiftly as she'd charged, she cooled off and got friendly, or at least calmer. She fondled and hugged Lana, patted the window, licked her expressive lips and escorted Lana down the hill.

Then Lana's other daughter, three-year-old Mchumba, cartwheeled up to greet me, rubbing her eager little rump against the glass. I rubbed back in response, but before I could say "bonobo handshake," Mchumba swung off on a rope and Lana was back, re-establishing our special connection and giving me the eye like a knowing butch in a chic lesbian bar. With my big straw hat and relatively hairless body, I fancied I was the femme in this erotic interspecies interface. I lowered my lashes, returned her gaze and smiled.

She kissed me. This was no quick 'hello' kiss nor a smattering of sweet little pecks like before. This was a long, slow, dramatic, downright tantric tongue smooch right on the glass in front of my face, those big, brown, assertive, inquisitive eyes of hers boring right into mine.

Again, I was thankful for the windowpane, because I'm sure I would have been aghast at ape saliva all over my face. But with the glass safely and squarely between us, I was utterly enchanted and irresistibly drawn into this very close encounter. It was a spiritual and yet infinitely playful call to the wild through the electrical connection that ignites us all.

At least, that's the way it felt from my side of the glass. Feeling the pull of that bond, I couldn't help but kiss her back, our lips meeting without touching, a modern interspecies same-sex version of Pyramus and Thisbē, with a shatterproof, transparent wall drawing us together while simultaneously keeping us apart.

Our kiss lingered voluptuously for several timeless seconds, then stopped as suddenly as it started. Lana pulled back from the window, licked her lips, turned and slipped away to munch on what looked like a big piece of halva, while gymnastic Mchumba jumped up like a jack-in-the-box to take her place, doing several exuberant handstands and rope swings as her mother and I watched, Lana from the stream, me from the window.

Long after we parted, Lana's presence tingled within me. I felt like I

---

[32] Please don't hold it against me, but my Yale theater education included a pantomime class, which, after graduation, I parlayed into a paying gig as a New Haven "City Mime," knocking on imaginary doors for politicians and school kids K-12, as well as annoying the pedestrians and providing a perch for the pigeons while pretending to be a statue in front of City Hall.

had just had sacred (and very safe!) sexual outercourse[33] with a bonobo cousin. This was the "Chivers Effect" on steroids. Once again, Max wasn't there to witness, but his sexy smile widened as I told him all about it, and when we made love that night, the "magic" of *The Nature of Sex* came rushing back again like a great river, replete with images of expressive ape lips and leathery hand-like feet pulling, sucking, squeezing and swirling us into Gaia's gargantuan, multi-orgasmic web of life.

In "On Tortoises, Monkeys and Men," Dr. Tony Rose (another very special guest on RadioSuzy1) writes about "profound interspecies events" (PIEs) which he describes as "natural epiphanies… reunion[s] of humanity and nature" that occur when "humans experience profound connections with animals."

My encounter with Lana was the closest thing I'd ever experienced to a PIE, but what did it mean? I can only imagine what it meant to Lana, but for me, it was a physical affirmation of a powerful connection between bonobos and humans that I believe can help us both.

---

[33] "Outercourse," which I describe much more thoroughly in Step 4, is any kind of sexual activity between two or more people that doesn't involve penetration or intercourse of the vagina, anus or mouth

Chapter 13: An Alternative Great Ape Paradigm for Humanity

"I sometimes try to imagine what would have happened if we'd known the bonobo first and chimpanzees only later or not at all. The discussion about human evolution might not revolve as much around violence, warfare and male dominance, but rather around sexuality, empathy, caring and cooperation."
— Dr. Frans de Waal, *Our Inner Ape*

So... what's it all mean to us? What does the Bonobo Way signify to human psychology, sexuality, anthropology, sociology, endocrinology, wellness, relationship counseling, ecology and community? By looking through current research on bonobos and other primates, we can infer deep and far-ranging insights into our humanity and our place on this wild and very sexual planet Earth, even within this 14-billion-year-old cosmos. In essence, the Bonobo Way offers an alternative great ape paradigm for human behavior, especially (but not exclusively) sexual behavior. This isn't just about grooving on some sexy beasts who swing through the trees. Nor is it Utopia through sexual liberation. What it represents is a revolutionary, very real and sustainable step forward in human awareness that also brings us back to our primal roots.

Is War Wired Into Our Genes?

Take war. Traditional science, along with the culture it informs, has long maintained we have murder and war wired into our genes. "Our bloody nature is ingrained," proclaims eminent biologist Dr. E. O. Wilson. But how do we know this, aside from our apparent love of cheap horror flicks and expensive perma-wars?

"Our closest ape relatives," explains Dr. Steven A. LeBlanc, "have always engaged in ferocious acts of warfare," chillingly reminiscent of human conflict. Dr. Jane Goodall famously observed this among chimpanzees in the jungles of Tanzania, where rival chimp gangs plotted, ambushed, gleefully tortured and ferociously killed their adversaries to acquire new territory.[34] Dr. Mitani's studies of common chimpanzees in Uganda deliberately murdering members of their own species, and even waging war on each other with strategic, lethal attacks further reveal *Pan troglodyte* being worthy of their Latin name, a *troglodyte* being "a creature of degraded, primitive or brutal character." In 2012, an adult male chimpanzee mauled a 3-month-old to death at the Los Angeles Zoo, grabbing the baby chimp from her mother, holding her away from the rest of the troop and repeatedly hitting her head as zoo visitors, staff and the murdered baby's mother watched in horror.

Are We Killer Apes?

Philosopher/archeologists like LeBlanc and evolutionary psychologists like Dr. Steven Pinker have long used the "killer ape" behavioral paradigms of common chimps, first devised by Dr. Raymond Dart, to account for the prevalence of violent behavior among humans. They suggest that people innately love to rape, pillage, bomb and behead each other, and always will.

This hugely popular notion comes to cinematic life in the opening of Stanley Kubrick's *2001: A Space Odyssey*, when one of our chimp-ish ancestors murders another with a zebra bone and victoriously tosses the weapon into the air where it morphs into a spaceship. More recently, *Dawn of the Planet of the Apes* presents an apocalyptic, dystopian vision of genetically enhanced warrior apes ruling the world, conveying the message that murder, war and the military mindset are wired so deeply within our DNA as apes that we can't possibly evolve beyond it.

For years, many scientists chimed in on this bleak, relentlessly male-dominated, "might is right" perspective on humanity, pointing to common chimps, rhesus monkeys and baboons to explain the purportedly primal roots of human murder and mayhem. These primate models, along with the warrior ape movies, reveal important aspects of human nature, but do they tell us the whole story?

---

[34] Dr. Goodall's team provisioned wild chimps with something to fight over—a limited supply of bananas—which may have stimulated at least some of the killing. In similar studies, however, primatological teams (such as Dr. Kanō's) have provisioned bonobos, and they didn't kill each other. All those ripe, yummy bananas might have just caused the bonobos to have a little more sex.

No—thank Gaia, Pan, Aphrodite, Ares and Eros![35]—they don't. We humans are at least as genetically close to the lovey-dovey bonobos as we are to the bellicose common chimps, and far closer to them than we are to those bloodthirsty baboons (Sapolsky's Forest Troop notwithstanding). Few experts acknowledged this until very recently. Many scientists still prefer to marginalize the bonobo who disturbs their Hollywood-friendly, military-supportive, sexy-but-not-too-sexual view of Man the Warrior whom they present as having obviously evolved from a warrior ape, not a peace-through-pleasure-loving ape. I can't even begin to count how many articles and books I've read that compare the violence in humans to chimps, but completely ignore or, worse, utterly misrepresent bonobos... and sex. Slowly, but surely, this is changing.

Obviously, humanity has its murderous, militaristic, common chimpish side. Thanks to the fracturing effects of property ownership, religious indoctrination and the human ingenuity that's gifted us with H-bombs, pipe bombs and automatic weapons, we humans are capable of violence beyond what any mere (non-genetically enhanced) chimp could dream of. However, unlike our *Pan troglodyte* cousins, *Homo sapiens* (at least those of us who aren't psychopaths or fanatics) tend not to relish our murders and wars. When chimpanzees kill, they appear to really enjoy themselves. Of course, we don't know exactly what's going on in their minds when they rip a fellow chimp to shreds. Watching a Wildscreen Arkive video of a troop of common chimps approach, attack, murder, dismember and lustily devour a fellow chimp from another group, it certainly looks to this human viewer like the killers are having a ball.

On the other side, bonobos refrain from killing each other entirely. Humans seem to fall somewhere between our two closest cousins. We do kill each other, but we tend to mourn, regret, condemn or at least try to excuse the taking of life, even when on the so-called "right" or winning side.

According to Dr. de Waal, there's even a critical bit of DNA involved in "bonding" that is found in both humans and bonobos, but not in

---

[35] In Greek mythology, Gaia is Mother Earth. Pan is god of the wild. Aphrodite is goddess of love, sex and beauty. Ares is god of war. Eros is Aphrodite's son, who may have been sired by Ares or one of his mother's many other lovers (though certainly not her husband, Hephaestus, the classical cuckold). Eros also rules the realms of sexual desire, shooting his victims with the arrows of love. But Eros is more than that. According to the ancient Greeks, erotic passion is the life force itself, and Eros was one of the original creators of the

common chimps. More proof our emotional wiring is closer to the peaceful, sexual bonobo than to the brutal, militaristic chimpanzee.

"It's worth noting that nobody suffers from post-traumatic stress disorder (PTSD) from helping a stranger," *Sex at Dawn*'s Dr. Ryan points out in a *Humanist* interview. "Now when we kill other people and hurt other people we suffer from that…it hurts us. So that does indicate that we're not neutral, that we are closer to the bonobo than to the chimp in terms of our reaction to violence and our ability to tolerate high levels of stress."

What might happen if we could somehow reorient ourselves toward our more loving, bonobo side rather than our inner mad chimpanzee?

Being "Humane" Is Actually Very Bonobo

Led Zeppelin needed a "Whole Lotta Love," and we great apes got a whole lotta love to give. The Good Samaritan who gives to the less fortunate, whether giving a hug or an anonymous hundred-million-dollar donation, is actually quite bonoboësque.

We can see the seeds of what we call our "humanity" in Hare and Woods's research which notes marked differences in the way common chimpanzees and bonobos interact with strangers of their own species. A chimp treats the newcomer as a rival or adversary and if food is available, the chimp will hoard it for himself. Under the same circumstances, studies by Hare and Jingzhi Tan in a controlled laboratory environment show that most bonobos will treat strangers as if they're already friends, often even better than friends. If a new companion is locked out of the enclosure containing food, the bonobo will find a way to open the door in order to share the meal.

Why? Apparently, bonobos understand that good food always tastes better with company, especially when sex is involved. And there usually is in Bonoboville. Perhaps the pleasure and satisfaction bonobos get out of sharing food and sex with strangers is at the root of human charity, altruism and social networking... not to mention mercy sex.

Compare bonobo values to the human war machine, global gun cultures, the cold greed of Wall Street, the cynical hypocrisy of K Street, Hollywood's glorification of high-definition violence, the corporate raping of our ecosystem, the brutal subjugation of women in patriarchies around

---

universe. Here, in our human Bonoboville, we celebrate "Eros Day" when the planetoid Eros is closest to Earth.

the world, the gangs of disaffected young men turned murderous by their elders, the ever-expanding Military-Industrial Complex (MIC) and Prison-Industrial Complex (PIC), the Army-Surplus policing of our citizenry and… you just have to wonder which animal is really "humane."

Chapter 14: 50 Shades of Bonobo

"The truth is that if bonobo behavior provides any hints, very few human sexual practices can be dismissed as 'unnatural.'"
— Dr. Frans de Waal, *Bonobo: The Forgotten Ape*

When bonobos first frolicked across my TV screen in 1993, I felt like I'd rediscovered long-lost relatives who, unlike my own rather upright clan, knew how to party hardier than the swingingest swingers in Swingtown.

I realize that's a very anthropomorphic thing to say, almost like a kinky version of what Disney and Warner did to mice and ducks. Some primatological purists frown upon any anthropomorphic comparisons of *Pan paniscus* to human swingers or polyamorists, contending that it ignores important human/bonobo differences and draws prurient attention to their intense sexuality.

My King Kong

But another opinion, which I share, is that a little animal-centric anthropomorphizing never hurt Flipper. In fact, the old TV show created tremendous human awareness of dolphins, their amazing abilities and their endangered plight. The highly imperiled bonobos desperately need this kind of special, focused and empathetic consciousness to help save them from imminent extinction.[36] So a little anthropomorphizing may just be in their best interests. It might rattle the primatological purists, but one of the major reasons many human laypersons (who are, as the term implies, preoccupied with getting "laid") deeply care about bonobos is because their playful sexuality reminds us so much of our own.

My personal fascination with apes began with the biggest ape of all, the classic King Kong, whom I "met" as a toddler through the original silent version on late-night TV. The giant gorilla seemed so human! He even threw tantrums like I did, though he was a lot more violent. For years, I dreamt of a big hairy hand reaching through the curtains of my bedroom

---

[36] See Step 12 for more about the bonobos' endangered status, what's going on in the world of bonobo conservation, and how you can help.

window. These were mostly nightmares, but sometimes King Kong took me away on a fun adventure. When I was about seven or eight, I created my first "porn:" a series of pen drawings of Kong ape-handling a half-naked woman who was a cross between Fay Wray (whom I was honored to interview on my show years later), my anatomically incorrect Barbie doll and me.

When my mother, an art teacher, found the drawings, she was intrigued and even praised their primitive artistry. But I was mortified to be so discovered, being just old enough to have learned that "society" (and my more conservative relatives) would consider such erotically anthropomorphic illustrations taboo or at least jeer-worthy, no matter what my artsy mom said. Fearing further exposure and feeling like throwing one of my Kong-like tantrums, I grabbed the drawings from her hand, tore the paper to shreds (an action I later regretted) and promised myself I would never again create such embarrassing ape erotica. Ah, how we humans torture and destroy ourselves and our art in the name of shame! Luckily, no amount of tearing and swearing could destroy my childhood passion for the archetypically anthropomorphic King Kong and my other fellow apes that resurfaced years later when I discovered bonobos. Could have been my "inner bonobo" who drew those pictures.

Are You In a State of Anthropodenial?

Anthropomorphizing non-human animals is as natural as a child's love for a big old Hollywood gorilla. Moreover, it may not be as unscientific as the old guard maintains.

"Given that the split between the ancestors of humans and chimpanzees is assumed to have occurred a mere five to six million years ago, anthropomorphism should be less of an issue than anthropodenial," points out Dr. de Waal in *The Ape and the Sushi Master*.

Are you in a state of "anthropodenial"? Do you, consciously or subconsciously, reject the scientific evidence that we humans are great apes closely related to other great apes? Some anthropodeniers cling to religious tracts that give people "dominion" over animals. Others assert human superiority through our ability to alter our environment to suit our immediate needs—even though that very ability tends to pollute that environment, often killing us with cancers, traffic jams, nuclear leaks and a myriad of other ills. Others just aren't comfortable thinking of themselves as apes, naked, furry or otherwise.

"The sentiency of non-humans remains problematic for us, given that we lack the tools and opportunities to perceive it," writes Deni Béchard in his soul-searching book, *Empty Hands, Open Arms: The Race to Save Bonobos in the Congo and Make Conservation Go Viral*. "In all fairness, the same has been true historically among human societies, who have demonized each other and been incapable of recognizing similarities across the boundaries of language and culture. But just as we increasingly understand foreign societies, our observations of gorillas, orangutans, chimpanzees and bonobos have provided us with enough information that we can begin to understand their social and interior lives… Do humans, as several authors of *The Great Ape Project* suggest, perceive the animal kingdom as a hierarchy that culminates in human superiority, and has the way we self-servingly defined superiority blinded us to our similarities with our great ape cousins? Some scientists even emphasize the violent traits of chimpanzees in order to distinguish them from humans… Bonobos, on the other hand, challenge our sense of superiority."

Indeed they do. Watching bonobos at play, observing bonobo politics, communicating with sentient individuals like Lana and Kanzi and practicing the Bonobo Way tends to crack the false veneer of anthropodenial, revealing the inner core of our deep evolutionary connection.

Humans Swing Too

In that spirit, let's swing back to swinging, this time from the other angle. Call it "bonobomorphism," if you will, but whether or not bonobos are like swingers, there's no doubt that the most active human swingers, a.k.a. "playcouples"[37] in the Lifestyle, are very bonoboësque. A good swing party is a human Bonoboville with lots of sex in various combinations and females in charge of most of the action—plus no killing (*Boogie Nights* is just a movie, folks!).

Swinging is not for everybody, not even for everyone who follows the Bonobo Way. It's too kinky or crass for some tastes and still quite taboo in most neighborhoods. But for many, the Lifestyle fulfills a very natural desire that bonobos and humans share: the need to partake in erotic, orgasmic experiences with multiple friends, loved ones and attractive

---

[37] "Playcouple" is a term coined by Lifestyle Organization founder Dr. Robert McGinley to identify a committed couple who likes to swing, watch, be watched or just "play" with others.

strangers.

Like bonobos, people swing for all kinds of reasons, including the desire for something different and someone new. Being part of an erotic community is another benefit. In a world that increasingly demands compartmentalization and sexual isolation, there are few arenas where humans can share the experience of communal ecstasy.[38] A friendly neighborhood orgy is one of the few.

Not that every swing scene is a utopian blast for all. Toes may be stepped on, literally and figuratively. Feelings may be hurt. Tempers may flare. Tears may flow. Wedding rings may be flung across the mattress room. Marital drama, usually private, is on display, along with sexual prowess. But deliberate, lethal violence is extremely rare. More often than not, a mood of erotic bonhomie prevails. In fact, a classic "swing party" looks a lot like a gathering of bonobos—with less hair and more hairspray.

Dr. de Waal says he doesn't "believe [the bonobos'] free love would necessarily suit us." With all due respect to the sage primatologist's breathtaking knowledge of both our sexy species, perhaps he's never had the eye-opening pleasure of attending a Lifestyles convention. Lucky for him, he has a standing invitation to be a guest on my show, and if he ever accepts, he should stay for the after-party, where he can observe humans engaging in very bonoboësque play.

Ryan and Jethá contend that prehistoric humans participated in various forms of bonoboësque "free love," group sex and multi-partner arrangements (depicted in some Paleolithic cave art) for tens of thousands of years before the advent of farming and our current ownership-oriented, property-based, paternity-obsessed society. The shift from bonoboësque arrangements to patriarchal families could have come about when hard-working husbands, fearing cuckoldry, needed to be reassured that their farms and flocks would be passed down to their own sons and not the progeny of some smooth dude down the road. Thus came about the increasing social pressure upon people, especially women, to be (or at least pretend to be) sexually monogamous.

But just because human society changed and people began trying to squeeze the wildly flared, polygonal peg of our promiscuous sexual nature into the neat, round, reassuring hole of traditional monogamy doesn't mean human nature has changed. Monogamy works for some, but from the looks

---

[38] "Communal ecstasy" is my erotic, orgiastic extrapolation from Dr. Barbara Ehrenreich's term "collective joy" in her wonderful book *Dancing in the Streets*.

of our high cheating and divorce rates, many of us are still pretty nonmonogamous. If you throw in watching porn and lusting after your hot brother-in-law, it seems that a human's sexual desire is as promiscuous as a bonobo's.

According to the American Psychological Association, 40 to 50 percent of married couples in the United States divorce (which doesn't imply that the half that don't are happy in their marriages). The divorce rate for subsequent marriages is even higher. It's tough to measure cheating rates, since most cheaters lie. But if the success of Ashley Madison, the "dating" site whose motto is "Life is short. Have an affair," is any indication, it's on the rise.

Not that humanity is all one-way. We are nothing if not diverse in our sexuality. Some of us can keep our natural desires for erotic novelty, variety and community under control more easily than others and live happily in monogamous marriages. Others suffer heart attacks, eating disorders, loneliness, cancer, insomnia, crippling insecurities, garden-variety neuroses and a host of other civilized ills, bravely attempting to force wild, promiscuous pegs into traditional, monogamous holes that often turn into sinkholes.

Another term for sinkhole is "depression." Whether it's in the earth or in your heart, it brings you down.

Are Women More Monogamous Than Men?

Women appear to be more naturally monogamous than men, mainly because we tend to be able to hide our true desires more effectively, especially when there are babies to burp or reputations to uphold. But if and when the timing's right, we can be more sexually voracious than men. Swingers and poets have known this for centuries, but sexperts are just now catching on.

"One of our most comforting assumptions, soothing perhaps above all to men, but clung to by both sexes, that the female eros is much better made for monogamy than the male libido, is scarcely more than a fairy tale," observes Daniel Bergner in his probing book about studies of the female libido *What Do Women Want?*

So apparently, we're *all* turned on by variety just like our bonobo cousins. Only we civilized humans don't get to satisfy our desires at casual lunchtime orgies with friends and interesting strangers.

At least, most of us don't. Despite society's sanctions against it, some clever or lucky folks have always found ways to enjoy various forms of free love, group sex and swinging, with and without persecution from society at large. The famously decadent orgies of ancient Greece and Rome come to mind, some presided over by eminent philosophers like Aristippus of Cyrene. In the 18th century, during the period known as the Enlightenment, European intellectuals (including the proudly promiscuous and ingenious Mary Shelley, author of Frankenstein, her husband, the poet, Percy Bysshe Shelley and leading Romantic literary figure Lord Byron) commonly enjoyed partner swapping.

In America, swinging rose in popularity during World War II, most notably among U.S. Air Force fighter pilots (the job which had the highest fatality rate in the armed forces), who swapped wives with the implicit understanding that if one of them were killed in the line of duty, the others would continue to love and take care of the widow. This arrangement is said to have continued through the Korean War and then, when the pilots took peacetime jobs, into the suburbs of America where they spawned the famous "Key Club" Bonobovilles of the 1960s and 70s. At these "key parties," like the one portrayed in Ang Lee's film, *The Ice Storm*, husbands are said to have dropped their keys in a communal bowl and the wives would draw keys and leave with whomever owned them.

Not to be confused with *Wife Swap*, the harrowing 21st-century reality TV show, in which two wives from different families "swap" every aspect of their lives *except* sex, the old form of "wife-swapping" (an archaic, somewhat sexist term) was mainly about switching partners for sex. This seems to have been, all in all, much more fun and less stressful for both the wives and their families, though complications did arise, sometimes breaking up a couple, other times bringing them closer together. It was all part of the ongoing sexual revolution[39] and an ever-increasing interest in nontraditional, bonoboësque arrangements and communities.

Polyamory & Designer Relationships

Some say that polyamory takes swinging to the next level. Like swingers, polyamorists also enjoy erotic relations with more than one partner, but they prefer lasting sexual relationships to swinging with casual

---

[39] The term "sexual revolution" is said to have been coined by the brilliant and tragic Dr. Wilhelm Reich, a star pupil of Freud and a big fan of orgasms. Also credited with starting the "sex positive" movement, Dr. Reich created a controversial "orgone" box that landed him in a U.S. prison where he died of a heart attack.

friends or strangers at parties. Polyamory is trending in the 21st century, metamorphosing from a marginal kink into a mainstream relationship model with a dizzying multiplicity of variations and spin-offs. Some people create what Dr. Kenneth R. Haslam, developer of the Kinsey Institute's polyamory collection, and others have called "designer relationships," customizing levels of commitment, freedom, boundaries and communication among partners. Sometimes a dedicated threesome calls itself a "trouple" to convey the idea that the three lovers are as devoted to each other as a couple. Committed foursomes and variously configured tribes are also gaining in popularity.

How can someone deeply love more than one person at one time? In *Sex at Dawn*, Ryan and Jethá remind us that many mothers who have more than one child don't have a problem deeply loving each of them, often pretty equally. Polyamorists feel the same way, or at least they try.

It's not easy when society pressures us to march in line, two by two. But more and more trouples and tribes are making it work, some of them inspired by the bonobos. On somatic sexologist Jaiya Ma's first appearance on my show, her partner Jon accompanied her, while her other partner Ian stayed in the Topanga home that the three of them share with their toddler son. Her second time on the show, Jaiya brought Ian, and Jon babysat. Their polyamorous[40] relationship is inspired by their vision of a better society, the bonobos and their own personal needs and desires. It has its ups and downs that, since my show, have been dissected by the likes of Anderson Cooper and Cynthia McFadden. Through all the media scrutiny, Jaiya, Jon and Ian are showing the world that being a trouple can be just as intimate, passionate, sustainable, familial and complicated as being a couple.

The Bonobo Way of sharing sex, deeply-held affection and the other joys and sorrows of life with various members of one's long-term fission-fusion tribe reflects the polyamorous desire to cultivate lasting, meaningful erotic connections with more than one partner.

Bisexuality Keeps the Peace in Bonoboville

These partners may be from the same or different genders. Which brings us to, for want of a better word, bisexuality. Some prefer less commonly used terms like "pansexual," "omnisexual" or, as actress Asta

---

[40] Some would call it "polyandrous" since it's two men and one woman.

Paredes described her sexual orientation on DrSuzy.Tv, "Kahlo-sexual" (inspired by artist Frida Kahlo, said to have had male and female lovers). But most use "bisexual" with caveats. Whatever box you prefer to check, more and more men and women are opening up and owning up to their complex sexual feelings for both sexes. This doesn't mean bisexuals are equally attracted to men and women at all times, just that their erotic interests are more fluid than "straight" and "gay."

For millennia, major religious groups and other human authorities have railed against bisexuality and homosexuality as "unnatural," so it's empowering to see evidence of these so-called "perversions" throughout nature, most notably among bonobos. Watching bonobos shows us that whether we believe we are "born this way" or that we "choose" our erotic orientations, our sexual diversity is utterly organic and natural, adding to the richness of our individual lives and the ecology of our society. Those of us who are "queer" or different shouldn't be discriminated against, as long as our actions don't infringe on the rights of others.

Of course, the bisexual nature of bonobos doesn't exactly parallel human bisexuality or queer inclinations and not every human Bonoboville is open to all variants of same-gender sex. For instance, most human bi girls would rather 69 than hoka-hoka, and many human swing clubs support bisexual behavior among the gals but not the guys.

Regardless of the differences, witnessing the fluid sexuality of bonobos helps bi-inclined, as well as transgender folks feel more at ease with their sexuality, and provides therapists and other experts with great insight into these expectation-defying bi, trans or pansexual feelings and behaviors. Whenever my clients worry that their bisexual feelings are unnatural or abnormal, I suggest they check out their kissing cousins, the bonobos.

Bisexuality seems key to keeping the peace in Bonoboville. This hypothesis requires more research, but it appears that when male bonobos engage in penis fencing and other erotic interactions, they're less likely to kill one another. And when the females do the hoka-hoka, they're more apt to look out for each other. This is great fodder for peace studies departments and bisexual anti-war activists.

Tantra & The Tao of Bonobo

Tantric sex, neotantra and other forms of "sacred sexuality" are quite popular among certain soul-searching, body-stretching humans these days. Bonobos might not know a chakra from a mantra (though bonobos like

Kanzi could probably learn), but their "spiritual," soulful nature shines through their eyes and actions in a way that is obvious to anyone but a dogmatic clergyman who insists that "animals" don't have souls. A few years ago, French Channel 5 interviewed me about bonobo "soulfulness" in conjunction with a clip from a Catholic priest declaring that bonobos and other nonhuman "animals" were most definitely lacking in the soul department. Unfortunately for the Father, he was not very telegenic, as he wrinkled his nose in apparent disgust, and came across as having less of a soul than a monkey, let alone a bonobo.

Whatever you may believe about such theological metaphysics, tantric sex techniques can help you slow down, breathe deep, spend more time on "foreplay" than intercourse, get in touch with your feminine and masculine sides (yin and yang), focus on your partner's pleasure, synchronize your breathing and your movements, delay male ejaculation, multiply female orgasms, gaze into each other's eyes during sex, relax your defenses and wake up your senses.

Taoist or Daoist sex practices, during which lovers "join energy" via the Tao (ancient Chinese for "way" or "path"), are fairly similar to tantra, with some cultural derivations and variations.

Though these techniques tend to be quite challenging for humans, it's all stuff that most bonobos do pretty naturally. The neotantric and Taoist philosophies of utilizing sexual energy to achieve spiritual enlightenment, personal growth and oneness with all of life is, in some ways, a similar path to the Bonobo Way, a.k.a., the Tao of Bonobo.

Bonobo BDSM

Moving along the kink curve, the Bonobo Way also complements many of the principles and practices of BDSM (Bondage and Discipline, Dominance and Submission, Sadomasochism and related kinks). Does it seem odd that masters, slaves and dominatrices wielding whips, chains and torture devices could be inspired by the peace-loving bonobos? Not when you consider that both the Bonobo Way and BDSM involve transforming violent, potentially destructive urges into consensual, non-lethal erotic play.

Bonobos don't kill each other, but they're not above a fight and they combine various forms of roughhousing with sex. As with human BDSM players, their play demonstrates that (consensual) pain and pleasure can be next-door neighbors. They just have to be managed.

Like most primates, bonobos have a dominant/submissive hierarchy, though their chain of command is much more fluid than that of their chimp cousins, and, as de Waal points out so succinctly, "Common chimps resolve sexual issues with power, bonobos resolve power issues with sex."

There is a lot of "sucking up" involved, in all senses of the term. Much of the sexual servicing and slavish grooming that subordinate bonobos perform for the alphas bears resemblance to a human submissive's body worship of his or her mistress or master.

BDSMers who believe in the value of a female dominant society, whether for ideological, fetishistic or just plain old prurient reasons, will find much to enjoy and even emulate in this matriarchal great ape culture.

But does anything resembling what human BDSMers call "erotic discipline" exist in Bonoboville? At the risk of getting über-anthropomorphic, I say yes. The fact that bonobos are so physical and emotional, but never kill each other, demonstrates an important type of discipline: *restraint*.

Of course, common chimps also can and often do restrain their violent impulses, but their form of discipline appears to be enforced through the constant fear of being beaten or killed by bigger, stronger males. Bonobo discipline involves being schooled in a gentler, more playful fashion. The elders steer younger members of the tribe toward controlling their violent impulses by giving pleasure, along with some pain, most often meted out by alpha females. This kind of erotic discipline appears essential to keeping the peace in Bonoboville.

Human Perversion or Sexual Diversity?

The Bonobo Way can inspire all types of fetishists because of the wide diversity of sexual practices bonobos embrace. I haven't yet heard of a bonobo with a fetish for nylons, but Lana loves her rubber ball and there have been reported cases of chimps developing shoe and boot fetishes. Maybe it's just a question of exposure.

Acceptance of your fetish is often the first step to coping with it and reducing its compulsive power over you. Seeing a bonobo merrily self-pleasuring with a rubber ball reminds us that solo sex and erotic play with inanimate objects are not twisted and "unnatural" human perversions as many religions and other organizations preach. There's no way to prove this, but I often wonder if solo sex, whether with a well-shaped twig or a stone, might have been the first motivation for primate tool use. Bonobos

The Bonobo Way

love to masturbate alone or with a partner, with a toy, or over snacks, especially in zoos.

I have to confess, despite my experience with wild public sex among humans, I'm still sometimes startled by just how far bonobos go. On one of my visits to Bonoboville in San Diego, Lana and a male bonobo named Junior squatted opposite each other and then proceeded to anally finger themselves. And they were not subtle about it! It was as if Lana was in a *Buttman* movie and Junior was in *Bend Over Boyfriend*.[41] All this in full view of a large late-afternoon family crowd!

This time, I had Max with me as my witness. "I can't believe they're doing that!" I squealed like I'd never seen a naked anus before, all while the other tourists stood stiffly in shocked anthropodenial or hustled their kids over to see the hippos. Max couldn't stop laughing.

What were those kinky bonobos really up to? Were they mocking us—our ogling eyes, our chirping phones, our gaily-colored *Bonobos* shorts, our freedom to come and go as we pleased—by giving us the finger up their own butts? Then again, maybe Junior was giving himself a P-spot (prostate) massage, while Lana was just giving herself a good time, as well as giving Junior, and us human gawkers, quite an exhibitionistic auto-anal performance. I wonder what they might do with a couple of butt plugs and some lube.

But you don't have to be an extreme masturbator, a fetishist, BDSM player, tantric yogi, swinger, polyamorist or even bisexual to enhance your sex life by unleashing your inner bonobo. Many of my clients, readers, colleagues and friends in conventional, conservative, even religiously observant marriages have been inspired by facets of the Bonobo Way to live with greater eroticism, sensuality, sensitivity, reciprocity, cooperation, tolerance, playfulness, honesty, openness and compassion. Whatever level of openness you bring to the table, the bonobos will fill it with love.

My Monogamish Boho-Bonobo Marriage

For more than 23 years, Max and I have dabbled in, and continue to enjoy, almost all the sexual arenas described here (at least the legal ones), though we're not hardcore swingers, fetishists, tantrics or BDSM players. In many ways, we're a traditional husband and wife, saving our most intimate sexual moments for each other. But we're ethical hedonists,

---

[41] With appreciation to Dr. Carol Queen.

exhibitionist/voyeurs, and we thrive on erotic play with friends and lovers, especially in our Bonoboville. So what does that make us? Sexpert Dan Savage would call us "monogamish." Some dub it "soft swing" or "bohemian plus." How about "boho-bonobo?"

It's not for everyone, but after almost a quarter century, Pr. Max and I have found that it continuously invigorates our private sex life, which might otherwise have collapsed into the stagnant sinkhole of monogamous monotony years ago. The intensity of our extra-marital relationships—from our erotic work with the artists, technologists and therapists-in-residence at the Institute, to our sex parties at the Speakeasy—varies with our moods and seasons. But the two of us are always at the core, no matter what, whether we're deliriously happy or madly shouting at each other, whether we're in each other's arms, sharing our most intimate feelings that no one else understands, or on opposite sides of an ocean, each in the middle of our own orgy. We are one another's witness in the great, seething sex party of life.

Lifelong pair bonding may not be so natural for most humans or bonobos, but it's still an ineffable joy to share "everything" with someone you love. The Bonobo Way helps you to do that without killing each other, literally or figuratively.

Bonobos Are Single But with Lots of Company

What if you're single? Welcome to the club! Like all the apes (except gibbons),[42] bonobos are not pair-bonders. In a sense, they're all "single." The Bonobo Way has helped many of my single, socially challenged clients and friends accept themselves, whether they're deeply shy, sexually confused, religiously repressed or recovering from first-degree relationship burns. This, in turn, inspires them to break out of isolation and "reach out and touch" others, in one way or another. Bonobos might be single, but they do not live alone. Marriage is not the only arrangement in which people can live together.

Unlike some other paths, you can't really follow the Bonobo Way all by yourself. You need others. And believe it or not, others need you, one way or another. Bonobos' closeness to each other reminds us of how close we,

---

[42] The pair-bonded gibbons are "lesser apes," as opposed to the great apes (common chimps, bonobos, gorillas, orangutans and humans). Ironically, gibbons are the best literal swingers, masters of "brachiation," swinging from tree limb to branch, using only their arms.

too, are probably meant to be.

Chapter 15: Release Your Inner Bonobo

"Sex is a part of nature. I go along with nature."
— Marilyn Monroe

Remember that couple that came in for a little BLT when the French were filming? Like most healthy human couples, when they first fell in love, husband Charlie and wife Phoebe (not their real names) had an active, orgasmic, laughter-filled sex life. But after eight years, a second mortgage, a third child and a 35-pound weight gain between the two of them, their conjugal relations went from X to R to PG-13, and before they knew it, they were in a rut, slip-sliding down that sinkhole that little by little sucks the desire out of so many marriages, like quicksand pulling down a pair of unsuspecting fellow travelers.

They were losing their sexual spark, their patience and their sense of humor. Gripes bubbled up to the surface of the sinkhole like toxic foam, each bubble containing a cry for help. Phoebe wished Charlie would be more sensitive to her changing erotic needs. Charlie yearned for Phoebe to be more aggressive in bed. Though they were stressed and nervous, they were also excited because they had come to the Institute ready for an erotic adventure.

After their intake interviews, we watched a film of bonobos engaging in various activities, including sex. We talked about the sensitivity of the males and the females' assertiveness in pursuing whatever kind of sex they wanted. Phoebe and Charlie giggled and elbowed each other as they watched, each trying to get the other to "take notes." Neither did, though midway through the movie, they started holding hands.

As the film ended, we talked about how the Bonobo Way might recharge their listless love life. When the cameraman asked Phoebe if she found watching the bonobos arousing, she wrinkled her nose and squealed, "Noooo!" and burst out laughing.

Not to cast doubts on her sincerity, but the onomatopoetic Chivers Effect, may have been the source of Phoebe's bubbling fountain of giggles and shivers. While she steadfastly maintained that the bonobos did not turn her on, she confessed to being intrigued by their "attitude," wondering aloud how she could get what she wanted in her relationship as effectively as the female bonobos did. Charlie didn't find the bonobos sexy either ("The ladies are a little too simian for me," he deadpanned), but was impressed with the sheer amount of erotic activity. "Those dudes get a lot of action," he marveled.

Their next step was to spend a couple hours together doing whatever they wanted to do in a private room at the Institute with a California king, lots of fluffy pillows, various lubricants, sex toys, their favorite music, aromatic candlelight, champagne on ice and a pipe which they could use with the prescription cannabis they brought. Then we left them alone—except for the camera and the winking French cameraman behind it.

The Bonobo Liberation Challenge

The cameraman did present a challenge since his constant looming, winking presence seemed to make sex much more difficult. I call this kind of obstacle, one in which a problematic situation can be turned into an erotic opportunity, a "Bonobo Liberation Challenge" (BLC). Charlie and Phoebe's first BLC was to tune out the cameraman and tune into each other.

Phoebe requested a back massage. We praised her assertiveness, and she quickly added, "Nothing more!" Off went her top as she lay down on her front. Charlie knew how to give his wife a good backrub (something he hadn't done in quite some time), and for 10 very quiet minutes, that's just what he did, nothing audible except Phoebe's soft sighs. Then he stopped and whispered into her ear, "Isn't it nice to finally get some private time, just the two of us?" and laughter burst from her lips. "Shh!" he hushed her like they were naughty kids, putting his hand over her mouth, which she bit down on, wiggling her tongue through his fingers, then passionately sucking on the middle one. So much for "nothing more," I thought as the rubdown broke down into white-hot bonobo sex—according to both of them, not to mention the French—*ooh la la*!

With a little push from *Pan paniscus*, plus that winking cameraman (making it a kind of *ménage à trois)*, Charlie and Phoebe pulled themselves out of the sinkhole and released their inner bonobos into the wild side of love... at least, for that afternoon. But it was an afternoon to remember, and the erotic exercise gave them hope for their future and helped them chart a newly energized love/life course on the Bonobo Way. Plus, now they had a new hobby: filming themselves making love.

The Unexpected Aphrodisiac of Shame

Although the BLC inhibited them at first, the whole encounter wound up boosting their marriage to a new level of eroticism. It's ironic, but breaking through inhibitions is often a key aspect of human arousal. With no inhibitions at all, there's not much to break through.

One of the great erotic philosophers of the mid-20th century, Georges Bataille, pointed to an ongoing struggle between sensuous pleasure and shame that creates eroticism. Shame, that awful feeling of self-blame accompanying a perceived failure, or the fear that something we do could be considered disgraceful tends to cripple and inhibit us. But, Bataille maintains, shame is also an essential component of the forbidden boundaries that we find so exciting to transgress, tease, crisscross, break and overthrow out the window.

"People tend to be aware of the positive emotions 'energizing' their peak sexual experiences—love, tenderness or affection," writes Dr. Katherine Frank, who credits Bataille as one of the kings of "transgressive literature," in her fascinating study of group sex, *Plays Well in Groups*. "But the 'unexpected aphrodisiacs'—anxiety or fear, guilt, shame, hostility, anger and vulnerability—also intensify arousal, though most successfully in low doses or controlled situations."

Many great thinkers in different disciplines have tried to put their philosophical fingers on this "naughty" aspect of human desire. In *Immortality*, novelist Milan Kundera calls it "the art of ambiguity," maintaining that "the stronger the ambiguity, the more powerful the excitement."

Psychoanalyst Joseph Lichtenberg puts it this way: "The interplay between desire and prohibition creates an experience of tension in sexuality not present in sensuality." Guided by their BLC and the Bonobo Way, Phoebe and Charlie mixed their desires and prohibitions into higher levels of conjugal rejuvenation than they'd experienced since they were newlyweds.

Go Bonobos!

Could the Bonobo Way work that way for you? More or less, yes. I'm not a fan of most one-size-fits-all lingerie, let alone solutions to anyone's love life. All of this can mean different things to different people in different cultures at different ages and stages of life. But we've got to start somewhere. So here's essentially what it means to liberate your inner bonobo:

- Discover your erotic, evolutionary connection with bonobos, and all of nature.
- Tune in to your personal, primal "inner bonobo."
- Free your inner bonobo from its psychological cage of societal and self-imposed repression, "going bonobos" in some safe, sane, consensual manner that *won't* get you arrested (and thrown in another cage) and *will* give you a new lease, or "re-lease," on life.
- Share your bonoboësque pleasure and knowledge with others.

You can get the process rolling by asking yourself a few personal questions that only you can answer. What made you open this book? What's gotten you this far? What really interests *you* about bonobos? You may resonate to the Bonobo Way of bisexuality, female solidarity, their athletic physicality, deep compassion, curiosity, generosity, reciprocity, their appealing youthfulness, the way they swing or combine food with sex, the sense of play that infuses almost everything they do, the "sperm wars" system of sexual competition, their relatively shameless expression of sexual feelings, or that seemingly magical knack the bonobos have for making peace through pleasure. Or maybe, like me, you feel that a combination of some of your loftiest, noblest aspirations and deepest, kinkiest desires converge in the Bonobo Way.

It can occur in an instant of insight, maybe even while you're reading these words. It can happen in the course of one transformational, slightly transgressive afternoon like Charlie and Phoebe experienced at the Institute. Most often, it evolves over time. You can instigate that evolution via BLT, in which the therapist guides the process. Or you can follow the 12 Steps in your own way, letting them revolutionize your whole existence or just allowing them to influence certain aspects of your life. Everybody has a unique situation and, unfortunately, this book is too slim to include even a fraction of all the different kinds of people who have benefited from the Bonobo Way, though I'll try to weave in a few.

Real 40-Year Old Virgin Gets Laid & Finds Love (In That Order)

Jeff was a real 40-year-old virgin (actually 42) who had repressed his sexual desires all his life in keeping with his sincere devotion to God. His particular faith happened to be Catholicism, but almost every organized religion maintains that a good person must "just say no" to sex before marriage. Though most modern people don't follow those rules so strictly, Jeff was serious about his faith and wanted to only have the "right" kind of sex in the eyes of his all-powerful God.

According to his religious upbringing, he shouldn't have sex until he fell in love and married. That seemed like a simple enough rule to abide by when he swore as an altar boy that he would remain "pure" until his wedding night. But over the years, he found himself falling in love with women who were already married, had boyfriends or just weren't interested. He dated a bit, but marriage eluded him, which didn't bother him so much as he saw many of his married siblings and friends cheating or getting divorced. But he began to wonder about his sexual destiny. Was he supposed to completely forgo his powerful, innate desires to connect sexually with his fellow humans just because he wasn't married?

Now, at the ripening age of 42, he no longer believed (intellectually, at least) in the Catholic doctrine that required him to be married before experiencing sexual intercourse. This realization alone was a tremendous BLT break-through for him, but he was painfully shy about sex, still religiously inhibited and unable to connect with women. I often suggest that shy middle-aged virgins who don't date but want to experience sex go to a professional sex worker, at least to get started. But when I mentioned this to Jeff, he cringed. He felt his first time should be with a woman who physically wanted him as much as he wanted her.

He yearned for true love, or at least genuine lust. To find it, Jeff needed to release his inner bonobo, which was still locked up in a cage of sanctified dogma. As we watched a bonobo video together, we talked about how natural his sexual feelings were. He admired the athleticism of the bonobos at play, and he wished he could experience that kind of physical, erotic energy exchange with an attractive woman, whether or not it led to sexual intercourse. Jeff had been a bit of a basketball star in high school, and still enjoyed an occasional pick-up game at the local courts. This kept him in great shape, but it wasn't high school anymore, and scoring on the court didn't help him score off it. He needed to put himself in an arena where he was more likely to meet eligible women.

So I told Jeff to quit dribbling and take up ballroom dancing. He laughed until he realized I was serious. Then the laughter dissolved into a frown, as if I'd offended his masculinity. I advised him to suck up his concerns and sign up for a class. He did and, within a few weeks, he went from being the shy guy to a man-in-demand due to the perpetual shortage of tall men for the dance-hungry women in his class. He also discovered an activity where he could experience the kind of physical energy exchange he'd seen among the bonobos, though in a "civilized" and uniquely human way.

Thanks to excellent posture, coordination and an ease of motion honed on the basketball courts, he became a fairly good dancer. Then, lo and behold, one of his partners, the attractive 46-year-old Cara, asked him to go for coffee after class. He wasn't as wildly infatuated with her as he'd been with some of his married would-be paramours and he rebuffed her first advances. During our following session, we talked about how one of the reasons Cara might not appear to be as exciting was that she was unmarried and available, exhibiting the genuine lust he'd supposedly been seeking. She wasn't the forbidden fruit he yearned for, but she was a peach he could reach. I reminded Jeff that he didn't have to marry Cara, and that he wouldn't be taking advantage of her if he just followed her lead.

As Robert Frost famously observed, "Dancing is a vertical expression of a horizontal desire," and it wasn't long before Jeff and Cara went from vertical to horizontal, releasing Jeff's inner bonobo as he "gave" his much-prized and anguished-over virginity up to her. Their sexual relationship lasted eight months, but their friendship continues to this day. A few dance partners after Cara, Jeff really fell in love, had even better sex, and finally got hitched. True, he'd gotten it backwards from the way his Catechism had dictated, but this real 40-year-old virgin *did* find love (though he found sex first—which might have helped!) via the Bonobo Way.

Phoebe, Charlie and Jeff are just a few of the thousands of individuals, couples, trouples and more who have followed the Bonobo Way. Some do it just for a few fun hours, others, for a lifetime. It's really a very simple philosophy, if you can even call it a philosophy. Its principles aren't inscribed on tablets like the Ten Commandments or on parchment like Plato's Symposium. They're encoded deep in our hearts and DNA. We already know them well, but we often bury them under inhibitions, prohibitions and superstitions in the heat of our busy, civilized lives.

We'll discuss these principles through the upcoming 12 Steps, but three of the most basic ones are: Pleasure heals pain. Doing good feels good. And you can't fight a war very well if you're having an orgasm.

Amen. Awomen. Abonobos!

Human Bonobovilles Must Be Adults Only

Caveat: though the Bonobo Way draws upon bonobos to inspire humans to lead better, freer, sexier and more empathetic lives, before you sue me because you fell out of a tree or got busted for having some kind of illegal sex, let me make clear that I'm not suggesting that you live just like a bonobo. There are some significant aspects of bonobo behavior that simply should not or cannot be aped by humans, and I'm not just talking about tying three out of four of your limbs into a pretzel while dangling from a rickety branch.

Much as we might love and feel close to them, bonobos *aren't* us. The less-than-2% genetic difference between us makes a big difference in certain aspects of life. Despite our many similarities, our distinct genetic regulatory mechanisms make the "expression" of that DNA diverge considerably between our species. Our cultural differences also help to make comprehensive "aping" impossible, ludicrous or dangerous. So please use common sense when practicing the Bonobo Way, and don't get *carried* away... okay?

To cite a controversial example, adult bonobos constantly nurture their young, virtually never excluding them from any aspect of life, including sexual activity. For various reasons beyond the scope of this book, this behavior works for bonobos, but it does not for humans, especially considering the laws and ethics of most human societies. Unlike bonobos, responsible human adults absolutely cannot include children in their sexual activities. The big BLC here is keeping the kids out of your Bonoboville, especially if your life is centered around your children within a conventional nuclear family. If you're an active parent, you have to be creative, resourceful and discreet when it comes to releasing your inner "adults only" bonobo. In these situations, it often helps to have a network of Bonobo Way-friendly parents who can take turns watching the kids while the other adults play.

Obviously, it's not always so simple. In fact, somebody should write a Bonobo Way manual just for active parents. Usually, you can't even let the kids know what you're up to, lest they tell the neighbors or their teachers who then alert the authorities who then proceed to ruin your lives, all done with the best intentions. As Michael Donnelly, a discreetly "poly" member of the bonoboësque "Monkey Clan" of Oregon, puts it, "'My Bonobo Parents' sure wouldn't go over very well as a school report."

That's an understatement. Yet, when we witness the tender care a bonobo mom gives her little boy (the only bonobo relationship that contains incest taboo), we can see they could probably teach us as much about parental primate love as the sexual kind. We just have to put these lessons through a human social filter.

"Bonobos Hold the Key to a World without War"

Though *Pan paniscus* behavior is no blueprint for *Homo sapiens* conduct, the Bonobo Way can help us better understand our own wild ways. Then we can better decide what to keep caged, what to tame and what to release. Our kissing cousins have so much to reveal to us about ourselves. As Vanessa Woods writes in *Bonobo Handshake*, "Bonobos… hold the key to a world without war." It's a key that we humans cannot afford to lose.

We have no time to waste. Time is running out for the bonobos, and in some critical ways, for us too. Now that you've met the bonobos, would you like to help save them from extinction, as well as learn how you can use the Bonobo Way to improve your love life—and your *life* life? Then let's swing on through to Part II.

PART II
The 12 Steps to Releasing Your Inner Bonobo

"Lots of people talk to animals. Not very many listen, though. That's the problem."
—Benjamin Hoff, *The Tao of Pooh*

So… are you ready to take the first step? This "12-Step Program" will guide you toward unleashing and cultivating your bonoboësque powers on a variety of interconnected, personal, interpersonal, sexual, social, political and ecological levels.

It will also serve as a manual for staying (or pulling yourself) out of the sinkhole and having more fun than a proverbial "barrel of monkeys." After all, monkeys are pretty cool, but not as cool nor as fun nor as close to us as bonobos.

Each step (if you actually follow it) will open you up to a different aspect of the Bonobo Way, partly by presenting you with information, examples and various BLCs designed to help you more fully release your inner bonobo via concrete actions in your private and/or public life. Some of the challenges I suggest might not be all that challenging for you. Others will be quite difficult, and thus all the more worthwhile.

BLCs vary according to the person. For some, talking about your fantasies to your lover presents a bigger challenge than stripping naked before a stranger, and for others, vice versa. Of course, it's up to you whether or not you meet these challenges, but the more you do, the greater, deeper and more powerful your release will be. It's up to you. You can let bonobos revolutionize your life. Or you can just let them touch parts of your life in small but powerful ways.

A Different Kind of "12-Step Program"

A word to the wise: this is not your typical 12-Step Program (obviously). This is the Anti-Program Program. Following it, or even just thinking about it, will help you deprogram from all those other programs. Like everything, deprogramming has its pros and cons. As you'll soon discover, liberating your inner bonobo is the very best thing you can ever do for yourself, your loved ones and your community. But it can be dangerous. After all, liberation tends to shake—and sometimes break—your cage.

The good news is that the Bonobo Way is a philosophy whose time has come... and keeps on coming. Even our violence-loving media[43] has to admit that the pendulum of sociopolitical discourse is swinging toward peace, erotic tolerance, female empowerment and the very bonobo notion that "we are all in this together." This great wave of change is supported by studies emerging from top universities around the world. Ever more frequently, anthropology, primatology, psychology, political science and sociology departments are tempering their old common chimp and baboon-oriented views of "Man the Warrior" to accommodate the genetic proximity of these feminist, sexual and peaceable bonobo apes.

Even beyond the echoing halls of academia, more and more individuals, couples, trouples, families, communities, movements, tribes and nations are changing the rules of social and sexual engagement. As we "occupy" the public squares, reaching out through the Interwebs of our "flat world,"[44] hooking up and opening up to each other with a new technical know-how and cultural tolerance, many are releasing their inner bonobos without even knowing what a bonobo is. Yes, indeed, there has never been a better time in civilized history to practice the Bonobo Way.

But there is a dark side to all this progressive peace, love and commerce. There are backlashes of various kinds, some of them quite vicious, exploding like bombs in different areas of the globe, from the extreme right wings of the world's most entrenched religions to the international MIC, the growing American PIC, corporate oligarchies, tribal patriarchies, sexually frustrated youth and attention-seeking psychopaths fanned by a media that gifts them with instant megawatt-attention for their telegenic atrocities.

Despite the great sex-positive strides being made all over the world in

---

[43] Everyone knows sex sells, but so does violence, and violence is much more acceptable in our society. No matter how much murder and mayhem is actually happening on any given day, the media is likely to "lead" with violence to catch eyeballs, magnifying and multiplying the carnage in our minds.

[44] From Thomas Friedman's best-seller *The World Is Flat: A Brief History of the Twenty-First Century*, the term is a metaphor for viewing the world as a level playing field in terms of commerce and perception, in which all players have "equal opportunity" in global markets, and where historical and geographical divisions are becoming increasingly irrelevant.

the media, social media included, nudity is still censored, while uninformed sexual judgment is rampant, often posing as political discourse. Want to shut someone up? Paint them in sexual terms or, even more effectively, make them out to be sexually "deviant." Many people and organizations are mired in these judgmental, gawking, squawking, superstitious, paranoid and stultifying attitudes about sex, love and life in general. There are probably more than a few of these people and organizations in your neighborhood, workplace, government, house of worship or backyard… maybe even in your bedroom. You should give them each a copy of *The Bonobo Way*. Some just might read it.

Or maybe they won't. But even if they burn it and tell you you're going to hell, rest assured that the world is going bonobos. As human societies around the globe move further from working on farms, plantations and factories into a kind of cyber-age version of hunting and gathering, we are loosening many of the traditional restrictions upon women and opening up more erotic possibilities for all.

Cultural and sexual attitudes are relaxing in many places around the world, and the isolated nuclear family with one exclusive patriarchal Dad and one sex-avoidant, submissive Mom is giving way to more fluid communities of various caring people, some of whom engage in sex with each other. "In terms of sexuality, history appears to be flowing back toward a hunter-gatherer casualness," foresee Ryan and Jethá in *Sex at Dawn*. "If so, future generations may suffer fewer pathological manifestations of sexual frustration and unnecessarily fractured families."

But just in case *your* family hasn't gone with that "flow" just yet, this 12-step program to releasing your inner bonobo is paved with lots of little baby steps. This gives you a chance to stick a tentative toe in the rushing waters of bonobo liberation—so as not to alarm your mate, your kids, your mom, your imam, your minister or the media—before diving headlong into the naturally intoxicating, healing, free-thinking and slightly subversive sea of bonobo love.

Enough warning! Time to step it up and stick your toe in the flow… Time to start going bonobos!

Step 1: See the Bonobos.

We begin with the first, simplest baby step you can take to liberate your inner bonobo: observation. It's an easy step, but it's a vital one. Bonobos must be seen to be believed. And just seeing them is a revelation, the likes of which the prophets could only have imagined.

Of course, the ideal situation would be to visit the bonobos in their native habitat in the DRC. However, the country is still in great turmoil and unsafe for most conventional sightseeing. At the time of this book, the western Congo around Kinshasa, where the marvelous Lola ya Bonobo sanctuary for orphaned bonobos is located, has become a little less hostile. The eastern section, which contains the rainforest, is still exceedingly dangerous and difficult for garden-variety tourists. But if you've got the money and moxie, give it a go!

Having enough cash is critical for most travelers, as it is extremely expensive to get from point A to point B even once you get there, especially when you factor in the bribes you have to pay to half the people you meet. If you're worried about Ebola, remember that you're more likely to get hepatitis, typhoid, yellow fever or malaria[45], so don't forget those critical shots (along with a host of other remedies) if you're still game for the journey. I myself haven't even been there yet, but you can bet it's pretty high up on my bucket list.

The good news is that you don't have to journey to the Congolese rainforest to see bonobos. You can visit them at one of the eight zoos in the United States or at one of the 20 zoos around the world[46] that house bonobos. Oh, and if you want to boost your chances of seeing them have sex, go during mealtime (theirs, not yours),[47] preferably when it's not too hot.

Then again, who needs first-hand experience in the Information Age? Though I still believe there's nothing like the real thing, you can at least

---

[45] At the time of this book the World Health Organization reported that the number of Ebola cases worldwide had passed 10,000. However, it is important to remember that 4,665 of those cases were in Liberia, the worst affected country, while only 67 were in the DRC.
[46] Check out the list in Appendix II.

start with the cyber thing: just type "bonobos" into your search engine, and you'll find a wealth of videos and pictures. You can even find some photos from *Bonobo Handshake* author and researcher Vanessa Woods in this book.[48]

Seeing Bonobos May Arouse Deep Feelings

Observing *Pan paniscus* in person or on film arouses different kinds of feelings in people. If you're like me and many others, it will inspire and entertain you, putting you in touch with your erotic animal nature, making you feel more a part of the great chain of sexual being. Watching bonobos at play inspires us to loosen up, open up and enjoy our own strikingly similar bodies, explore new erotic activities, toys and positions, or just relax and savor more quality time with our partner(s).

"We might consider ourselves a naked ape, but we have the capacity to be, let's say, a godlike ape. We can do far more than we're doing," Dr. Sue Savage-Rumbaugh told Deni Béchard in *Empty Hands, Open Arms*. "We're just on the cusp of really understanding how brains interact…We have thought of ourselves as individual sacks of skin. We're far more connected than we've ever understood. And bonobos have almost a sixth sense. They have an understanding of their connectedness."

Ever since I saw bonobos on *The Nature of Sex*, I've tuned into their sense of connectedness. I don't know if it's "godlike," but I do feel exceedingly close to them as fellow apes, and I can observe their intimate, intoxicating closeness to each other. Looking into their eyes can be like taking a drug or hearing a song that makes it impossible for me not to dance.

Am I sexually aroused by watching bonobos? No, at least not that I'm aware. But like Phoebe in the previous chapter and the many ladies in Dr. Chivers' study, I may be influenced by the "Chivers Effect" and unconscious of just how turned on I get from watching bonobos. I know I enjoy it, and I believe that my sex life is better for it, one reason being that after I watch them, I'm usually more interested in having sex—with humans.

---

[47] While you're more likely to see bonobos having sex when *they're* eating, if you munch something while watching them, you might find that they like to creep over and see if you'll share some of your goodies.

[48] That is, if you have the e-book or the print edition with photos.

What If Watching Bonobo Sex Creeps You Out?

If you don't get those good vibrations, if you feel disgust, shame or just really silly as you watch bonobos getting it on, don't be alarmed. I know the feeling. Remember my embarrassment at seeing Lana and Junior anally finger themselves at the zoo? We're all at some level of "anthropodenial," balking at the recognition of our closeness to other animals and our "dirty" intimacy with Mother Earth.

If you experience such negative feelings while watching bonobos, consider what they might be able to teach you about the beast within you, the beast you'd be without your high heels, cool wheels, smartphone and blinders. How much does your disgust reflect the well-entrenched efforts of civilization to distance you from other animals and nature, despite the fact that nature will reclaim you in the end?

Even if you live in a prison within the most sexually repressed of human cultures, the Bonobo Way can help you find a way. As you follow this step and simply observe the bonobos, their magical warmth will eventually melt your protective layer of shame. You will find yourself smiling, getting a "contact high" from seeing them swing, making peace through pleasure and playing in the rich dirt of life.

Relax, Reboot, Press PLAY

This is the easiest of all the steps, and you can follow it at any time, whenever you need to relax, reboot, feel connected or get a playful perspective into practicing the Bonobo Way. Try watching bonobos have sex just before you have sex. The Chivers Effect might pack more power than your favorite porno.

Watch bonobos whenever you need a visual aid to release your inner animal, feel more interconnected or just think differently about your life, especially your love life. Throughout the next 11 steps, I will remind you to come back to this one for insight and grounding.

Your BLC is to bookmark your personal favorite scenes of bonobo love and play—on your computer, tablet, smartphone or in your memory banks—so you can refer to them whenever you feel the need to revisit this step. Unless you're keeping your inner bonobo totally in the closet, you'll probably want to share your favorite scenes with your lover(s) and/or friends, but that's another step for another time. For now, it's only between you and the bonobos. So just open your eyes and see.

Step 2: Be a Bonobo.

Having opened your eyes wide for Step 1, it's time to now let them close.[49] Step 2 takes you from observation to imagination and focused visualization. Take a deep breath. Like neotantric yoga, Tai Chi or belly dancing, many of these steps to releasing your inner bonobo begin with releasing your breath.

Breathe in a Rainbow

My favorite deep breathing technique is a mixture of Pranayama, self-hypnosis and my old Yale Theater teacher Nikos Psacharopoulos' pre-improvisational relaxation exercise. I can still hear Nikos' voice, like a high-pitched *Zorba the Greek*, telling us to inhale slowly through the nose with lips together and exhale through the mouth, lips apart, letting the exhalation last a little longer, imagining a sensuous warmth flowing into our bodies with each inhalation, all tension and anxiety leaving us as we exhaled.

For even deeper relaxation, you can try this "Color Hypnosis" technique I picked up at summer Camp Ramah when a secret cabal of my fellow campers and I put each other into "trances" (despite camp rules against such naughty, psychologically adventurous games): As you breathe deeply, go through the colors of the rainbow in your mind's eye: from red to orange to yellow to green to blue to violet. Despite its simplicity, this is such an effective calming technique that it might even lull you a bit as you read through the hues.

You can also incorporate more elaborate, hypnotic visualizations for deeper effectiveness. Always start with red, because it is the first color of the spectrum and the easiest to see. In fact, this is one reason stoplights and "sale" signs are red, also the color of the blood flowing through your veins. Breathe deeply in and out of blood red, crimson and scarlet, slowly letting the red change to orange, the next color of the spectrum. As you breathe in, imagine a radiant pumpkin-colored sun setting behind your eyelids.

---

[49] Obviously, you can't close your eyes while you're reading this book, unless you've got the Braille edition. So do this exercise after you finish reading this step, or in between sentences. You'll figure it out...

As you breathe out, let the orange sunset turn into a yellow sun, its golden rays melting all your tensions, warming every cell as you lie in a meadow of yellow buttercups, a soft breeze fluttering sweetly across your skin. Breathing in, let the breeze grow a little stronger and turn into a wind that blows all the buttercups away like a flock of golden butterflies, leaving you lying in a field of cool green grass surrounded by emerald trees and rich verdant foliage. Breathe out, letting the wind gust up, blowing you down a lush, green hillside. Feeling light and free as tumbleweed, you roll down through the trees with the greatest of ease. As you come to the end of the grass green hill, you find yourself diving off a cliff and into the deep blue sea, as everything turns crystal clear azure blue. You dive down deeper, water rippling all around you, and yes, you can breathe underwater. Inhale, and feel yourself becoming one with the sea as it gets darker, cooler shades of blue, from cobalt to sapphire to midnight to indigo.

Deep down at the bottom of the ocean, the water turns dark violet, the last color of the spectrum. It retains the cool calm of blue, but with a hint of blood red to keep you awake and aware as you swim through this very relaxed yet vibrant trance state.

As you inhale, you may find yourself swimming effortlessly through the deep violet currents of your consciousness like a fish. On the exhale, move ashore with your fellow amphibians, from reptiles, mammals, primates and onto bonobos. Breathe millions of years of evolution in and out of your flow.

When you get to bonobos, revisit the images you've seen at the zoo, online, in this book or, if you're lucky, in the wild. Continue breathing deep as you imagine yourself as one of them, and open your unwinding mind to that wild bonobo energy streaming through your blood-red veins from your brain. Visualize yourself swinging, flying, as you free your mind to play the way you really love to play. That's the Bonobo Way. Play.

Have You Forgotten How to Play?

Over the centuries, play has gotten a pretty bad rap from our puritanical, work-focused culture as being frivolous and beside-the-point. For bonobos, play *is* the point.

Professor Isabel Behncke, whose vivacious personality is as playful as her theme, has gained international acclaim for her TED video featuring what she calls a "trust game." In it, a female bonobo holds onto a male's testicles—kind of like a dominatrix clutching her submissive's helpless but happy package—as both of them move around in circles.

As Behncke puts it, "This bonobo has literally got her man by the balls. But there's actually an important point here—trust requires vulnerability. The male needs to trust the female because she could rip them off. But she doesn't. In turn, she trusts him when that vulnerability is offered back. Playing with the relationship between trust and peace is something very prominent in bonobo society."

Bataille extolled play as the essence of "sacred" eroticism. For Bataille, *le sacré* isn't associated with an organized religion or even "spiritual" feelings, but with creating or participating in something that is outside of the realm of work and everyday life. He defined play as the *transgression* of work for pleasure, a primal state wherein things and actions are temporarily stripped of their everyday meanings. He thought the eroticism of transgression was what separated humans from other animals. But Bataille probably didn't know bonobos and their love of teasingly transgressive, erotic play. Bonobos retain their "juvenile" characteristics well into adulthood and even old age. Maybe their bubbling Fountain of Youth springs from all that play.

Oh, to play as a bonobo plays! Perhaps that would help us stay younger longer too, but it's tough for most adult humans. Falling head over heels in love opens you up to your inner playground where you and your beloved can play different kinds of "trust games" for endless hours, as if you were kids again. But the euphoria never lasts and the playground closes down... unless you work hard to keep it open. But isn't work supposed to be the opposite of play?

In order to learn to play in the Bonobo Way, your BLC is to transgress time and flip through your memories, reaching back into your playful childhood or adolescence. You don't have to open your eyes for this unless you want to look at old photos or videos for inspiration. You can keep your "eyes wide shut"[50] in the misty rainforest of fantasy.

As the English philosopher John Richter said, "Fantasy rules over two-thirds of the universe, the past and the future, while reality is confined to the present." Memory, as it filters through the mind's eye, is a kind of fantasy that gazes backward into the past. Hope and anticipation, fear and desire are fantasies that look toward the future.

But we'll get back to the future later. For now, turn your internal crystal ball to your earliest memories and ask yourself: *How did I play?* Focus on the kind of play you really relished, not the kind you were forced to endure. Did you enjoy quiet pleasures, rough sports, competitive games, dress-up fun or mischievous pranks? Did you imagine you were a princess, a fire fighter, a movie star or a superhero?

What about sexual play? What were the first erotic games that you played by yourself or with others? Did you play "doctor," "post office" or Spin the Bottle? How did they fit into your general experience of childhood? In *Your Brain on Sex*, psychotherapist Stanley Siegel, LCSW writes, "Behind every sexual desire is an unmet need or conflict that grew out of our childhood experiences... Children discover the world and themselves through fantasy play."

You might try digging even deeper, excavating DNA "memories" of an evolutionary past long gone when your promiscuous, pre-human ancestors might have moved and played somewhat like bonobos, wild and free of the pressing concerns, property issues and plastic mechanisms of modern civilization. How do you imagine your forebears played?

Or just stick with your personal recollections. Consider how your favorite forms of play may have evolved, for better and for worse, along with you. Have you "forgotten" how to *lose yourself* in play the way you did as a kid (and the way bonobos do pretty much all their lives)? Consider incorporating more of your favorite forms of childhood play, and the innocence with which you once approached games, into your sex life and your other daily activities, including your work.

Play at Work

For Bataille, "play at work" would be the ultimate oxymoron. But with the growing omnipresence of work in human lives, the virtue of play (reported to increase productivity and creativity, as well as job satisfaction) has seeped into business philosophy. Clever managers integrate game mechanics into projects, humor into memos and bananas onto desks, attempting to foster a more playful, bonoboësque environment at work.

This brings us back to our hunter-gatherer ancestors, who, according to psychologist Peter Gray and others, maintained collective harmony in part by cultivating their silly side. This "suppressed the tendency to dominate and promoted egalitarian sharing and cooperation by deliberately fostering a playful attitude in essentially all of their social activities," including

---

[50] With appreciation to the inimitable Mr. Kubrick once again.

everything from the "work" of hunting and gathering to the mysteries of religion to the pleasures of sex and the passions of love. A teasing, trickster, don't-take-yourself-or-anyone-else-too-seriously approach helped to keep the "strong men" from getting too strong, Dr. Gray says. Playing with others—in the bedroom, the boardroom, on the wrestling mat or in the rainforest—requires a suspension of lethal, hurtful aggression with a heightened sensitivity to the needs and capabilities of the other player(s). Whether you're jamming with the band or just getting the job done in an upbeat office, "playing at work" can be ecstatic.

This is work so enjoyable and meaningful that you're literally getting paid to play. As Dr. Jared Diamond says, "I'd rather spend my leisure time doing what some people call my work and I call my fun." *Nice work if you can get it.*[51] If your boss lets you release your inner bonobo through play-at-work, you just might.

Erotic Theater of the Mind

Thankfully, in the realm of the sexual imagination where you can really go bonobos, there's no boss but you. Of course, most of us are our own worst bosses in this department, which is why we may really need to take this step.

Close your eyes, breathe deep, and let the curtain rise on the Erotic Theater of the Mind. Like the mystical Magic Theatre in Hermann Hesse's classic *Steppenwolf*, where the protagonist interacts with his own dreams and reveries, you can enter the erotic theater of *your* mind anytime you want to break the rules of the everyday and play within the limitless world of your sexual fantasies.

Most people's inner theater is a multiplex, so if what's playing on one screen starts to bore, there are always others to explore. These erotic movies in your mind may seem crazy or weird, but they serve a vital psychological function as keys that unlock the doors of your repressed personal history. They can help you to cope with your real-life problems just as your dreams do, giving you a "stage" to work through past trauma or abuse, or like an erotic painkiller on negative, hurtful memories. Fantasizing about the past can also lead to problems, such as wanting to "act out" in a way that perpetuates the abuse that you may have experienced onto someone else. But it doesn't have to. On the contrary,

---

[51] With a tip of the top hat to George and Ira Gershwin.

sexual fantasies, especially when accompanied by orgasm and perspective (not necessarily in that order), can help you to release the stress and suffering of the past without acting out at all.

Moreover, it's not all about stress and suffering. Within the erotic theater of your mind, you can also relive good sexual memories. Like fine wines or old classic movies, many erotic recollections get better with age. This is something you appreciate more as you get older and you are less physically capable of bonking four different lovers in three different places in one fine day. *Ah, memories!*

But the fantasies that play in your internal erotic playhouse aren't just reruns from your past, especially if you're young. They might also prepare you for the future. Such fantasies can be hazy or detailed mental rehearsals for sexual acts you yearn and burn to indulge, but haven't yet experienced. Just as athletes imagine playing and winning the Big Game before it actually happens, so you might imagine seducing or being seduced by your lover before the Big Date, the Big Hook-Up or the Big Wedding Anniversary. Some Casanovas and Cleopatras combine fantasy with strategy to entice the partners they desire. If you can dream it, you can do it... sometimes.

Other times, your fantasies might seem like more of a hindrance. Some secret sexual fantasies are very perverse, enhancing your insecurity even as they arouse your passions. If you tend to fantasize about being humiliated by people you desire or admire, then you might have a hard time, so to speak, psyching yourself up in a positive way for a date with someone you want to impress.

Perhaps you'd like to get rid of your more troublesome fantasies. Maybe you fantasize about being embarrassed when you'd like to be confident, having gay sex when you'd like to be straight, or doing your partner's sister when you'd like to focus on your partner. But deleting a secret sexual fantasy from your mental hard drive is much easier said than done. In fact, it can't really be done. The more you try to repress a fantasy, the more it tends to play, over and over again, growing larger and larger, obsessing you. So don't make like the Thought Police[52] and bust yourself for your fantasies. You simply can't control these erotic movies in your

---

[52] The Thought Police or *thinkpol* are secret cops who investigate and punish "thoughtcrime" through omnipresent surveillance in George Orwell's classic dystopian novel *Nineteen Eighty-Four*.

mind, at least no better than you can control your dreams[53].

But your fantasies don't have to control you either. Just because you imagine doing something crazy doesn't mean you have to do it. Though you can't control what you imagine, you can control what you actually do in real life. Hold yourself accountable for your actions, not your thoughts. Your favorite, secret, sexual fantasy is a gift you can't return, though sometimes, with time, it fades.

"Have faith in the healing power of your desires," Dr. Siegel advises. "Some schools of society tend to treat fantasies as pathological (and) many Christian (and other religious) groups preach that sexual fantasies are sinful... Both systems of thinking have contributed to our feelings of sexual shame and confusion."

Whatever your school or system, your fantasies are always with you, forever playing hide-and-seek with reality, whispering wild ideas into your inner ear, stirring your passions mysteriously, yet so powerfully. If you are imprisoned in any way—by your work, your family, your religion, your government—fantasies become your path to freedom. Sometimes, your ability to fantasize is the only freedom you have.

So relax and enjoy the show!

Bonobo Medibation

Since this step is all about play, your next BLC is to "play" with yourself. You could call it masturbation meditation. I like the term "medibation," which sexperts Dr. Annie Sprinkle, Barbara Carrellas and others use to describe a neotantric path of self-exploration and highly individualized sex education, a back road we all need to drive down to learn what we really like.

Find a quiet, private space, turn the lights down low and light an aromatic candle or your favorite incense. Then get naked (or in your lingerie, PJs, monkey suit or whatever you like), say OOOOMMMM and *medibate*, breathing into the rainbow as you mindfully touch your body. If you feel odd saying "OM," try "SEX," another mantra[54] or a positive

---

[53] You can exert some control over your dreams when in a state calling "lucid dreaming," in which you are not only aware that you're dreaming, you consciously direct the course of your dream. Some of the principles of lucid dreaming can be applied to erotic fantasy play, though it is more challenging to control what turns you on.
[54] From the Sanskrit word for "sacred utterance," a *mantra* is a sound, word or group of words that has spiritual or emotional power for the person uttering it. A sexual mantra has erotic power.

affirmation that helps you stay in the moment and aware as you touch yourself where it feels good.

Obviously, this is not the kind of difficult-to-master meditation where you have to sit perfectly still while attempting to corral your naughty, wandering mind into focusing on the present moment only. With bonobo medibation, you can concentrate on the pleasurable sensations you feel from touching yourself, let your mind enter your Magic Theater, or a combination.

Just stay relaxed, awake and *aware*. You might notice that, besides fantasies of the past and future, the erotic theater of your mind plays wild dreams that never happened and that you don't even *want* to have happen, but that haunt and stimulate you like a kinky parallel universe.

Rape & Other Disturbing Fantasies

Some of these fantasies might upset you, even though they turn you on. For instance, as a sex therapist, I talk to a great many clients who fantasize about rape. Some imagine they are the rapist, but most (both women and men) visualize themselves as the victim. None of these people want to be raped in real life. Nobody does! Real rape is the opposite of the Bonobo Way. But the fantasy of rape can be very compelling. Some people can only come when they imagine they are overcome.

Sexperts and sex researchers attribute various motivations for the common rape fantasy. One is that we feel so guilty and ashamed of our desires, we'd rather someone force us (in fantasy or in roleplay[55]) than admit to, and take responsibility for, what we want sexually. Of course, this "someone" has to be very attractive. After all, he (or sometimes she) is an idealized character, not a real rapist who smells bad or looks really abhorrent, though certain types of "scary" can be appealing.

Another reason for the rape fantasy is that this type of fear tends to *transgress* our comfort zone and heighten erotic tension, or so Bataille might say. Still another is that so many of us are seriously overworked, and being raped is (in a twisted fantasy way) the opposite of work. Someone else is doing the "work" of raping, dominating, controlling and ultimately pleasuring you, making you relax and enjoy the sensations, like a strong masseuse taking control of your body.

Another analysis, put forth by psychologist Dr. Marta Meana, holds that

---

[55] See "Ethical BDSM" under Step 8: Practice Ethical Hedonism for more on negotiating consent for rape fantasy and other forms of taboo roleplay.

the rape fantasizer is essentially "narcissistic," and what they really want is to be *really wanted*. The fantasy is that this sexy, lust-driven rapist *wants you* so much that he (or she) throws caution to the wind, seizes you against your will, overpowers your feeble protestations, rips off your clothes, throws you on the bed, kitchen table or hayloft (forcefully but without breaking anything really important) and takes you to the heights of orgasmic passion. *Oh my!*

Real rape is a terrible, traumatic, unconscionable act. But fantasy rape is an aspect of play, and it's important to remember that. The fact that the reality is so terrible is part of what makes the fantasy exciting and worth playing. Keep this in mind if your medibation practice takes you into rape fantasies or any territory that is counter to your real-life values.

If you don't act on it, a fantasy, whether disturbing or comforting, is just a movie playing in the erotic theater of your mind. It can be a romance or a horror flick, a long-drawn-out soap opera or a quick-n-dirty clip of "cumming attractions." Whatever form it takes, you can think of your favorite fantasy as the G-spot[56] of your psyche.

Once you know the location of your G-spot, or the nature of your favorite fantasy, you have a map that tells you where to go when you want to get aroused. Just as a map comes in handy when you're lost on the road, the map to your G-spot (both physical and mental) can come in handy when you want to make love, even if you're feeling distracted or "not in the mood." It enables you to focus your mind on something that will get you excited relatively quickly and easily, if that's what you want to do. Whether your "G-Spot Fantasy" involves sweep-you-off-your-feet forbidden love or indulging an obscure fetish, the sky's the limit, at least in the realm of fantasy.

Puritans, Like Poachers, Shoot to Kill Your Inner Bonobo

Which brings us back to that other realm, the one we call reality, where limits are much lower than the sky. In fact, those limits take us all right

---

[56] The physical G-Spot, i.e., the *Gräfenberg* Spot or Goddess Spot is an area about the size of a nickel with a raspberry-textured bumpiness located just an inch or two inside the vagina under the roof of the vaginal cave. When stimulated properly (one method is through fingering with the "come hither" gesture) swells and triggers tremendous orgasms as well as female ejaculation. Some say the G-Spot is the internal side of the clitoris. Some relate it to the Skene's gland, a.k.a., the female prostate. Others say it does not exist. However, many women claim to have experienced powerful, squirting, G-Spot orgasms, this author included!

down to our poor, over-plowed, over-drilled, over-farmed and abused Mother Earth. Dr. Jared Diamond called farming "the worst mistake in the history of the human race." Most of us wouldn't be here without it, however, so who are we to complain? But with agricultural development came a litany of limits on human freedom, including the life imprisonment and solitary confinement of our inner bonobos, often without so much as a conjugal visit.

Interestingly, the Internet (as long as it remains neutral, open and free) stimulates the hunter-gatherer in us, releasing our inner bonobos to come out and play in many ways like never before, especially when it comes to "sharing" ideas, apps, images and information. We are opening up to each other around this great flat world of ours, spreading the "likes" and the love in an orgy of international communication.

But the backlash to all that love and sharing is on the march, and the world's "great" religions are leading the charge from the military academies, to the villages, to the streets and to the Internet, fighting each other as well as natural human sexuality. Those of us who try to free our inner bonobos are often slapped and trapped by the slurs, snubs, hypocritical castigations and nonconsensual punishments of this jealous, erotophobic crusade. Whether they're thumping Bibles, Korans or Bhagavad Gitas, dropping bombs or leaflets, pointing fingers or guns, throwing acid on unveiled faces, slut-shaming pop stars or taking children away from good parents who happen to be swingers, the effect is always deadening. Socially active puritans are spiritual poachers shooting to kill our inner bonobos as surely as bushmeat hunters gun down the real bonobos in the rainforest.

Your BLC is to protect your inner bonobo even as you release it into a hostile world. After being caged for so long, stepping beyond the bars can be scary and even dangerous. That's why this program is a series of baby steps. Virtually anyone, even a devout nun in a convent, can take Steps 1-2 without fear of exposure. These first two steps require minimal action, being passive activities focused on discovering your inner bonobo without necessarily doing anything about it, except private medibation (which can be done under the covers with the door locked). You can even fantasize that you're a prisoner of the Pope, being sexually tortured for your sins by a well-endowed Cardinal, and no one ever has to know. Not even your Mother Superior.

But life is for living and interacting in the world, not just watching and fantasizing under the covers. Steps 3-12 gently guide you out of the convent toward unleashing your inner bonobo into your real life *with others*. We (bonobos and humans) are highly social creatures. We're "people who need people," which makes us "the luckiest people," but you can't test your luck without some risk. So, unlike the first two steps, these next ten are more likely to challenge your game. From Observation and Imagination, it's time to get outside your head into Imitation.

Step 3: Go Bonobos in Bed.

Ape your fellow apes! Your Step #3 BLC is to roleplay your wild side. After all that watching, feeling and fantasizing, it's time to *learn by doing*. Unleash your enlivening bonoboësque passion into the bedroom with your consensual partner(s)... if you dare.

Going bonobos in bed is erotic alchemy. Ancient alchemists were said to turn lead into gold, so taking Step 3 transforms fantasy into reality—at least to the extent your reality allows. Where does fantasy meet reality? When a dream or fantasy is so vivid that it "seems real," or when your real life flows along "like a fantasy," you're in the zone... the "Bonobo Liberation Zone" (BLZ).

Unleash the Erotic Animal Within

Physically, "going bonobos in bed" can range from athletic porn star sex to almost-motionless tantra. Mentally, it also runs the gamut, from roleplaying crazy cartoon scenarios to just "being in the moment," breathing in synch, relishing the touch and taste of each other.

What do these different ways to go bonobos have in common? They all involve embracing your authentic, organic, animal nature without worrying too much about being "normal." After all, bonobos reveal that an incredible range of sexual diversity *is* normal for animals like us.

There are infinite ways to release the sexual animal within you. One fun, slightly silly, but amazingly effective approach to getting into "the zone" is to imagine that you and your partner(s) are non-human animals. You could be bonobos. But you could also be tigers, pandas, eagles, kangaroos, peacocks, bulldogs (boola-boola!) or any other animal with which you feel an erotic affinity.

Maybe you already do this. Many of us identify strongly with nonhuman animals. We name our sports teams, astrological signs and cars after our favorite creatures. We wear leopard print, zebra stripes and teddy bear hoodies. We love our dogs and kitties more than our mates sometimes. Most of us grow up cuddling and sleeping with pets and/or stuffed animals. Some of us fantasize about having sex with an animal (okay, now we're getting past kinky) or watching someone have sex with an animal. But then there's having sex *on* an animal…

One of my own most exhilarating erotic experiences was having doggy-style sex with my male lover behind me as we rode bareback through the Connecticut countryside on a big, beautiful stallion. Though it was only my lover thrusting inside me, the sensation of the horse's powerful muscles spreading my thighs as we galloped through fiery fall trees made me feel as if I was having sex with some great "humanimal," like the ancient half-man half-horse centaur of Greek mythology. Needless to say, I released my own inner animal that crisp New England afternoon, and I often tap into that memory when I want to better understand my sex therapy clients' animal sex fantasies.

Bestiality is one of the great human taboos, probably even older than civilization. Nevertheless, shepherds have long found comfort in their sheep… literally. Mythology is filled with gods transforming themselves into beasts who mate with humans. The Greek god Zeus (Jupiter to the Romans) is said to have morphed into a bull, a swan, a goat and a small rain-drenched bird to facilitate his seduction of various fair maidens.

So it's well within the realm of "normal" human fantasy to imagine sex as, or with, a non-human animal. Though I certainly don't advocate anyone actually engaging in bestiality (partly because it's likely to involve some form of animal cruelty), I usually validate such fantasies when my clients reveal them to me, worried that their wild imaginings indicate sex "addiction" or "perversion." Sometimes I roleplay the animal sex fantasy (I love pretending to be a wild bull!) with them or guide them through it via erotic hypnosis.

Many people need to imagine themselves as nonhuman animals in order to get out of their heads and into their bodies. It doesn't have to be a real animal. One of my clients, a rather stressed-out tax attorney, imagines that she becomes a werewolf as she makes howling hot love to her girlfriend.

Romp & Wrestle or Cuddle & Groom

Whatever animal or fantasy beast you choose to become, you can enter the BLZ through its skin. Romp around in your jungle of sheets and pillows, play-wrestling, biting, sniffing, pawing, tonguing, tickling, love-smacking, rolling, undulating, rubbing, thrusting, penetrating each other, synchronizing your strokes, climaxing together or one after the other, falling exhausted into each other's arms, creating a nest, snuggling up, inhaling each other like intoxicants, listening to your hearts beat hard, your limbs intertwined so you don't know whose is whose, your bodies merged, intimately attuned to each other, as well as to the entire animal world and the great Gaian ecosystem from which we humans religiously cut ourselves off, but that feels so damn good to rejoin.

Then again, you might want to skip the romping and other erotic athletics and just groom each other, cuddling close and breathing your lover's essence deep into your lungs and heart. Soft sex like this is especially important if one of you is disabled or fatigued, because being "too tired" or "too old" should never be an excuse to forego going bonobos in bed or tuning into your inner animal.

Remember, "going bonobos" might sound like extremely energetic group sex while swinging through the trees and/or chandeliers (and it can be that!), but it can also be lying serenely in each other's arms. It certainly doesn't have to include sexual intercourse. Bonobos skip it all the time. In fact, going bonobos doesn't have to include any particular activity. It just has to feel good, preferably *really* good.

Feeling really good is usually accompanied by sounds of joy, desire and euphoric satiation. Whether you have wild upside-down anal intercourse or you're just nestling close to each other, give your feelings a voice. Try an animal voice. Draw a breath so deep you feel it in your diaphragm, filling your lungs from bottom to top. Open your throat and let the dogs out—or the horses, wolves or Siamese cats. Howl. Moan. Grunt. Groan. Purr. Giggle. Sigh. Bonobos hoot at each other in a high-pitched squeal. They also pant. But any sounds will do, and if those sounds become words ("dirty" or divine), so be it. You don't have to scream "Hallelujah," but try not to be silent, unless you don't want to wake the baby or alert the warden. If you're worried about the neighbors, turn up the music. Or just whisper something sex-positive to let your partner(s) know when you like what they're doing and they'll probably do what you like more often.

What about "dirty talk"? Best to float in test balloons, one word at a time. Talking "dirty" is naturally edgy, so try incorporating the word "love" to soften the edge, i.e., "I love your cunt." Spill your fantasies a drop at a time as you play. Interweave your *Pan paniscus* dreams with the reality of you and your favorite *Homo sapiens* in bed.

But why confine it to bed? Bonobos make a new nest every night, and our hunter-gatherer ancestors did something similar. So shouldn't you get out of the same old bed once in a while? Do it up against the wall, on the kitchen counter or in the bath. Do it in the car. Check into an upscale hotel or a no-tell motel. Do it in the great outdoors, especially if you can find a good spot where you can see the stars without alarming the locals. Again, "doing it" can be anything from bucking-bronco humping to serene holding. The idea is to share your erotic nature... in nature.

What to wear to enter the BLZ? You can dress up or strip down. If you tend to take this stuff literally, go ahead and put on an animal costume, don a mask or go all out in a bonobo furry suit.[57] However, bringing out your animal nature doesn't have to involve resembling a wild or anthropocentrically Disneyfied animal. Not at all. If lingerie and high heels make you feel not just sexy but sexual, or if the texture and smell of real leather (with apologies to PETA) puts you in touch with your mammalian spirit, go for it. Sometimes, it's the opposite of animal that makes us *feel* animal. Latex, anyone?

Of course, simple nudity, allowing for all-over, skin-to-skin, oxytocin-enhancing contact, is usually the most direct way for most humans to go bonobos in bed. Not that it's always so simple...

The Ideal is The Enemy of The Real

Going bonobos in bed is, essentially, erotic play with your beloved partner(s), and it's one of the most exciting steps of the 12. It's also one of the riskiest. What if your beloved partner(s) can't (or won't!) go bonobos with you?

Ideally, you'll both free your inner bonobos in erotically compatible ways. Unfortunately, Goethe was pretty much right when he cautioned, "Love is an ideal thing, marriage a real thing; a confusion of the real with the ideal never goes unpunished." Or as my darling Pr. Max puts it, much more succinctly, "the ideal is the enemy of the real."

Your partner(s) may feel threatened by your bonobo liberation. They may have a different idea of what liberation means or may not want to go bonobos at all. These "kinks" need to be worked out, or played out. Even if your partner's desires appear to be the antithesis of yours, it is not the end of the world. In fact, *vive la difference*! Remember, without a little erotic

---

[57] A furry suit or "fursuit" is an animal costume made of plush materials. It can range from just ears or a tail to a full-body suit. Furry suits are often worn by "furries," people who love anthropomorphic animal characters. The suits allow the wearer to adopt their interpretation of the animal's character while in costume. Though controversial within the larger community of "furry fandom," some furries enjoy having sex or just "yiffing" (sniffing, rubbing and dry-humping) each other while in costume. I haven't seen a full bonobo furry suit yet, so if you do, send photos!

tension (or, as Bataille might say, transgression), there is no release.

Sharing fantasies isn't usually necessary when you first have sex together. So much is new in reality, your mind doesn't have to go much farther than the present moment for stimulation. But after a while, when you've been together a few years, your bodies become so familiar that your minds are bound to drift... into fantasy. After all, there are only so many physical positions into which you can bend your bodies, but there is an endless array of mind-games you can play or roleplay. But what if your secret sexual desire turns off, upsets or even disgusts your lover? One person's favorite fantasy can be another's worst nightmare.

Empathize as You Fantasize

So... to share or not to share? It depends on you, your partner and your desires. In general, proceed with caution, but by all means, do proceed. If you've never shared a fantasy with your lover, and you'd like to try, start by sharing a memory, a thrilling erotic experience you actually had together. Reminisce about it in bed, then embellish the memory by fantasizing about something that could have made the experience even more exciting. For instance, you might recall having hot sex outside in a secluded garden. Then imagine if someone were peeking through the bushes, watching you.

You can also stimulate the sharing of fantasies by reading or looking at erotica together. Be poetic, be explicit, be romantic, be outrageous, be honest, but be sensitive. Try tossing out small parts of your secret fantasies one at a time. If it floats, keep embellishing, if you can see it sinking by your partner's negative reaction, switch gears. This exercise challenges your ability to empathize as you fantasize. It's risky business, but nothing great in life comes without taking a chance.

Can you ride the erotic tension between you and your partner(s) like a surfer traversing a wave until a fantastic orgasmic wipeout whooshes you into the BLZ? That kind of pure flow involves body-mind-and-soul connection and control that is beyond most mere mortals. However, the "kinky but noble" bonobos can help you stay on top of the wave and out of the sinkhole through the rest of these steps. And remember, more good sex boosts those brain cells, so that'll help too.

It goes back to what Drs. Salovey and Mayer dub "emotional intelligence" (EI or EQ). That's what gave bonobo Djonoa the edge over the common chimps to win the Ape IQ competition. EQ is your ability to identify, assess and deal productively with your emotions and those of others without sulking in a corner or throwing a fit like a mad chimpanzee.

Being emotionally intelligent means knowing when to freely go bonobos, and when to keep the raging King Kong within you on a short leash. Cultivating a high EQ gives you the power to live a passionate, pleasure-filled, peaceful life even if murder, mayhem, insanity and stupidity are erupting all around you. In the Great Ape EQ Olympics, bonobos win the gold. If they can survive a war-torn jungle (as they have *so far*), maybe we humans can make it through this erotophobic world and enjoy satisfying sex with someone we love.

Applying the emotional intelligence theory specifically to sex and love, Dr. Marty Klein identifies "sexual intelligence" in his book of the same name as "the set of internal resources that allows you to relax, be present, communicate, respond to stimulation, and create physical and emotional connection with a partner." Sexual intelligence gives you the emotional tools to have great sex, regardless of your partner's or your age, physical ability, genital function or so-called dysfunction.

Fortunately, the most vital BLC of "going bonobos in bed" doesn't require much intelligence at all. For some, though, it might require courage. The challenge here is simply to wrap your arms around the one(s) you love, look into their eyes, and (before it's too late!) let them know you love them in any and every way you can.

Not that you must always look your lover(s) in the eye and think of nothing but them when you make love. After all, the erotic theater of your mind is a multiplex and there's nothing wrong with that. Another BLC for going bonobos in bed is to make your sexual fantasies your allies, not your enemies. Just as your dreams are vital to your emotional health, your erotic fantasies are an important aspect of your sexual health as an individual and as a part of maintaining relationships. If a fantasy keeps recurring in your mind, despite your efforts to "think of something else," your inner bonobo is trying to tell you something, even if the rest of you would rather not hear it.

That doesn't mean you have to share all your sexual fantasies with your partner(s). You don't, and sometimes you really shouldn't. But it's always easier to go bonobos in bed if you can accept them within yourself.

"She's Everything I Want! What's Wrong with Me?"

Nate, a career-driven and physically fit young investment banker, came to me at the end of his sexual rope. Actually, he was as limp as a rope.

He'd already seen two sex therapists, a psychiatrist and a urologist about the "performance anxiety" that had plagued him since his first sexual experiences as a teenager. One minute he'd be fine, granite-hard and raring to go. Then suddenly, he'd start sweating, his heart racing and every part of his body stiffening up *except* his penis, which wilted like an orchid after prom. It didn't happen all the time, but sometimes it would "fail" him at the worst moments. And now his inability to "perform" was threatening to ruin his brand-new marriage to Nadia, a woman he adored.

The urologist couldn't find anything physically wrong with Nate. The psychiatrist was ready to prescribe various medications, from antidepressants to Viagra, but Nate, to his credit, chose not to medicate the problem away. The sex therapists gave him ejaculation control exercises, breathing and relaxation techniques to help calm his nerves and sensate focus to help him stay in the moment.

Nate enjoyed all of these excellent exercises but ultimately they didn't "work." That is, he kept going soft at critical moments. When one of the therapists wisely counseled Nate to stop worrying about his erection, he worried about it even more. Plus, his lovely and otherwise-patient new wife, excited about starting a family with her new husband, was getting just a little bit *im*patient. This put Nate under more pressure than ever, and the anxiety left him feeling like he was trying to shove a marshmallow into a parking meter... as the meter maid rolls her eyes and writes him a ticket.

When he heard about BLT, Nate figured he'd give it a shot. I asked him what he usually thought about just before he got anxious. He hesitated, muttered something to himself and let out a big sigh. "Not my wife," he confessed slowly. "I love Nadia, and I know I should focus on her when we make love. I feel very guilty because sometimes my mind just wanders into these fantasies. I can't help it. I mean, Nadia's beautiful and wonderful. She's everything I want! What's wrong with me?"

I said I didn't think there was anything wrong with him for having fantasies. But if *he* chastised himself for having the "wrong" fantasies, that might chase his erection away. And the more he tried to control and police his thoughts, the more these unwanted, transgressive fantasies, whatever they were, would tease and torment him, like mischievous Merry Pranksters[58] tricking and confounding the thought police of his mind.

"Amazon women," he blurted in the middle of my little lecture on the

---

[58] The Merry Pranksters were a group of psychedelic drug-lovers who formed around American author Ken Kesey during the 1960s.

futility of fighting fantasies. "Since I was five years old, I've thought about dominant Amazon superwomen stronger than me, pinning me down and forcing me to have sex with them. I know it's crazy. I can't stand it! But I can't help it."

Crazy or not, Nate had not divulged this vital piece of information to his urologist, psychiatrist or either sex therapist. I'm not sure if they didn't ask, but he certainly didn't tell. However once he started talking about "her," he couldn't stop. We went back to his earliest childhood dreams of this Amazonian superwoman overpowering his resistance: how his strict, upwardly mobile upbringing denigrated such unmanly thoughts, how he got extremely aroused by her anyway, and how he thought he could finally rid himself of the Amazon now that he was in love with Nadia. At that point, we discovered the real cause of his performance anxiety.

"As sex begins, I get an image of this Amazon woman overpowering me and I get so super hard," he told me. "Then I realize I should focus on my wife, so I try to stop thinking about the Amazon. And then, after a while, my erection just dies."

"Well, don't try to stop the Amazon," was my suggestion. "Don't make her your enemy. Make her your ally. Surrender to her power. Make her a team member. She's already on your member's team."

"But shouldn't I be thinking about my wife?"

"Sure, just don't stop the Amazon. Go with her flow." I really meant this, puns and all.

But Nate was so tough on himself. The sex-negative perfectionist in him insisted he be "pure of mind" before he could enjoy sex and he was rarely pure enough. His eager, but terrified, young sexual psyche had conjured up the image of an archetypal supergirl to overpower that part of him that was a harsh, judgmental, repressive, erection-wilting purist, and "force" him to set his inner bonobo free.

Of course, the Amazon woman was just a character in the erotic theater of his mind, so he could always overpower her and stop the fantasy, which he did out of a sense of guilt and duty to his bride. But when his Amazon fantasy woman left, she took his erection with her, leaving his performance anxiety to ultimately "win" the game. Nate's BLC was to let the Amazon win, so she could overpower the sex-negative perfectionist within him and free his inner bonobo. Then maybe his cock would get hard for sex with his wife.

Unraveling a mental knot like that can take a while, but in Nate's case it happened literally overnight, which he relayed to me the next day, going bonobos with joy. That morning, as he was making love to Nadia, the Amazon surfaced in his imagination, flexing her strong, scary, seductive muscles, as usual. But instead of trying to push her out of the ring of his mind, he surrendered to his lifelong fantasy of her subduing him, along with his "performance anxiety," making room for his erection, now growing and flexing into a powerful muscle of pleasure which he used to make love to his wife who was orgasmically happy to see her husband hard again, even if it was 6:30 a.m. and their eyes were still foggy with dreams.

Then an amazing thing happened: once Nate let the Amazon within him "win," she faded from his mind, and Nadia filled it. And there they were, "in the moment" more than ever—going bonobos in bed! Traversing that blissful, buoyant BLZ together, Nate heard Nadia howling like a mountain wolf, sensed her delicious contractions all over his still-hard pleasure-muscle as he felt her coming like crazy, and then suddenly, within the most deeply thrilling three seconds of his life, so was he.

Two years later, Nate and Nadia are the proud parents of a beautiful baby boy and, thanks to Nate's mom being the "world's greatest babysitter," they still find time for bonoboësque sex. These days, Nate only fantasizes about his Amazon goddess every few weeks or so (usually when he's very stressed). Most of the time, he finds it easy and natural to focus on Nadia as they make love. Giving himself permission to fantasize has given Nate the freedom to go bonobos in bed.

Step 4: Outercourse Is In

The idea of "going bonobos" might conjure images of non-stop humping, and sometimes that's just what it is, but most of the Bonobo Sutra doesn't even involve intercourse. Actually all the fondling—or as they say *en Français*, "frottage," i.e., massage, licking, stroking, erotic wrestling, rump-rubbing, ear-tonguing, hugging, kissing, bonobo handshakes and even the highly orgasmic GG-rubbing and penis-fencing—are more accurately considered forms of sexual "outercourse."

"Outercourse" is a neologism which wiggled its way into Anglo-American discourse toward the latter part of the 20th century. I had to instruct my spell-check to recognize "outercourse" as a word, but then again, I had to teach it "bonobo" too. The first time I heard the term was from my former erotica editor, pioneering sex therapist Dr. Lonnie Barbach, when the advent of AIDS caused many sex-positive people to search for various forms of "safer sex." Outercourse can be any kind of sexual activity between two or more people that doesn't involve penetration or intercourse of the vagina, anus or mouth. Kissing, spanking the behind, touching the breasts or caressing the outside of the genitals or other erogenous zones are all forms of outercourse. Many people, especially women, also enjoy being touched, massaged, tickled, teased, squeezed and licked in many other zones that are not conventionally considered erogenous, such as the ears, knees, elbows, ribs, feet and the nape of the neck.

"Cuddle Parties," founded by sex educators Reid Mihalko and Marcia Baczynski, are "non-sexual," no-kissing, clothes-on, outercourse events where people go to find that basic physical touch and affection that sometimes goes missing from so many human lives, without the pressures of sex and dating.

Like intercourse, outercourse releases positive, healing hormones, endorphins and oxytocin. Unlike intercourse, virtually no semen, vaginal fluids, or blood is shared between outercourse partners, though saliva sometimes is, and there are the occasional drops of sweat, pre-cum and feminine juices.

No activity is risk-free, but outercourse protects against pregnancy and most sexually transmitted diseases (STDs) far more effectively than intercourse with even the finest condoms. It can be tough to just stick to outercourse sometimes, especially when you're going hot and heavy. But a true outercourse orgy is a safer sex party indeed, raising those pleasurable hormone levels, just by scratching (and caressing) the surface of things.

Eroplay, Chero & the Art of the Tease

My old friend and one of my mentors, the late, great Frank Moore, was an outercourse orgy master. Frank was the Stephen Hawking of erotic theater, a revolutionary "wounded healer" for artists and seekers all over the world. Physiologically speaking, he was a spastic quadriplegic with severe cerebral palsy who couldn't walk or talk. But he never let what others would call his extreme disability get in the way of his illustrious career as an award-winning artist, poet, musician, theater director and shaman, nor his good time as a great luver.[59] On the contrary, he proclaimed his body to be "perfect for performance art," and then he proved himself right. Talk about making the lemons of your life into limoncello!

Frank coined the term "chero," combining "chi" and "eros" to express the physical energy of life, which I call bonoboësque. He also created the word "eroplay" to describe the physical interaction between people released from the linear goals of sexual intercourse, often in the context of long, 5-48 hour ritualistic nude performances. These intense outercourse happenings, in which I was privileged to participate when he and his happy, hippie, bonoboësque family were my guests, were transformative experiences that melted the barriers between performers and audience without penetrating physical orifices.

Or did they? As Frank says, "Foreplay is eroplay, but eroplay does not have to be foreplay." Outercourse without intercourse could be considered a form of *teasing*, which may or may not lead to anything else. That can be part of the excitement—not knowing where things are going. Will boundaries be transgressed, or won't they?

Everyone benefits from a little teasing, at least sometimes, as any burlesque artist well knows. Men need to be teased because it makes them slow down. Women need to be teased because it makes us come around. Without the art of the tease, we'd just be rutting dogs. But even dogs tease!

---

[59] LUVeR radio is the name of Frank's Internet radio station.

Look at the stop-start, pounce-retreat mating dances of canines, cats, birds, snakes and even insects. Of course, bonobos are experts at erotic teasing, which is an integral aspect of play. They do it all day, every day, in a myriad of ways.

Trust Kills Lust

Teasing generates lust through denial and delay. The essence of flirtation, teasing may last a few seconds or forever. Whatever its length in time, it stokes the fires of desire.

According to *Kosher Sex* Rabbi Shmuley Boteach, a three-time guest on my show, "Lust is enhanced through an inability to attain the object of your longing, the failure to satiate human yearning." Though I differ with Rabbi Shmuley about some things, like masturbation and open marriages, I'm right with him here. Lust thrives on tease, denial and transgression, which the good Rabbi enticingly and Torahically dubs "sin."

Trust is a vital aspect of love and friendship but, ironically, *trust kills lust* with kindness, familiarity and easy access. This sad truth sends many good marriages down the sinkhole of sexual boredom. In a way, falling into this sinkhole is as easy and "normal" as falling in love.

Visionary psychologist Esther Perel (whom I was fortunate to interview when her best-selling book *Mating in Captivity: Reconciling the Erotic and the Domestic* first appeared) puts the great marital conundrum this way: "Love seeks closeness. Desire needs distance." Moreover, "excitement is interwoven with uncertainty, and with the willingness to embrace the unknown rather than to shield ourselves from it."

But how to create that excitement when you feel you "know" your partner better than you know yourself? There are many ways to trick your erotic mind into "forgetting" what you think you already know so that you can enjoy the true mysteries of lust with someone you love, and this book is filled with them. One very physical solution is to engage in frequent, teasing outercourse that doesn't predictably lead to intercourse, allowing you to be ultra-close while delaying gratification and giving desire the space it needs to grow, at least every once in a while.

When outercourse precedes more serious sex, we call it "foreplay," which sounds rather subordinate, like an appetizer with intercourse as the main course. Lots of people like to skip the appetizer, especially if they aren't hungry. That's fine for food. But skipping foreplay is rarely a good idea for sex, even or maybe especially when you're not very horny. The right foreplay can send you from zero to a thousand on the horniness scale.

Foreplay is (or should be) "coreplay," according to *She Comes First*, Ian Kerner's fine guide to becoming an exceedingly proficient cunnilinguist. It can involve tasting, touching, talking or even just texting a sexy message or hot selfie when you can't be together. The Ninth Commandment of a Lady's Pleasure[60] is "Thou Shalt Have Foreplay." It also happens to be the longest commandment, just to remind you to take your time.

"Slow down" is also the mantra for the international "orgasmic meditation" (OM) movement. This tantra-style two-person yoga, in which the active partner (male or female) ritualistically lubes and strokes the clitoris of the passive partner (always female) for 15 minutes, was developed by OneTaste founder, *Slow Sex* author and orgasm revivalist Nicole Daedone. Many women find OM's largely external stimulation to be "better than sex," a meditative form of clitoral outercourse that can also be great foreplay for good old PIV.

Women often protest that they don't get enough foreplay (which usually means some form of outercourse) from the men in their lives. They want to devote more time to romance, intimacy, conversation, massage, frottage, external clitoral stimulation and other kinds of outercourse, while most men prefer to "plunge into plunging" (i.e., hard-thrusting intercourse, or maybe a blowjob) as soon as any woman will let them in. In wild Bonoboville, females rule the bedroom (which is everywhere), so there's plenty of outercourse and foreplay to go around.

Though "not enough foreplay" is typically a woman's complaint, there's another side to the sexual story. Many of my male sex therapy clients would love to linger endlessly on foreplay, but the women in their lives are uninterested, disgusted, exhausted or in a hurry. Perhaps these ladies are preoccupied with work or family matters and just want to get sex over with. Then again, it could be that the husband or boyfriend's idea of outercourse involves fetish play, mutual masturbation, oral sex, cross-dressing, reading erotica or looking at porn that the wife or girlfriend doesn't enjoy.

Can a Chimp Be a "Porn Addict"?

Yes, in a way, watching porn, or any kind of voyeurism, could be a

---

[60] Check out the other nine commandments of a lady's pleasure in my book, *The 10 Commandments of Pleasure*.

form of outercourse, though you can also watch it while having intercourse. Indeed, erotica viewing is one of humanity's most popular and effective aphrodisiacs. It's a turn-off for some, but most are aroused by images of people they find attractive engaged in various sexual activities. Viewing pornography is a safe (most often private) way to get that feeling of communal ecstasy without actually participating in an orgy.

Of course, porn is demonized, and porn stars are the victims of much public posturing and corporate hypocrisy (often from some of their most avid closet viewers!) that they even have trouble opening bank accounts. Yet pornography continues to grow in popularity and public acceptance with individuals and couples around the world, developing more and more niche audiences in every fetish, genre, body type and orientation. It may change shape or name, and in some places it may be forced underground, but porn will not go away.

Unsurprisingly, some bonobos and other great apes go ape over porn while others favor a different approach. Just as some male humans prefer *Vogue* to *Playboy*, Kanzi, the genius bonobo, is said to pleasure himself while looking at women's fashion, especially ladies in fur coats. Gina, a common chimp-in-residence at a Spanish zoo, loves hardcore human porn. In fact, she enjoys it so much that she's developed a reputation (among humans) as a "porn addict."

It's interesting that the most famous chimp porn-lover is female and Gina's preferences should make you wonder. If our simian cousins enjoy it, is it any surprise that we do too? Obviously, looking at porn is not unnatural, and like anything enjoyable, you can seriously overdo it. You can watch too much porn just like you can eat too much pizza. But that doesn't make pizza or porn evil. Plus, all other things being equal, too much pizza will kill you a lot faster than too much porn.

Watching porn is an escape for some, but it's also an important, albeit unreliable, way to learn about sex in a society like ours that doesn't provide much real sex education. Not that porn is very realistic about sex, but its purpose isn't educational (unless it's educational porn), responsible or realistic. Porn or erotica is a type of art, specifically, the type that turns you (or somebody) on. It might be bad art, but every art form has both Picassos and pretenders.

The odd thing about porn is that oftentimes something we feel is in "bad taste" will turn us on. This can be very disturbing. Going back to Bataille and that unnerving, transgressive feeling that accompanies much eroticism, we tend to get even more upset when something we feel is in bad taste turns our partner(s) on.

The Power to Give Pleasure

Which brings us back to you and your loved one(s). What if you loathe, or just aren't interested in, the type of porn, fetish play or other forms of outercourse that your partner desires? What do you do when your liberated inner bonobo crashes headlong into your partner's hang-ups?

We all have our erotic likes and dislikes, and none of us should have any kind of sex, inter or outer, that we really don't want. No means no, and the ability to say no to something we don't want is as vital to sexual intelligence and practicing the Bonobo Way as the courage to say yes to the things we actually (often secretly) desire. Interestingly, studies from the Max Planck Institute show that bonobos shake their heads, in the exact same manner as most people do, to say "no." But if you say "no" *a lot*, especially to the one(s) you love, whether human or bonobo, rejection becomes cumulative and backlash is inevitable. When you constantly reject, belittle or ignore your lover's desire for a particular kind of outercourse, foreplay, fetish or fantasy, it doesn't just go away. Sometimes it gets even stronger and more urgent, transgressively rattling its cage inside your partner's head, pushing for release, possibly through infidelity, alienation or both.

Your disgruntled partner, trying to respect you and sidestep your negativity, will simply seek outlets outside of you, such as secret love affairs, clandestine phone sex, discreet porn viewing, obsessive social media networking, hiring an escort, serving a dominatrix or engaging in an embarrassing affair with your hot and unhappily married sibling, to name just a few common possibilities. Or perhaps he or she won't be so sexually adventurous and will simply curl up into a big, seething ball of erotophobic resentment and bitterness toward you, without ever mentioning the sexual problem. And both of you will be left wondering how "that lovin' feeling"[61] got flushed down the sinkhole-loo.

One way to avoid this is to say "yes" a lot, at least to discussing things, watching a little of the porn or exploring some of the outercourse your partner craves. Open your mind, your heart and maybe your legs. See if you can find common ground, something you like, or at least find tolerably

---

[61] With apologies to the Righteous Brothers.

intriguing, about what he or she clearly loves. Part of following the Bonobo Way means giving each other a chance to enjoy one another's favorite forms of outercourse, as long as they're legal and consensual.

That doesn't mean you always have to share the same foreplay. For instance, hubby can watch a bit of porn while the missus warms up with her vibrator, reads erotica or goes out dancing with friends. Then they can meet in the middle of their marriage bed for a hot bonobo handshake, climactic sex and/or blissful cuddling. As every sexpert knows, spending ample time on outercourse (whether you do it separately or together, before or after) helps make intercourse all the more orgasmic and rewarding... if intercourse happens.

Your BLC is to reduce jealousy or judgment of your partner's preferred form of outercourse. Practice compersion and be grateful they're sharing their turn-ons, instead of hiding them from you. Learn what you can about them and how you can get involved in a way that feels good for you. The power to give pleasure is the greatest power you have. You might be surprised how you learn to like your lover's favorite forms of outercourse, at least a little, if only because they please your lover.

Your Step #4 BLC is to make a list of what types of outercourse you enjoy or wish you could explore. You may share this list with your partner(s)... or not. You can write it down, tweet it out or just medibate on the subject. When is outercourse even better than intercourse? What kinds of outercourse make you crave intercourse like crazy? What do you like to do by yourself, and what do you prefer with a partner? Are you actually exploring the activities on your list, or are you stuck in a foreplay rut? Is your taste in outercourse limited by your experience or a jaded frame of mind? If so, go back to Step #1: See the bonobos. Watch how they relish so many types of foreplay and outercourse and all that good stuff that comes before cumming... and sometimes after.

Then again, your own experience is often your best teacher. What kinds of outercourse did you enjoy once or twice that you'd like to do more? What do you think could make your sex life more "gourmet" and less "fast-food"?

Speaking of food—yum... Let's eat!

Step 5: Mix Food and Sex.

Bonobos are great gourmands. They love to combine food and sex, two of the most vital and delectable elements of life. Humans can relate. In his famed 1943 "Theory of Human Motivation," Dr. Abraham Maslow put both food and sex into the basic foundation of his "Hierarchy of Needs," along with water, sleep, excretion and breathing. Like all animals, we eat to survive, and we have sex so our genes might survive. But there's so much more to food and sex than just survival for us humans, and the same goes for bonobos.

We humans often use food and sex as metaphors for love. After all, love is pretty abstract. You can feel love in your heart... or is it all in your head? But you can't hold love in your arms or savor it in your mouth. This is where chocolate kisses, hot buttered buns, sweet creamy pies and thick juicy sausages come in. Food and sex bring love to life. Recipes and positions vary, but the basic cravings hold true.

There's something very sweet and savory about the way bonking and brunch can represent love... in theory. But the reality can have treacherous consequences, like when you inhale an entire carton of double fudge ice cream because you're lonely or hook up with someone you don't really like... because you're lonely. In both cases, you feel all kinds of stupid afterwards, not to mention nauseated and often even lonelier.

If it gets really bad, you might go into an actual 12-Step Program that may or may not help you get a handle on your "problem." Whatever you do or try to deny, you can't just cut food or sex out of your life the same way you might be able to stop drinking alcohol, smoking cigarettes or doing narcotics. That's one reason neither food nor sex qualify as true "addictions." Both are just too inseparable from essential existence. Basic need is not addiction. We need to breathe incessantly, but we're not air addicts.

Why Are We So Emo About Eating?

Why do so many of us humans have such messed up eating habits? Going back to Step #1 and observing how our closest non-human relatives eat and have sex, often at the same time, might give us a few clues. Among bonobos, food and sex are used not just as the way to handle hunger and horniness but also for entertainment, barter, celebration, consolation, as a reward for social accomplishment and much more. Is it any wonder we humans do the same, sometimes (when we have the opportunity) to unhealthy excess?

Our intimate, sometimes confused food-and-sex association has its roots in the beginnings of life itself. As Drs. Lynn Margulis and Dorion Sagan so eloquently suggest in *Origins of Sex: Three Billion Years of Genetic Recombination*, the first "meiotic" sex acts were a kind of cannibalism on the cellular level. Consuming led to reproducing, which led to more consuming, and here we are now, reenacting that primal cellular scene, eating each other up with love.

The Oral Sex Diet

In this step, your BLC is to combine healthy, sensuous food and sex for a delicious, decadent breakfast in bed. If breakfast isn't your thing, make it dinner. If bed isn't your thing (too much mess on the sheets?), take it to the tub for easier clean up or do it right on the linoleum floor in front of the open refrigerator like that classic wild strawberries-honey-and-hot-peppers scene from *9 ½ Weeks*. The kitchen table also makes a great "bed" for a food-and-sex banquet for two or 22, and it's much easier to clean up afterward than a real bed or couch. Stick peach slices in orifices and slurp them out, tonguing all the way. French kiss while passing a seedless grape back and forth, mouth-to-mouth, until one or both of you can't help but bite the fruit, juicing up your kiss with grapey sweetness. Suck down fresh lemon-soaked oysters between licks of labia and discover the hidden pearl of female pleasure. Eat organic icing off perky nipples or a hard throbbing rod for the best birthday cake ever. Revel in the faux cannibalism of oral carnality.

Just be careful you don't bite or chew too hard, and if you're prone to yeast infections, avoid getting the sweet stuff inside your vagina. But do devour your lover's mouthwatering body parts like fine cuisine. Yum! Giving oral can be as pleasurable as receiving, like eating your favorite dish, without the calories. Indeed, the time-honored "Oral Sex Diet" is a proven weight-loss "system." If you're busy eating your lovers' goodies, you won't be so hungry for fattening snacks… unless, of course, you spread junk food on your lovers' junk.

If you like group fun, you could throw a "splosh" soirée: an erotic, messy food party. For a more elegant affair, serve sashimi off your lover's wasabi-ed and soy-saucy, nude body, entertaining a convivial polyamorous supper for six. Even the classic romantic dinner date can have its bonoboësque aspects, especially at a cozy bistro with discreet tablecloths to veil naughty under-the-table activities. Or how about trading food for sex... dinner in for being eaten out? It's the Bonobo Way.

Not that you should eat constantly and voraciously *during* sex like bonobos do. The rate at which bonobos chow down while they get down is bound to give most mere mortals a wrenching stomachache. This is one of those cases in which aping our fellow apes definitely has its limits.

Don't Let the Kids Eat Up Your Holidays

Seeing bonobos share food and sex with such gusto reminds us that enjoyment of sex can be like that of food: a fundamental pleasure to be shared. Just as enjoying special foods is an essential component of any holiday celebration, special sex can be a vital part of the festivities,[62] even if the tenets of the religion associated with the holiday are mostly sex-negative. Jewish law even commands married couples to have sex on most holidays. In any religion—even a very repressive one (and they're all pretty repressive in their most dogmatic and fundamentalist forms)—holidays are a good time for sex, if only because they tend to break up our workaday routines.

Just try to make sure those adorable little anti-aphrodisiacs known as children don't overwhelm the sexy side of your celebration. Christmas (or its equivalent) isn't just about giving the little ones all the gifts they want, it's also about giving each other the gift of romance. Halloween isn't just costuming the kidlets and stuffing them with candy, it's a chance to roleplay your freakier fantasies and stuff each other with love. On the 4th of July (or the 14th if you celebrate Bastille Day), between family BBQs and kid-friendly pyrotechnics, make sure to make time to set off some sexual fireworks too.

This is a big BLC for parents. In many modern households, the kids' needs reign supreme, especially around holidays or just ordinary mealtime. It's fine to be child-centric, but beware of losing your identity to theirs lest you lose yourself to the sinkhole, that deep rut of parental resentment, which is just as unhealthy for your beloved offspring as it is for you. Most experts say children grow up to be happier and healthier when their parents

---

[62] More about this coming up in another one of my future books: *Erotic Holiday Making.*

are personally and sexually fulfilled (preferably with each other).

"We are afraid that our adult sexuality will somehow damage our kids, that it's inappropriate or dangerous," writes Dr. Perel in *Mating in Captivity*. "But whom are we protecting? Children who see their primary caregivers at ease expressing their affection (discreetly, within appropriate boundaries) are more likely to embrace sexuality with the healthy combination of respect, responsibility, and curiosity it deserves. By censoring our sexuality, curbing our desires, or renouncing them altogether, we hand our inhibitions intact to the next generation."

Wise words, though it's not easy to be your sexual self or even express physical affection in most family environments. Of course, there are many "appropriate" G-rated ways to release your inner bonobo (a few of which are in this book) that you can share with your children. But when you need to express your sexual wild side, you've got to do it without the kids around. For your sake and theirs, make some grown-up time and space to go bonobos, even around holidays. Again, this involves organizing those babysitting networks, carpools, code terms and getaway plans that are way beyond the scope of this book. But whatever you do, don't let being a good parent completely bury your inner bonobo. Otherwise, you'll find yourself resenting your kids as well as substituting food *for* sex, especially around the holidays.

The Bonobo Rainforest Diet

Bonobos in the wild rarely get fat (in zoos and primate centers, however, it's a totally different story). Their diet of raw greens and fresh fruits, with a little meat every so often, keeps them svelte and swinging. All that sexercise doesn't hurt either.

How can you make your diet more bonoboësque? It's utterly wondrous that Kanzi can roast marshmallows and hotdogs over a campfire, demonstrating how intelligent bonobos can be. However, regarding health (ours and the planet's), we'd probably be better off if we learned to eat more like bonobos instead of teaching them to eat like us.

Most overweight, undersexed humans would benefit from skipping the franks and s'mores and going on a modified "Bonobo Rainforest Diet" or "Paleo Plus," including lots of fresh fruits of all kinds, seeds, sprouts, raw leafy greens, roots, organic honey, herbs and mushrooms, complemented by small portions of meat. Be sure to include fruits and veggies that improve the taste of your body fluids. Though no official studies have proven it, my personal experience and anecdotal evidence indicate that pineapple, celery and cinnamon are effective ejaculate sweeteners. Alternate between the Bonobo Rainforest and Oral Sex Diets, and you've got the ultimate recipe for slimming down and sexing it up.

Then again, bonobos also love to eat those nutritious termites and plenty of other bugs too. Despite the great source of low-fat protein most insects offer, not every item in our cousins' cuisine need appear on our own Bonoboville menus.

Bonoboville Communion

Sometimes when we eat, we also drink. Other times, we just drink. Assuming we're all adult humans here, there's no doubt that imbibing "spirits" can assist uptight, stressed-out *Homo sapiens* in releasing their bonobo spirit, especially if sipped or swallowed in an erotic, bonoboësque manner.

Here at the Speakeasy on Saturday nights, we often practice "Bonoboville Communion," doing body shots (boobs, butts, bellies, backs of necks and the occasional courageous cock being the most popular body parts) with salt and the appropriate libation (usually a sponsored liqueur or a mysterious concoction we call Bonobo Juice). If you'd like to see how it's done, you should watch us perfect it to a fine sloppy art on DrSuzy.Tv. Learn how you can put the "cock" and/or the "tail" into cocktails, turning any private party into your own version of Bonoboville.

Of course, too much of a good thing can turn it into a bad thing, sometimes a very bad thing, and alcohol is the perfect example of a good thing that can go bad. As Shakespeare's Macduff explains in *Macbeth*, "it provokes the desire, but it takes away the performance." Worse yet, it can release your inner chimpanzee or raging baboon, creating that most unbeloved of characters: the angry drunk.

The same goes for most other recreational drugs, with the general exception of cannabis, which rarely makes anybody angry, just dopey. Hemp also happens to be one of the most versatile and sustainable products the Earth has to offer, and many people attest to the wonder weed being a rare, true aphrodisiac, helping them to relax and focus on pleasure and sensation without rendering them incapable of sexual activity. Other popular mind-altering substances are not as benign. So always imbibe and ingest in moderation or sex *won't* be bonobo or very good at all. And never drink and drive. Under the influence, the only heavy machinery you should be handling is a Sybian!

Prozac, Sex and Love

What about non-recreational drugs? Many prescription and over-the-counter medications affect your sexuality, usually for the worse. Antihistamines don't just dry up your sinuses, they can also turn an otherwise moist yoni[63] into the Thar Desert. High blood pressure medications often cause erectile problems. Painkillers don't simply mute your pain, they can also put a muffler on your pleasure.

The most insidious medical effects on human sexuality tend to come from the drug of choice for tens of millions of Americans: antidepressants, a.k.a. selective serotonin re-uptake inhibitors (SSRIs), such as Prozac, Zoloft, Paxil, and Lexapro or their generic versions. "It is well known that these medications can cause emotional blunting and dysfunction in sexual desire, arousal, and performance in upward of three of every four patients," Drs. Helen E. Fisher and J. Anderson Thomson Jr. write in *Prozac and Sexual Desire*.

Many of my sex therapy clients who take SSRIs complain that they lack libido, can't get erections or have difficulty climaxing. Sometimes it's just a question of asking their doctor to adjust their prescription so that they can enjoy sex. Physicians who prescribe antidepressants generally won't discuss sex unless the patient asks. So if you want to go bonobos while on Prozac, you have to be proactive.

But it's not "just" sex. Drs. Fisher and Thomson speculate that "serotonin-enhancing antidepressants can actually jeopardize one's ability to fall in love," challenging the mammoth, multi-billion-dollar SSRI industry as well as outside scientists to conduct research into the complex effects of these powerful, emotion-flattening medications on the "neural systems that govern desire, mate choice, romantic love and attachment, perhaps even mechanisms that detect facial attractiveness, immune system compatibility, and other neural systems we unconsciously use to mate, breed and rear our young."

Antidepressants can be lifesavers for folks suffering from chronic depression or severe anxiety disorders. But more and more doctors are prescribing SSRIs to patients who are just having a tough time coping with a bad break-up, the death of a loved one or job loss. If you're wondering

---

[63] "Yoni" is a Sanskrit term for female genitalia. Its male counterpart is the "lingam" or penis.

what SSRIs are doing in this step about food, it's because some doctors give the stuff out like candy. Then, even after the trauma has passed, many patients continue the medication, afraid to face their real feelings, preferring a state of prescriptive calm.

The problem is that good sex isn't very calm and neither is deep love. Your BLC is to get off the antidepressants if you're on them, but only if you really don't need to be. Be sure to gradually phase them out. Do not try to kick SSRIs cold turkey or without guidance. At the very least, tell your doctor you'd like to have your prescription adjusted to accommodate your love life.

The good news is that the bonobos themselves can be an excellent, organic inspiration for recovering prescription or recreational drug addicts *and* alcoholics since *Pan paniscus* are truly high on life. No hootch necessary for those hootchie mamas!

Step 6: Explore the "Opposite" Sex Within You.

The peace that reigns in Bonoboville is, at least in part, a matter of gender equilibrium. That is, the male bonobos aren't bullies, and the females aren't doormats. You might say that bonobo guys are in touch with their feminine side, which Jung called the "anima" and which Taoists refer to as "yin" energy. The gals tend to have well-developed masculine aspects, the Jungian "animus" and the Taoist "yang" force.

This is especially remarkable considering how dominant male common chimpanzees and gorillas are, while the females are notoriously submissive. Not that bonobos are "unisex," but compared with other great apes, they have a particularly balanced take on gender roles.

The Sexes Aren't Really "Opposite"

What about us humans? Being a "he-man" or "all-woman" makes for an awesome comic book character. But it tends to be bad for your health, not to mention the health of society, fostering stereotypes, bigotry, slut-shaming, harassment, rape culture, brutality, environmental exploitation and war.

The sexes aren't really opposite anyway. Men aren't from Mars, and women aren't from Venus. We're all from the same beautiful, wild, sexual, planet Earth, and we're far more alike than we are different. As Dr. Siegel writes in his *Psychology Tomorrow* column, we have many more "exquisite similarities" than dissimilarities. Just as very few BDSM players are utterly exclusive tops or bottoms, virtually nobody is all-man or total woman.

In *Sex at Dawn,* Ryan and Jethá call our hunter-gatherer ancestors "fierce egalitarians" in every way, including their treatment of the genders. In prehistoric hunter/gatherer times, men hunted together, but there was not much to fight over and great incentive for cooperation. With the advent of farming and property ownership about 12,000 years ago, suddenly, the stakes became higher.

Hunters morphed into fighters. Women morphed into possessions to be fought over, along with all the other things that became "private" property. Thus, the sexes began to assume their positions as "opposites," with men forced to be super-strong (or be killed) and ladies compelled to act ultra-meek... or be killed.

Bonobo Boys Aren't Brutes & the Gals Aren't Pushovers

In many ways documented in numerous studies, human civilizations in general, and patriarchal cultures in particular, have exaggerated the differences between genders throughout recorded history. This can be very exciting and romantic... the image of the swashbuckling superhero seducing the sweet, soft damsel comes to mind. But a little too much swash in the buckle and the hero turns into a macho brute. Likewise, if a sweet damsel gets too squishy, she becomes a pushover and a victim.

Bonobo gals are not pushovers and bonobo boys are not brutes. With that in mind, we will now diverge onto somewhat different branches for men and women. Transgender and other gender-nonconforming individuals can follow both. Actually, everybody should follow both. Release your inner bonobo by letting the so-called "opposite" gender within you breathe, move, groove... and maybe even dress up and play!

LADIES:

Your BLC is to get in touch with your "masculine side" and assert your desires, both when you want sex and when you don't. You have to be able to clearly say no before you can fully say yes. Of course, if you always say no, the Bonobo Way isn't going to work too well for you.

What if you are one of the many women who suffer from low sexual desire? Maybe you've felt this way all your life, or since you had kids, or just because your otherwise perfect marriage has slid down the sexual sinkhole. Before you toss out the bonobos with the bathwater, consider the possibility that your personal lack of lust might be, in part, the effect of 12,000 years of agriculturally inspired female sexual oppression. That's a tough row to hoe, but if your libido hasn't bought the farm just yet, there's hope.

"Before the war on drugs, the war on terror, or the war on cancer, there was the war on female sexual desire," write Ryan and Jethá in *Sex at Dawn*. Like other wars on the forces of nature, this one is utterly unwinnable, but its victims number in the gazillions, and might very well include your sex drive.

Adding insult to injury, for the past few decades, there seems to have been a call to sacrifice female sexuality on the altar of feminism. Influential feminist theorists like Andrea Dworkin, Dr. Catharine MacKinnon and their acolytes have employed verbal weaponry in this war, categorically rejecting most expressions of sex as hopelessly male-dominated, rather than asserting female sexuality as a source of power, as well as pleasure, for women in the bedroom and the boardroom.

Sociologist Dr. Catherine Hakim calls this sort of sexual power "erotic capital." The kind of feminism that encourages women to repudiate our own erotic capital and that of our sisters is not the Bonobo Way, any more than is old-style, misogynistic patriarchy.

Bombarded by sex-negative messages from the right and the left, many of us ladies conclude we're simply "not sexual," especially if we happen not to be turned on by what our partners desire, or by what our culture tells us we should desire. What about what *we* desire? Do we even know? Freud wasn't the only one to wonder, "What do women want?" Nor was Daniel Bergner. Most of us women haven't even solved that little riddle for ourselves.

The mysteries of female sexuality rise like a rainforest mist from the steamy concoction of nurture (civilized repression) and nature (female biology). *Yes, Virginia, there is a biological component to the feminine mystique.* Dr. Chivers' meta-analysis reveals women's minds and genitals respond differently to sexual arousal, whereas in men, the responses of the body and mind are more in synch with each other, showing that we gals tend to be more oblivious to our own erotic feelings. But *why* don't we know what we want? Is it due to our having less testosterone? Is it because we don't have erections straining at our pants, telling us in no uncertain terms *what we want*?

Or is it due to our being the more fluid gender, literally and figuratively? Is it because, thanks to our more adaptable anatomy and physiology, we women don't *need* nagging boners, high testosterone, fancy fetishes, erotic triggers or *any arousal at all* in order to mate and procreate? To put it in crass but clear terms, we just need to "spread our legs" to stay in the reproduction game. We don't even need to have a good time! Lucky us.

Sexual Tupperware & the Plastic Fantastic Female

This is what neuroscientist Dr. Keith Kendricks calls the greater erotic "plasticity" of the female. It sounds like Tupperware, and in a way it is, since our plastic adaptability allows us to become physical and mental containers for male sexuality, as well as the social pressure of other females, the demands of our parents and children, and all the various sex-manipulative rules, commandments, commercials, pop-up ads and pop culture enticements of human civilization, often without our even noticing.

As "containers," according to Kendricks, we women feel we need to be "filled." We want to be wanted, so we want what you want. At least, we think we do… sometimes. It's not always so simple, is it? And it's not our lovers' fault. But thanks to our fabulous feminine plasticity, the sexual needs and desires of "others" tend to fill up—and drown out—our own.

Then there's that old gender stereotype: Women *shouldn't* initiate sex. After all, we're the containers, not the container fillers. That makes a certain physiological sense, but my experience as a sex therapist tells me that both men and women tend to prefer for the "other" to initiate sex. As long as they're "in the mood," most people would rather be the object of need than the needy one. It's easier, more flattering to the ego and minimizes the risk of painful rejection.

So if both genders would rather not initiate, who will get the job done? Since guys have those driving testosterone surges and nagging erections longing to fill our plastic vessels, causing them to lust mightily more often and more obviously than women (Hakim calls this the "male sex deficit"), men wind up doing most of the initiating.

Sounds like a great deal for women, and ideally, it could be. But the reality is that many of us gals just wind up fending off or passively enduring—yet deeply resenting—sex we don't really want, sometimes from guys in whom we're not really interested. We might be "plastic" and physiologically aroused enough to tolerate sex we don't desire, but *arousal is not consent.* And it's not the Bonobo Way. Sadly, it is the human way for a lot of women around the world who experience a lot of horrible sex, from selfish husbands to subway rapes.

Your BLC is to turn this around in your life, and maybe the world will catch on. Sure, it's great to be wanted. It's an honor to be chosen. That's the feminine way. But an overdose of femininity paves a path to passivity, doormat treatment and abuse. Don't expect your partner to read your mind like an all-knowing *pater familia* in the sky. Learn to ask for what you want when you want it—in the bedroom and the boardroom.

Too many women don't ask for what they want in sexual relationships or in the workplace (higher pay, promotions, benefits, child care), at least not nearly as often as men do. What you don't ask for, you generally don't get. As Hakim says, "Women must learn to ask for a better deal in private as well as public life." Bonobo girls tend to ask for what they want, sexually and otherwise. And they get it, at least some of the time. If you ask, there's a chance you'll get what you want. If you don't ask, chances are you'll never get what you want.

Back to what *you* want. Have you figured it out? Why is it often such an enigma? Unlike most guys, we ladies usually have to *learn* what turns us on, and if we don't make that effort—and go for it with the passion and openness of a bonobo gal—many of us remain ignorant and unhappy victims pretty much all our lives... like Tupperware filled with someone else's leftovers.

Take a Bonobo Moment

If that sounds like you, your BLC is to take a "bonobo moment" to get away from the madding crowd of mates and playmates, parents and pets, church and children. Find private time (even just five minutes, though more is better) to explore your desires without the needs of your partner(s) horning in on your exploration. Medibate (as discussed in Step 2). Find the sexy, self-assured, libidinous bonobo girl within you. What makes her shriek with delight? What arouses her erotic power? What inspires her desire? What gives her life meaning, passion and satisfaction?

Set the mood for your bonobo moment with your favorite music or nature sounds, low lighting, aromatic candles, dildos, vibrators, bondage clamps, rubber duckies, porn or whatever you like. If you're one of those ladies who has difficulty getting "into the mood" and you don't care for porn, you might try reading erotica before or even while you medibate. Though male sexual energy tends toward the visual, female sensibility often craves a good story as at least a side dish to the sex, and written erotica, from the best-selling-but-badly-written *50 Shades* series to the more literary erotica found in Cleis Press anthologies to classics like *Delta of Venus* or *The Story of O*, is turning on more and more women (and the men who love them). Try perusing a hot story on your next boring train-ride to get yourself in the mood by the time you get home, or just read as you strum, medibating on the meaning of the erotica as it swirls from your eyes to your brain to your fingers and back through the erotic theater of your mind. In this case, it's okay to move your lips while you read. And licking your finger to turn the page never tasted so good.

Whether you're inspired by erotica or your own pure desire, as you touch yourself, be mindful of your feelings, both mental and physical. Yes, just like "mindfulness" in regular meditation—that is, staying in the moment—but a lot more fun. Plus you get to move.

Keep at least one kind of lubricant nearby. Your own natural juices and saliva are best, but dry spells are normal, and there's no shame is using a supplement. Extra virgin coconut oil is my favorite lube, great for solitary scenarios as well as getting slippery with partners as long as you don't have to use condoms.[64] It's also one of the most eco-friendly lubricants on

---

[64] If you do have to use condoms, try Bonoboville's preferred protection: Condomania. And use water-based lube.

the planet.[65]

Let your fingers roam like hunter/gatherers across the terrain of your body, the hills and valleys, the foliage and wetlands. Hunt for your pleasure points[66] and gather information, from your toes to your elbows, your ears to your ass, your clitoris (still and always the hottest pleasure point for almost any woman, especially when wet) to your G-spot. Taste yourself, noticing the subtle flavors and notes as if you were sampling a fine wine. Tease your most sensitive pleasure points to the utmost edge of ecstasy. Discover (or rediscover) what arouses, what hurts or what leaves you cold, and how it might vary with your mood, the seasons or time of month. It's amazing how you can inhabit the same body all your life, yet there's always something new you can learn from it. Moreover, it's constantly changing. That's why the best way to get in touch with yourself is through touching yourself.

Kegel Yoga to Holy Water

Some say it's what's inside that counts and, sexually speaking, your internal, "Kegel" or PC (pubococcygeus) muscles are at least as important as what's on the outside. In 1948, Dr. Arnold Kegel was the first to prescribe the exercise of repeatedly contracting and relaxing the internal muscles of the pelvic floor to help women with the pain and urinary incontinence that often accompany childbirth. These muscles also happen to contract and release naturally and deliciously during orgasm. Moreover, doing consistent Kegel exercises increases a woman's ability to have an orgasm when she wants one, as well as a man's ability to control his orgasm, reducing occurrences of premature ejaculation. Who knows how long humans have been flexing these delightfully deep inner genital muscles for better sex? I wouldn't be at all surprised to learn that bonobos do it too.

Slowly squeeze and release your Kegels as you breathe deeply into your pelvic floor. Try using a Kegel exerciser or dildo to "train" your muscles (or just because it feels good). Doing this type of daily "Kegel yoga" gives women, men and trans individuals longer, stronger orgasms and greater genital health in general.

---

[65] If the woman uses coconut oil as lube and the man drinks pineapple juice to sweeten his ejaculate, the ensuing blowjob would be a "penis colada" (seen on the American Association of Sexuality Educators, Counselors and Therapists [AASECT] listserv).

Give yourself little tests and BLCs to keep it interesting: How many Kegel squeezes in your favorite position does it take to make you come? How about when you're in a different position? Don't strain yourself, but how long can you squeeze before you need to release? Now squeeze and release your sphincter muscle. Try going back and forth between sphincter squeezes and Kegels, and you'll soon be playing your inner muscles like an inside-out saxophone, a skill which is sure to make beautiful internal music for you and your lucky lover(s).

As you medibate, tune into whatever's playing in the erotic theater of your mind. Only when you know what excites you (physically and mentally), can you cultivate and share your pleasure with your partner(s). If past abuse, trauma or anything else comes up that's so distressing you feel you can't handle it, consult a sex therapist (AASECT members are some of the best). Don't imagine that you can just sweep it under the bed. Our demons tend to grow stronger when we try not to acknowledge them.

Everybody benefits from medibation, but for us ladies, it's an essential, often neglected aspect of sex education. Despite the fact we emerge from our mothers' wombs, nobody is born with a working knowledge of female anatomy. Quite the contrary. Many of us need to *learn* how to climax in different positions, experience multiple orgasms or discover the wonders of female ejaculation (FE). Yes, men are not the only ones who can hit their lovers in the eye with their cum. Women can squirt too, some shooting "holy water" like geysers of desire.[67]

Since schools can't give you this kind of sex education,[68] you often have to take matters into your own hands—literally and with literature. Like most Yalies without sports scholarships, I loved to read, so it's not surprising that I experienced my first voluntary orgasm at age 19 with the help of a book. But it wasn't one of my textbooks that showed me the way. It was a little pamphlet I'd picked up at a sex-positive feminist "consciousness-raising" group, Dr. Betty Dodson's revolutionary manual

---

[66] I describe a woman's (and a man's) pleasure points, the hottest erotic spots of our bodies and minds, in greater detail in *The 10 Commandments of Pleasure*.

[67] Because it's so light, warm, fresh, clear and mysterious, I call female ejaculate "Holy Water," especially when I'm being "baptized" by it. Check out my "Squirt Salon" to see the amazing Annie Body or "27 Squirts" to get drenched by FE Queen Deauxma.

[68] Though former U.S. Surgeon General Dr. Joycelyn Elders never suggested actually teaching students how to self-pleasure, she did recommend that sex educators mention masturbation when discussing different forms of safe sex. For that, she got fired. In retrospect, I bet former President Billy Jeff wishes he'd forgone Monica's blue dress *and* Dr. J's pink slip and taken the good doctor's sound advice.

Liberating Masturbation (since retitled *Sex for One*), which I highly recommend, especially if you're hesitant to try your hand at sexual solitaire.

For squirting, read Deborah Sundahl's *Female Ejaculation and the G-Spot*. Though award-winning director Axel Braun[69] made me squirt for my first time (and many times after), I'd never ejaculated on my own until Deborah's book broke it down for me into simple, easy-to-follow steps illustrated by anatomically correct diagrams that, thanks in part to strong yoni muscles from all that Kegel yoga, soon had me baptizing Max in my holy water. *Hallelujah!* Praise the Lord *and* the Lady!

What Makes You Thrive?

We ladies need to learn more about our anatomy for our own pleasure and our partner's pleasure, as well as for our own protection. In general, females are more vulnerable than males to sexual violence. Being "containers," we're also more likely to pick up most STDs from the guys than they are from us. And then there's the far greater likelihood that we'll be slut-shamed and bullied for being sexually experienced or sex-positive. Often it seems our Tupperware is made to hold a lot of crap.

But greater vulnerability doesn't mean we're better off narrowing our horizons, erotic or otherwise. After all, women are sexual beings, with greater capacity than men in some ways, even the most ladylike among us. We all need good sex for our health and well-being, and not just the kind our menfolk say we need. We all deserve the kind of sex that helps us thrive.

But how do you introduce what you want without coming across like a demanding bitch? In some cases, the bonobo bitch approach (direct and dominant) is ideal and pretty damn irresistible. The dominatrix has come out of the dungeons of human culture to take the stage as the sexy woman of modern times, so just strapping on your stilettos and sitting down on your lover's face without so much as asking could do the trick. In other situations, you might want to choose a different, more congenial tactic.

One way to introduce a new desire without much risk of rejection or

---

[69] Actually, the first time I ejaculated involved Axel's fingers and his sex revolutionary dad Lasse Braun's verbal guidance. What a father/son team! Later, Axel made me squirt on his own several times. He also almost lived up to his boast that he could make any woman squirt, coaxing the holy water from 10 out of 12 women at the Speakeasy (and of the two that didn't, one was purposely trying not to squirt and the other was taking antihistamines (notorious for drying tissues that would otherwise be moist).

embarrassment is to say, "I had this dream last night..." and then describe your desire as a dream. In a way, your desire really is a dream, so you're not lying, though you are being indirect, and you're certainly not being a demanding bitch. Dozens of my clients have used this almost transparent but still rather effective technique with great success and, in those cases where the partner reacted negatively, the dreamer could always say, "Well, it was just a dream!"

There are many other indirect "Weapons of Mass Seduction" you can wield, enough to fill a thousand issues of *Cosmo,* from dressing the part to laying your preferred sex toys or BDSM implements on your partner's side of the bed, to sharing an article from your news feed that alludes to the secret fantasy you're too shy to bring up. Your partner(s) might even think it was their idea. For additional inspiration on how to assert your desires, go back to Step 1. See how your bonobo sisters practice the most sex-positive feminism on Earth. Watch how they cultivate sexual power, wielding it with gusto, compassion, good grooming and playful teasing. See how they wrap those bigger, stronger males around their sweet, leathery, little fingers. Now you try it.

Do the Hoka-Hoka

One vital key to bonobo power is female solidarity. Individual bonobo females tend to submit to the larger, stronger individual males when it's just the two of them, but within a group, females join forces and dominate the males, much to everyone's benefit and satisfaction. Like bonobos, we human gals can't break the shackles of shame or the cycle of female oppression without sisterly support.

Whether you do the *hoka-hoka,* join a sewing circle, dance in *One Billion Rising,* protest injustice with *Code Pink,* volunteer at a women's shelter or get out on the front lines of a Slut Walk, part of bonobo-assertiveness involves being there for your sisters, especially the ones who aren't your actual, blood-related sisters, and yes, the proverbial "less fortunate." Share sexual knowledge with older and younger women, as well as your peers, in whatever way you can. Keep it legal, but keep it real.

Civilization often puts us at odds with each other, like some sort of endless, vicious Miss Universe contest. That's the common chimp approach, and it hurts us just like it hurts them. As the bonobo gals show us, cooperation is one of our gender's strong suits. We have so much to learn from and love about each other, and when women support and cooperate with other women, we become a force to be reckoned with.

But don't men lose power as women gain it? Isn't that why crumbling old patriarchies around the world are fighting feminism and sexual freedom tooth, nail, gun, bomb and acid-in-the-face? Yes and no. Again, back to Step 1: Check out those happy males. Bonobo gals take care of each other, but they also take care of their menfolk big-time. Most men would be happy too if they got laid as often as bonobo males do. All these macho dudes battling sex-positive feminism are just fighting against their own best interests (kind of like working-class Tea Partiers). Which brings us to the other branch of this step...

GENTLEMEN:

Get acquainted with your anima. Just as the ladies benefit by asserting themselves sexually, most gentlemen have much to gain from releasing repressed inner empathy, openness, fluidity and compassion... in bed, bath, and sometimes beyond. It's the Bonobo Way, and it's one way to look and feel years younger. In conjunction with their relatively high thyroid hormone levels, being "in touch with their feminine side" is at the source of that bonobo male Fountain of Youth, keeping these guys playful, young, virile and vital much longer than their grouchy, old-before-their-time common chimp counterparts.

It sounds pleasant enough. But too many human males are terrified to show vulnerability, admit they're wrong, "let" a woman have her way, wear pink or confess to enjoying prostate stimulation. It's like they believe that if they lose control in any way except a virile, penetrative, ejaculatory orgasm, some thundering patriarchal authority will take away their "man card" and condemn them to a lifetime on Wimp Row.

There is no doubt masculine strength and confidence can be very exciting to both women and men. They are also highly advantageous qualities in our super-competitive society. But if they're not tempered with some humility, humor and compassion, they become stubborn narrow-mindedness and/or obnoxious misogynistic bullying. That's no fun for anybody, not even the bully. It certainly doesn't lead to great bonoboësque sex.

Did You Marry the Wrong Woman?

My client Keith was so tough, he refused to marry his sexy, loving girlfriend, Ginger for whom he felt real passion, because he felt he couldn't "handle" her. Instead he settled down with meek Miranda whom he figured he could control. A few years and a couple kids later, Keith called me from the bottom of his marital sinkhole, wondering why his sex life was "the pits." He complained that his nice, sweet, obedient wife didn't arouse him in the least. Once a week, she dutifully complied with the sex that he half-heartedly initiated. It was the same ten-minute chore every Friday night, lights-out under-the-covers missionary that ended with a humdrum dribble of an orgasm for him and not much of anything for her. Ignoring my suggestions for spicing things up, Keith moaned, "I'm just not attracted to Miranda. I never really was. I just knew she'd make a good wife. But Ginger, she always turned me on. I wonder who she's with now."

Many of my male sex therapy clients tell me some variation of this sad story. It's sad because it's a lot easier to reignite passion that existed between partners in the beginning than start a fire where there was never a spark. Some desperate husbands, like Keith, have cuckold fantasies, not about their own wives, but about those hot ex-girlfriends they couldn't handle. Then they may fantasize about the kinds of porn-star-supermen or "alpha males" they figure could dominate the wild women they couldn't handle. Sometimes, they even imagine themselves sexually servicing these fantasy studs, who are almost always bigger, stronger and far more endowed than they are.

Only in the shame-shackled privacy of their imaginations do such men's men allow themselves to surrender, climax and relax enough to fall asleep or get on with their strong-man roles at work as well as at home. Only in fantasy do they find erotic freedom. Well, at least they have that. But it could be a lot better than that if they learn to let their hearts, hands and glands help their heads choose their partners. After all, a good woman can still be the wrong wife.

Does Your Soft Side Make You Hard?

Male or female, it's only human to enjoy surrendering to something or someone that turns you on. Even the most macho man has a soft side. My personal experience as a "Mother Confessor" to many different men has shown me that, psychopaths notwithstanding,[70] the harder the exterior of the human male, the softer the center.

It may be a skewed sample, but many of my male clients who love cross-dressing, submission and other so-called "feminine" activities are hard-driving CEOs, film directors, chief surgeons, five-star generals, cops, lawyers and firefighters. Recall how Nate, the ambitious young investment banker in Step 3, needed to "let" the Amazon of his fantasies overpower his deep sex negativity and defeat his performance anxiety so he could

---

[70] Though recent research shows there are quite a few psychopaths running the world these days as well as perpetrating the most horrendous crimes (these are not necessarily, though sometimes, the same people), they're still a rarity.

relax, get hard and go bonobos in bed.

For even more men, it's less a question of getting hard than softening up a little and practicing the fine art of erotic empathy. Tuning into your partner's feelings, whether through tantra or just being a better listener, is often considered "feminine," but it's essential to being a bonobo male. Sometimes "oral" means talking and listening... communication. If you want to go further in bed, be sensitive to how your lover likes and doesn't like being touched. Don't make the stereotypical male mistake of believing that the type of touch you enjoy will also bring pleasure to your partner.

"Partner" can spell "performance anxiety" for many men. One relatively safe way to get in touch with your erotic feminine side, without the pressure of pleasing a partner, is through medibation. This is not about jacking off as fast and hard as you can while flipping through your favorite porn scenes. This is about taking your time to explore what feels good mentally and physically. Practice delaying ejaculation with the stop-start technique[71] so when you're with a partner, you won't find yourself coming before s/he's even gotten going. Let your mind and body luxuriate in slow sensuality. Allow the sexy "yin" within come out and play.

Those men who can't or won't balance their yang with some kind of erotic yin (at least in fantasy) are candidates for secret affairs, volatile divorces, heart attacks, criminal activity, political gaffes (i.e., getting caught showing their Weiner on Twitter[72]) and other types of personal breakdowns. Nurturing one's softer, feminine side, even if only in strict privacy, is especially critical for the hyper-masculine, so-called "alpha" male.

Male Backlash & Female Whiplash

What about the so-called "sensitive male"? He may be the butt of some beer jokes, but he's the man of the future, if there is to be a sex-positive future for all of us. Like the bonobo male, he's empathetic, well-groomed, sexually fluid, youthful, open-minded, acknowledges erogenous zones other than his penis and is more likely to spar with his wits than his fists.

---

[71] The "stop-start technique" or "edging," fully described in *The 10 Commandments of Pleasure* and many other books, helps men who tend to ejaculate earlier than they'd like to slow down.
[72] Former New York Congressman Anthony Weiner was forced to resign from Congress in 2011 over a sexting scandal that broke when he publicly tweeted a photo of his erect penis distinctly outlined in tight underwear.

He may self-identify as sapiosexual[73] or even metrosexual.[74] Though the truly sensitive bonoboësque male is not narcissistic like the stereotypical metro male, he does tend to appreciate art, use skincare products and wear flattering fashions.[75] Thanks to various hunky athletes and rock stars publicly sporting jewelry, make-up and even kilts, most modern women think it's cool for a man to be metro.

But it's not just about fashion. After all, if it's so cool to be metro, why are men still killing other men, women and children, raping, shooting and blowing up innocents from Santa Barbara to Mosul? And some of these men are quite "metro" (though not very sensitive!), checking their hair and designer sunglasses in the mirror or adjusting their panties under their trousers before committing the most heinous crimes, then posting the videos on Youtube.

Back to the backlash. Just as many of us are going bonobos, others are going bonkers! These "mad men," include both the insane and the insanely angry. If that sounds like you, if you're feeling mad at the world, the woman in your life, women or people in general, and if you feel like you're getting madder and madder, please seek therapy... before it's too late.

Of course, it's not just the guys that go mad. There are plenty of crazy ladies out there too, though nowhere near as many willing to shoot up the neighborhood to express their distress. But some women can't or won't accept a man's feminine side. Unless you have a humiliation fetish, stay away from such intolerant women, or give them *The Bonobo Way*. Then there are the man-blaming women (both militant and passive-aggressive) who level false charges against men simply because they are male. Sometimes these baseless accusations are of the worst crimes imaginable, throwing many innocents into the hungry maw of the Prison-Industrial Complex (PIC) that feeds on the "bodies"[76] of men.

Between male backlash and female whiplash, it's tough to be a guy in

---

[73] "Sapiosexual" is a neologism combining the Latin root *sapient* (intelligent) with sexual, and is used to indicate a person (of any sex) who finds intelligence the most sexually attractive feature.

[74] "Metrosexual" is another neologism derived from the word "metropolitan" and "heterosexual," yet its originator Mark Simpson in *The Independent* says the metro male "might be officially gay, straight or bisexual."

[75] One stylish menswear company even calls itself "Bonobos" and uses imagery that evokes the swinging, easygoing, bi-friendly bonobo male.

[76] In American prisons and jails, the wardens and police call the inmates "bodies," and that's just what they are to the PIC which is now one of this country's fastest growing industries.

the 21st century, especially a tough guy. But don't let that make you "mad" or stop your bonobo flow. As fearless Frank Moore writes in *Eroplay in Life and Art*, "If you can ride out the backlash... you will be a stronger person, and you can modify the moral system to fit how you want to live." *Amen* and *Awomen* to that.

The backlashers are enraged by changes they see as detrimental to their rightful male privilege, often behaving like bands of bellicose common chimps defending their territories. Fear and fury against sexual freedom, women's power, men's softer side, male homosexuality or bisexuality and the Bonobo Way are entrenched in many patriarchal cultures, from rural tribes to frat houses to temples of God (usually a male) to the modern MIC.

It takes a lot of courage to honor your feminine side in these might-is-right enclaves, but more and more brave men are doing it—and loving it—every day, reaching out and reaching around, opening their minds and mouths as well as (sometimes) their butt cheeks, sharing information and pleasure, getting in touch with their feminine side (often leading to discovery of their erotic, youthful, virile, creative, confident, core masculinity) and releasing their inner bonobos.

Mama Mia

Honoring your feminine side includes acknowledging the importance of the first lady in your life. Love her, hate her or try to be indifferent, she's your mom. Most human males probably don't want to be mama's boys to the extent that bonobos take it. But there's no doubt that a man's relationship with his mother is a vital key to his happiness and success, sexual and otherwise, not to mention his sanity (consider Hitchcock's *Psycho* or Kay Parker in *Taboo*).

The "Harvard Grant Study," a longitudinal analysis following over 250 Harvard grads over the course of several decades, found that the relationship between the men and their mothers was a critical factor in determining their lifelong happiness and success. The study found that men who had enjoyed "warm" maternal bonding in their boyhood earned $87,000 more per year and were less likely to develop dementia in old age than those who had cold or poor childhood relationships with their moms.

According to my favorite developmental neuropsychologist, Dr. James Prescott,[77] who studied infant-treatment, child-rearing, circumcision,[78]

---

[77] Another mentor and guest on my radio show, Dr. Prescott's groundbreaking work inspired my philosophy of ethical hedonism years before I learned about bonobos.

violence and sexual behavior in forty-nine cultures, "maternal-infant isolation that leads to sensory deprivation can cause developmental brain damage… mother love has a neurobiological basis that is essential for life." In bonobos and humans, there may be nothing more crucial to male well-being than a mother's love.

But what happens when that love is laced with a bit of lust? What about incest fantasies? Lots of people have them, but merely having incestuous thoughts doesn't mean you have to act on them. Freud probably overstated the case with his Oedipus complex that has every boy lusting after Mommy. But my own experience plumbing the depths of the male erotic mind on a daily basis tells me that old Dr. Sig's understanding of the centrality of that Venus/Eros[79] bond wasn't so far-off. Maybe that's why one of Max's pet names for me is "Mommy." And isn't that what tough old cowboy Ronald Reagan called his beloved Nancy?

If your own mom was a terror, cold or absent in any way, and if you didn't have a good grandma, aunt or "surrogate mother," acknowledge your pain and the effect it must have on your erotic fantasies and sexual reality. If you need therapeutic help, don't be embarrassed to ask for and receive it. And remember we are all children of our great mother, Earth.

Nice Guys Sometimes Win

Of course, all this getting in touch with your anima can bring some guys dangerously close to feeling the next envelope they open will contain that dreaded bit of Kryptonite, the wimp card. Only a hardcore submissive with a humiliation fetish relishes being labeled a wimp—and even then, he doesn't *really* like it, he's just helplessly aroused by it. Most guys fear it more than an STD, especially if they've been raised in more conservative, male-dominant cultures.

It's easier to say "don't cross that line" into wimpdom than to even know where "that line" is because it's different for every guy, depending on his background, body type, upbringing, genetics and many other factors.

---

[78] Dr. Prescott and others consider male infant circumcision to be nearly as bad for a baby boy as the almost-universally condemned practice of female circumcision is for a little girl. The procedure robs men of over 20,000 nerve endings. Circumcised men who feel they were victimized may need to "heal" themselves psychologically from what Dr. Prescott and others call "cruel genital mutilation."

[79] In Greco-Roman mythology, Venus/Aphrodite is both mother and lover to Eros/Cupid. You never see or hear of them having sexual intercourse and they have no children together, but they are often portrayed petting, kissing and fondling, and appear to have a rather bonoboësque mother-son relationship.

Though the symbol of a bold, straight, well-defined line is a masculine one, the reality is that there are webs of lines and few of them are totally straight. Liberating your inner bonobo means not being afraid to stretch, tweak and cross those squiggly lines (mentally and physically) until you're reasonably comfortable and pleasantly aroused.

Forgive yourself... for not being as much of a "man" as somebody (Mom? Dad? Ex? High school gym teacher? Military recruiter?) said you should be. Ease up on your tough self and take the cape off once in a while! Remember you're a human being, not a human doing, so let yourself *be*, at least sometimes. Remember Sapolsky's "Forest Troop" baboons? The bullies went down and the nice guys survived.

Whether you enjoy cooking or cross-dressing, having sex with the woman on top or keeping house, marrying your boyfriend or being consensually cuckolded, receiving a bouquet of flowers or a deep P-spot massage, take pride in your feminine side. Get to know the yin within your yang. It doesn't make you any less of a man. It makes you more bonobo.

Step 7: Make Peace through Pleasure.

Making peace through pleasure could be the most socially significant step of the Bonobo Way. It's the step that could save humanity! If only world leaders would just do some penis-fencing instead of trying to obliterate each other's countries, countless millions would be spared. If only it could be so easy. Could it be? Sure, the idea of penis-fencing politicians is a bit over-the top.[80] But can't we find bonoboësque ways to share love, pleasure and resources to ease tension and keep ourselves and our fellows from bombing and beheading each other?

Once again, let's take a step back to Step 1 and watch how bonobos cultivate sexual and sensual pleasures with as much energy and purpose as we humans put into achieving fame and fortune. We often focus so much on these lofty, elusive goals that our own basic pleasure and that of others drops to the bottom of the to-do list. The bonobos show us that peace is a dividend when sharing pleasure is a priority.

"Bonobos may not be able to do calculus, but they can do something even more impressive," writes Vanessa Woods, "live together without killing each other."

Even with all our civilized cerebral know-how, that's something we humans have yet to learn. Could we be lucky enough to have discovered "the last ape"[81] just in time for them to show us the way? All of the other great apes—common chimps, gorillas, orangutans and, of course, humans—have been seen deliberately killing members of their own species. Not bonobos.

Bonobo Alchemy: Turn Anger into Desire

Part of their "secret" to keeping violent tensions low lies in the playful, erotic atmosphere of Bonoboville. Another part lies in how they prevent

---

[80] It's not like I haven't tried. In 2002, I suggested U.S. President G.W. Bush challenge Saddam Hussein to a "Cockfight at the Baghdad Corral," rather than invade Iraq. Obviously, George didn't take my advice. Not that I expected him to. I just thought that a Bush-Saddam penis-fencing contest made much more sense than the Iraq War.
[81] *The Last Ape: Pygmy Chimpanzee Behavior and Ecology* is a book by Dr. Takayoshi Kanō, its title referencing the fact that bonobos are the last of the great apes to be recognized by humans.

physical conflict from escalating into murder. In the midst of what looks like a serious fight, one of the two battling bonobos might turn around, sometimes literally, and engage the other in a sex act: evocative penis-fencing, GG-rubbing (hoka-hoka), oral sex, butt play, kissing, hugging or a feel-good bonobo handshake.

What does this kind of bonobo sex mean? It's hard to say. Sometimes it appears to be an act of contrition, and other times, consolation. It can be intriguingly formal, like fraternity brothers engaging in ritual combat that climaxes in a ceremonial embrace. Sometimes the stronger one demands sexual reconciliation, or the weaker one submissively offers it up in a bonobo version of BDSM. Or both fighters' rage seems to spin off each other into a lightning-quick orgasmic frottage.

This is bonobo alchemy. Instead of turning lead into gold, bonobos turn violence into pleasure. Anger, hurt, fear, brutality and indignation are transmuted into intense erotic energy or brushed off with a casual but meaningful sexual encounter. However you analyze it, it works, reducing violence and averting murder and war, at least for them.

Humans already do it too, in a way. It's the essence of make-up sex. The tension of having been in conflict and the release of reconciliation often produces an exciting, transgressive friction that sets off erotic fireworks. As we learned in Step 4, trust kills lust all too often. When you quarrel, you lose a little trust (hopefully not too much!), which leaves room for lust to come roaring back in when you reconcile. Some make-up sex is extraordinarily tender. Other times, residual anger spends itself with wild "animal" sex that leaves claw marks down backs. No doubt, make-up sex can be the hottest lovemaking ever, though a real scorcher can burn you out.

Too Angry For Sex

Jaquie, a vivacious transwoman, and her lover Bill were constantly fighting. At first, their courtship was a grand soap opera. Usually, their dates would start out with a fabulous evening, but would soon explode into a fight over some slight, actual or imagined. Name-calling would ensue, often topped off with someone storming out while kicking something over. Soon enough (sometimes even that same night!), they'd feel miserable without each other, tearfully apologize, and have hot make-up sex amidst passionate declarations of love.

If only they were filming a reality show, it could have been number one. But this was *real* reality, and the fights were draining their sanity. By the time they came to see me, their arguments had gotten so nasty they weren't even making it to the make-up sex. Jaquie was now "too angry for sex." Bill was angry about the lack of sex, adding that to his laundry list of grievances.

How did it get to this point? For many people, eroticism isn't just feeling good, it's being "bad." Back to Bataille and the erotic imperative of transgression. Passion often arises from the struggle between competing forces: desire and some obstacle. That obstacle could be a partner's unavailability, distance, taboos, power differentials, prohibitions, contradictions or even (and all too often) anger. The dance between safety and danger stirs up sexual desire. This can be great—until the danger gets too dangerous, the fights get vicious or the whole thing just drains you of all your energy, including sexual.

That's the boiling point that Bill and Jacquie had reached. They'd started out doing a hot samba worthy of *Dancing with the Stars* and now they were stepping all over each other's toes. Their conflicts had gone from playful sparring that stimulated arousal into emotional slugging that knocked desire out cold, leaving the two of them in separate corners.

In our first therapy session, we watched footage of bonobos fighting and then having sex. Bill and Jacquie laughed a lot, seeing themselves all too clearly. They decided to meet the challenge of their mutual anger management issue with eyes wide open, and over the next few sessions, we focused on various methods of reconciliation that had worked for them in the past, as well as new segues from conflict to make-up sex that they might try in the future. I also suggested they take some basic BDSM classes at their local sex toy store where they could learn how to channel aggressive energy into controlled erotic activities like spanking (Jacquie's favorite) and bondage (Bill's). As expected, neither wanted to be the top or the bottom all the time, but "switching" fit their personalities and relationship needs. Studying the ebb and flow of human conflict, they've learned to play off their own for erotic effect, as well as minimize it when it counts.

Now when Bill picks a fight with Jaquie, instead of taking the bait, she says, "Are you trying to turn me on?" Jaquie has also acknowledged how often her out-of-whack hormones made her lash out at Bill, triggering or exacerbating their quarrels. Bill confessed his ambivalence about committing to Jaquie was another trigger.

They now see how their two strong-willed spirits conflict in ways that both turn them on and tear them apart. But conscious sexual reconciliation, BDSM play and focused management of Jacquie's hormone levels with the help of her endocrinologist, have brought their raging arguments down to manageable erotic proportions. It's not perfect (is it ever?), but it's better.

Anger Management, Bonobo Style

At least, Bill and Jacquie never permitted their arguments to become physically violent. That would cross a line that cannot be uncrossed. But the Bonobo Way still applies. According to Dr. Prescott's study, of violence and sexual behavior in 49 cultures, "Our brains have a built-in reciprocal relationship between pleasure and violence. When the pleasure systems of the brain are activated, they inhibit the neural systems that mediate (and stimulate) violence." Thus, the best way to inhibit violence is to activate our pleasure centers.

This is anger management, bonobo style. It's the kind of revolutionary re-imagining that can turn guns into vibrators, swords into dildos, bullets into butt plugs and war into peace. That sounds pretty idealistic, and we already know *the ideal is the enemy of the real*, so we can't take it all that seriously... or can we? Maybe it's more real than the war profiteers would like the rest of us to believe. Many great thinkers and activists, from 20th century philosopher Jean-Paul Sartre to the bonoboësque ladies of Code Pink and *One Billion Rising*, as well as *Scientific American* writer John Horgan, David Swanson's *World Beyond War* campaign and many more agree that "the end of war" is within reach of humanity. There may be other ways to get there, but the Bonobo Way is the pathway to peace that's paved with pleasure. I don't know about you, but that's the scenic route I want to take.

Peace through pleasure is more than make-up sex. It's a way of life and a way of thinking about oneself and the world. Between the bombings and beheadings on the global stage and the domestic violence and police brutality on the home front, a new path for peace seems more essential than ever. "While military tactics can be effective in the short term, you can't bomb an ideology," opines the Reverend Paul Brandeis Raushenbush. "You have to combat it with better ideology."

Here in our Bonoboville, we put our peace-through-pleasure "ideology" to the test on a small scale every day. Utopia it ain't, but in a quarter century of wild orgiastic Saturday night shows and afterparties, I can count the number of nonconsensual physical violence incidents on one hand. This is one thing for which we tolerant folks have zero tolerance. Lame excuses like "She wasn't wearing panties," "He insulted my girlfriend," "She was wet" or "I was drunk" are not defenses. Such violators are not allowed in our Bonoboville, and if they somehow slip in once, they're not permitted back.

You can't have the same zero tolerance for verbal violence. And why should you? Sometimes a good argument can be very productive… and ironically erotic, as Jacquie and Bill discovered. For further proof, check out the sexually charged repartee in old Katherine Hepburn and Spencer Tracy films like *Adam's Rib,* made while they were real-life lovers. Of course, verbal violence is much more charming in the movies than in your face where it can really hurt (and not in a good way), whether you're on the giving or receiving end. So if you feel you must use verbal violence, proceed with caution.

Your BLC is to "alchemically" transmute your next stupid, petty and ironically erotic fight into hot, mutually satisfying, make-up sex—or at least a conciliatory embrace. Sometimes make-up sex just happens, even when you don't want it to. Sometimes you have to make it happen, even when you're seething mad. But how?

First, when you're not fighting, you might want to share the Bonobo Way, so you two (or three, or more) are on the same page. Talk to your partner(s) about how close humans are to bonobos and how they somehow manage to turn their crazy fights into sex and pleasure for all. Watch them together like Bill and Jacquie did. Acknowledge that the possibility of peace through pleasure exists and can work for you if you choose it.

Next time your partner pushes your buttons, try this classic, very bonoboësque, "nonviolent communication" technique: call "time out" for a few minutes or even just a second. Call it an "empathy break" if you think "time out" sounds too sporty. Close your eyes. Take one of those deep, cooling, clarifying, belly breaths. Let it out. Sip some water. Take another deep breath. Now imagine that you *are* your partner.

It's just like Step 2, where you imagine you're a bonobo, but here you are your partner. Even if you feel your partner is totally wrong, selfish, mean or crazy, it doesn't matter. Just take those transformative deep breaths, close your eyes, open your heart and put yourself into his or her shoes. Eventually, sometimes within the split-second it can take to do this visualization, you will establish a deep connection, and your anger will melt into love... or at least compassionate understanding.

Robert A. Heinlein called this kind of deep connection "grokking" in his free-loving science fiction classic *Stranger in a Strange Land* about a human born and raised on Mars who comes to Earth. In Heinlein's Martian, to "grok" means you are not superficially experiencing or communicating something, but profoundly understanding the thing or intimately connecting with the receiving person, drinking in[82] and empathizing to the extent that you feel as if you are the "other."

This is a skill that may take some time for Earthlings to learn. Applying it in the midst of fighting is even more difficult, especially for us humans who have spent our lives defending ourselves against the envy, anger, condemnation, terrorist threats and attacks of our own kind. But it's not impossible. It seems that this is how the ancient Greco-Roman Stoics (who were really more hedonic than sullenly "stoic" in the modern sense) immunized themselves, more or less, against insults and attacks. By cultivating bonoboësque compassion, they "grokked" that we are all "in this together," one way or another.

But back to you and your anger, which is, if you're grokking like a Stoic, already thawing into empathy. Now apologize! I know, it's not your fault. Well, not *all* your fault, so just apologize for the part that is. At least, apologize for arguing. If you can't bear to say "I'm sorry," use other words. But even more than regret, try to express gratitude. Say "thank you" for something you appreciate about your partner, even if it's not directly related. Find common ground. Surrender to love. In war, "surrender" spells defeat. But in love, surrender can be sweet. As the Taoists say, "In yielding, there is strength." In surrender, there is power. That's the Tao of the Bonobo.

In *The 48 Laws of Power*, Robert Greene gives sage, almost bonoboësque advice to underdogs on the battlefield, as well as in the boardroom and bedrooms: "If you run away or fight back, in the long run you cannot win. If you surrender, you will almost always emerge victorious."

Words of reconciliation are a good start, but we all know that actions speak louder. Here's where you could really go bonobos and offer a blowjob—or a hug, or at least a handshake (either kind). Foot massage is a

---

[82] In *Stranger in a Strange Land*, drinking is a very special activity on Mars where water is scarce, and the merging of bodies with water symbolizes how two separate entities can become one greater reality.

fantastic form of reconciliation. One of Max's favorite ways to bury the hatchet with me is to pull my feet into his lap and rub them. Even if I'm raging mad, if he can manage to get me to sit down for a foot massage, my happy feet instant-message my angry brain to quit complaining about the guy who's giving my peddies such pleasure.

Then again, sometimes a nice spanking (consensual, of course) or other BDSM act is what you need to release your inner bonobo(s) and fire up your innate ability to make active peace through erotic play. A rosy pair of buttocks tingling from a fresh flogging invites the soft caresses of aftercare, which for many Doms and subs leads to greater feelings of intimacy.

What if you just can't stop fighting? That old saying "never go to bed angry" is often self-defeating. Sometimes it's far better to go to bed angry than to stay up arguing until you're both exhausted, crankier and likelier to hit each other "below the belt" or worse. After a good night's shuteye, including at least a couple of hours of psychically healing REM dream sleep, you regain perspective (and morning wood doesn't hurt). So next time you find yourself up quarreling endlessly, take a break to "sleep on it," and you just might wake up to making love.

After all, the ability to make peace through pleasure is not just a bonobo trait. As Drs. Ryan and Jethá write in *Sex at Dawn*, "The evidence—both physical and circumstantial—points to a human prehistory in which our ancestors made far more love than war."

If you master the art of making peace through pleasure, you'll win every game you play. Greene quotes Abraham Lincoln's wise response to an elderly woman when she criticized one of his speeches during the height of the Civil War in which he expressed empathy for the "enemy," the Southern Confederate soldiers, as "fellow human beings who were in error." A staunch supporter of the Union, this lady thought Lincoln ought to condemn the South as incorrigibly evil and worthy of total destruction. "Why, madam," this wisest of U.S. Presidents replied. "Do I not destroy my enemies when I make them my friends?"

Can Jealousy Be an Aphrodisiac?

Many a lover's quarrel is fueled by the emerald flame of jealousy, an integral aspect of love and lust, often connected to fears of abandonment and loss, especially among intensely social apes like us. Since the dawn of agriculture and ownership of people and things, the green-eyed fiend has incited tremendous rage, endless bickering, harrowing abuse and lethal violence, even triggering the legendary Trojan War. It's not just lipstick on the collar, its blood on the saddle. As Dr. Christine Harris points out in *The Evolution of Jealousy*, "In various studies, jealousy is often ranked among the top three motives for non-accidental homicides where motive is known."

Bonobos are not immune to that witch's brew of fear, envy, insecurity, anger, anxiety and anguish we call jealousy. Our kissing cousins can get very upset and even violent when their friends ignore them as they share food and sex with someone else. But the pain of jealousy is often assuaged with a little of what the experts call "comfort" (another great primatological euphemism for sex). Like polyamorous wise ones trained at Esalen,[83] the most popular bonobos seem to know how to make their old lover(s) feel loved while cultivating new ones.

In humans and bonobos, one key to controlling jealous impulses appears to be high EQ/SQ, emotional and sexual intelligence. Of course, this EQ/SQ balancing act can be much more difficult for humans grappling with jealousy, especially when losing a lover can also be accompanied by losing your home or access to your children.

Jealousy always scorches, but the burns are rarely more than first degree in Bonoboville. Human property considerations turn an ember into a house fire that devastates everything. If we could somehow separate ourselves from post-agricultural concerns about thy neighbor coveting thy wife, thy farm animals and thy SUV, we might even consider jealousy to be a partial aphrodisiac, despite (or perhaps because of) the edginess it can induce.

Take the human husband. Many an otherwise sensible spouse may find himself both angry and aroused upon catching "his" woman flirting with another man. Such was the case when Gene noticed Lisa, his wife of 13 years, all dolled up and giggling conspiratorially with her handsome male co-worker at an office Christmas party. Despite his jealous fear and even fury, Gene couldn't help but want to make love to Lisa as soon as they got home, his erection stronger than usual, and his ejaculation more powerful. When he came, he hollered like he'd just won some sort of sexual competition against that other male for the prize of this valuable female,

---

[83] Esalen Institute is a venerable old human Bonoboville, a retreat center emphasizing humanistic alternative education and personal growth that has been in Big Sur, California for more than 50 years.

his wife. Lisa, for her part, had a couple of unusually powerful, reverberating orgasms of her own, soaking their marriage bed in her *amrita*.[84]

So go the sperm wars,[85] those microscopic games of reproductive life at which our big-bollocked friends the bonobos are the undisputed champs. But while bonobos might have the more capacious *cojones*, humans engage in sperm wars too, and in some ways we beat the bonobos.

Understanding how these microscopic "wars" work within us isn't just a sex geek's delight (thought it certainly is that), it really helps to keep the passion burning. Sometimes a pinch of jealousy can save your marriage from sliding down the sinkhole. And who knows? The energy it stirs up may even help us stop (or at least curtail) the wars outside of us and make peace through pleasure among nations.

The sperm wars theory shows that if you can breathe past the fear and rage of jealousy, you may find arousal and desire. This is *not* a matter of compersion or training yourself to feel pleasure whenever your partner feels pleasure. Gene certainly wasn't feeling compersion! It's a matter of seminal fluid volume—that damn green-eyed fiend actually increases it—and much more...

The Shape of Things to Cum

It seems that human males even have a special, built-in sex toy that bonobos don't have: a penis especially sculpted for pleasurable thrusting. A study conducted by Dr. Gordon Gallup, whose team used dildos to thrust inside containers filled with a flour and water mixture concocted to simulate semen, determined that the unusually thick shaft, bulbous glans and especially the coronal ridge running around the circumference of a man's penis are optimally structured by evolution to "upsuck" another man's semen before depositing his own in that urgent engine-piston motion so characteristic of hot human intercourse that really gets our motors running.

Wow. I can just picture Dr. Gallup's team thrusting away for science, panting with the exertion and excitement of controlled experimentation, as their floury concoction spews lasciviously all over their lab coats. Kudos to the University at Albany, State University of New York for funding this important and highly entertaining research!

---

[84] Amrita is a Tantric term for female ejaculate.
[85] See Chapter Eleven: "Sperm Wars: The Super Bowl of Sex."

Why Men Love "Sluts"

Between sperm wars and his super-scooper cock, the human male is wired to be aroused by sexual competition, jealousy being a side effect. This is one reason why so many men are turned on by so-called "slutty" women, even though they don't tend to want to marry them, and despite the fact that, throughout history, societies around the world have consistently and vigorously denigrated sluts, i.e., women who have (or appear to have) a variety of sex partners.

It also explains the popularity of typical straight pornography. If straight guys just wanted to see women, why wouldn't more watch lesbian porn or just a hot woman masturbating? Some choose that, but the vast majority prefers to see the hot woman with a man—or men, as in the popular gangbang genre.

Dr. Sarah J. Kilgallon and Leigh W. Simmons' study of how erotic imagery influences semen quality showed that images of one woman with two men elicits an even higher sperm count with higher quality sperm, proving that watching a woman with two men, and maybe more, incites the aphrodisiac of male competition, triggering a stiffer sperm wars-powered erection and more explosive ejaculation than the viewer would otherwise get. Watch out for your keyboard when viewing those MFM threesomes.

The sticky sperm wars theory and Dr. Gallup's thrusting study also explain why many husbands and boyfriends, even if they adore their monogamous wives or faithful girlfriends, get sexually bored after a few years. It's not just that they'd like some extra-marital sex (though yes, most probably would). It's just that many of these jumpy gentlemen would be even more excited if their not-so-lusty ladies were getting some too—at least in theory.

When a happily married man like Gene feels there is *no* possibility that his wife could be with another man, he might love her with all his heart, but his sperm count will stay comfortably low. Nature is sensible, and there's no sense sending out the whole football team with no opposing players on the field. A few inseminators can score the touchdown with ease. Gene's mind also transmits an unconscious message to his comfortably soft dick that energetic, super-scooper thrusting is not necessary since there are no rival sperm to scoop out of loyal Lisa's trusty twat. No wonder the sinkhole of monotonous monogamy doesn't feature a lot of hard thrusting sex.

But after Gene caught Lisa flirting with that audacious male co-worker, the slightest inclination that his wife might stray had his testicles aching with semen. He soon found himself thrusting in and out of his wife like a jackrabbit, harder than he had in years, his ejaculate shooting into her inner space like a rocket.

Lisa was also unusually excited that night. Laughing with her co-worker acted like a sort of foreplay for sex with her husband. Flirtation generates lubrication, especially when more than one man is involved.

Anatomy and physiology may give us further insight into some of the mysteries of the human female orgasm. The fact that most women naturally take a relatively long time to climax (an average of about 20 minutes of erotic activity, compared to a man's average of around 7 minutes), and can still have an infinite number of multiple orgasms (compared to most men's one ejaculation per encounter), seems to promote sperm competition too.

Perhaps men should slow down and study the art of foreplay or women should learn to come quicker, as most sexperts (including myself) valiantly try to teach. Then again, maybe if the typical woman had sex with two or three typical men and a couple of bonoboësque girlfriends, all would be satisfied and sleep very well.

Jealousy Edgeplay

This is not to say that couples can't enjoy hot monogamous (or at least monogamish) sex for many decades. Pr. Max and I have managed it for 23 years and counting. But couples like us[86] usually utilize the power of fantasy (together or individually, deliberately or spontaneously) to keep things hot and thrusting. A long-term marriage that never even entertains the possibility of swinging, power exchange, cuckoldry, exhibitionism or voyeurism (being watched or watching others), or some kind of transgressive, extra-curricular sex, is almost inevitably doomed to comfortable boredom in the bedroom. And down the sinkhole we go.

One way out of the sinkhole is through play. It's the Bonobo Way. Though never lethal and rarely hurtful, bonobos do sometimes play naughty. In order to further develop your EQ/SQ, you can try a form of "edgeplay" I call "jealousy play." Edgeplay is a term used by the BDSM community to describe activities that are considered too dangerous by most people because they push "the edge" of the envelope of the traditional safe,

---

[86] Okay, there are no other couples like us. But there are many other happily married couples who utilize the tremendous power of fantasy to supplement their monogamy.

sane and consensual (SSC) credo. Another term for edgeplay is Risk-Aware Consensual Kink (RACK). Usually, the danger involved is physical, such as breath play, knife play or fire play. Sometimes it is psychological, as in age play, rape play, humiliation play or, in this case, jealousy play.

Playing with jealousy is like juggling fire—you might get burned. But if you take precautions, you won't incinerate. And when you can keep those sparks of passion flying, it's just so exhilarating that, for many, it's more than worth the risk.

We return to that irony of marriage that goes against many of the relationship platitudes human society holds dear: Trust kills lust which thrives on mystery, desire, competition and yes, jealousy. Thus, a little fresh rivalry can excite an old husband, as it excited Gene, forcing him to see the trustworthy wife he might otherwise take for granted through her co-worker's laughing, lustful eyes, making him competitively hard and raring to stake his claim... literally.

Of course, there are risks—to your marriage and your sanity. It wouldn't be edgeplay if it weren't dangerous. Before you play this game, make sure all the players themselves aren't dangerous or mentally unstable. Jealousy can overwhelm a man to the point that the sperm war going on within his balls only adds fuel to his fear. This can involve retroactive jealousy over past lovers, fantasy jealousy over future lovers, paranoid jealousy over imaginary lovers and probably a few more toxic variations. Yes indeed, the sperm competition cocktail is a potent one, and can be quite hazardous in high doses or at inopportune times or places.

A wise wife always makes her husband feel special and irreplaceable, despite her extracurricular activities (real or fantasized), recognizing and respecting his limits. With bonoboësque sensitivity, she inflicts a playful pinch of erotic jealousy without upsetting his entire applecart of insecurities. The way she does this depends on a million tiny details. She needn't turn herself into a gangbang-a-week hotwife[87] (unless she really wants to and the hubby enjoys playing the cuckold) or even have any in-the-flesh sex with another man or men (or women)[88] to create the scintillating sperm wars effect. It is only necessary that her partner think

---

[87] A hotwife or hot wife is a married woman who has sex with lovers other than her husband, usually with her husband's consent.
[88] Some men experience the sperm wars effect when their female lovers have sex with other women. Also, many gay men feel it when their male partners have sex with other men.

that she might and that she could.

Indeed, for most civilized couples, the power of sperm wars and the experience of being cuckolded are most safely explored in the erotic theater of the mind… or the fantasy playpen of their own private bed. If you're fantasizing about the wife being with another man, but don't feel quite ready to deal with another actual flesh-and-blood *man* with needs and quirks of his own, try using a dildo as a "stand-in" for the man. This can work amazingly well, especially if the hubby is very visual, and if the wifey enjoys penetrative diversity. Some couples eventually "graduate" from the rubber toy to the real-life boy. Some utilize the services of a telephone sex therapist to roleplay as the other man, describing in explicit detail (from a safe distance) what he would do to/with/for the wife. Others are happier keeping their outside friendships platonic and wild threesomes dildonic.

Remember, Lisa and her handsome co-worker did nothing but laugh together… or did they? No matter how much Gene's brain wanted to fully trust Lisa, his balls had doubts. They traded a dash of trust for a whole lot of lust. Moreover, the lingering effects kept Gene and Lisa hot for each other for many months after that office party. Even now, years later, the Christmas season triggers a flood of erotic feelings that often translates into great holiday sex.

Sperm wars edgeplay mixes lust with trust in unpredictable ways. It's not for everybody, not at all. So if you find yourselves fighting over it, it's back to anger management, bonobo-style, and making peace through pleasure.

If Sapolsky's baboons can do it, we can too!

Step 8: Practice Ethical Hedonism.

Long ago, before Moses took down the 10 Commandments via divine dictation, and even prior to some visionary Sumerian cobbling out the Code of Ur-Nammu, our prehistoric ancestors lived by morals—or tried to—much as we do today. Though the religions of the world preach about charity and fairness, they didn't invent these concepts. We did. That is, they're part of our primordial animal nature.

After all, even non-human animals—including bonobos, chimps, monkeys, elephants and dogs—understand fairness. As Dr. de Waal and others have pointed out, a dog will do a trick for the sheer pleasure of playing, until he sees another dog getting a biscuit for performing the same trick, at which point he will demand equal treatment. The yearning for moral justice and fairness is not just a human trait.

Pleasure Is the Root of All Good

Empathy, compassion and helping the needy when it doesn't directly benefit the helper are considered cornerstones of human morality. But many nonhuman animals—especially bonobos and, to some degree, other primates—also exhibit these traits. In *Bonobo Handshake*, Vanessa Woods describes a young bonobo named Kata encountering newcomer Lomala who was scared by a squawking chicken. Kata's response, putting her arms around Lomala's shivering little shoulders to comfort and protect her, was a moral act of compassion.

"Bonobos are supremely empathic, and possibly more empathic than us," observes Dr. Harry Prosen, a psychiatrist who treated Brian, a mentally disturbed young bonobo (yes, bonobos can go bananas, just like humans). Traumatized by childhood abuse and isolation, Brian was vomiting, pulling out his fingernails and pacing, unable to socialize with his fellow bonobos at the Milwaukee County Zoo. Eventually, Brian made a full recovery, integrating with the group, fathering children and even becoming a troop leader, thanks to the good doctor (who treated the traumatized bonobo much as he does his human psychiatric patients) and the caring zookeepers. Oh, and let's not forget Brian's highly empathetic fellow bonobos who treated him with the tolerance, kindness and understanding he needed to heal.

As these stories indicate, and as de Waal, Ryan and others have pointed out, humans didn't become ethical by choice, reason or religion, but through our natural evolution and need for each other. Civilization isn't the only thing that makes us civil. We have an innate sense of morality that appears to be interwoven with our sensations of pleasure and pain. Nature rewards us with pleasurable feelings for doing things that we need to do for our survival or our genes' survival. That's why good food tastes delicious, especially when we're hungry, and good sex feels fantastic, especially when we're horny.

In the same way, recent studies show that nature rewards us with a feeling of emotional or "moral" pleasure when we share or help others, especially those we love or lust after. Emory's Dr. Rilling has illuminated how reward centers in the brain are activated when people and bonobos cooperate and share with each other, even with strangers, based on reciprocal altruism, empathy and gratitude. *Doing good feels good.* That's ethical hedonism in a kola nutshell.

So perhaps pleasure isn't the root of all evil, as the puritans and other sex-negative overlords have always told us. Perhaps pleasure is the root of all good.

Then again, life isn't always so simple and good. Sometimes doing the right thing goes against our selfish desires and/or financial considerations, and that's when we face a tough decision. But usually, on a very basic level, doing something good for someone else gives you a nice, pleasurable feeling, especially when you know the recipient of your largesse appreciates it. Of course, it's easier to enjoy doing good deeds in a small tribe like the bonobos, where you know everybody, and everybody knows you and the good you do, and nobody owns much of anything anyway.

Doing good doesn't feel quite so good nor imperative in large anonymous cities and spread-out suburbs steeped in alienation, banking, corporate franchises, private parking spaces and stockpiles of guns. That's when trying to harm and undermine others might feel right or even good, even when we know in our hearts it's not. History has shown us that many otherwise "normal" people can be persuaded to do terrible things, including murder, rape, torture and war, if they believe that the cause is right.

But even the bleakest dystopia doesn't entirely delete the joy of giving. Nor does it erase the gratitude of the receiver who feels a natural sense of appreciation and a desire to "pay back" the giver or, if that's not possible, "pay it forward," creating a network of empathy where the point is to, as Bonoboville's webmaster Abe puts it, "surround yourself with good," and always be grateful for the good that surrounds you.

Cicero may or may not have been first to say, "Gratitude is the mother of all virtues." Whoever said it, the bonobos know it. They live it. Studies by Hare, Woods and Tan show that when a bonobo goes out of his/her way to give another food, sex, a bonobo handshake or a helping hand in a tough situation, the receiver remembers the goodness of the giver with gratitude and is likely to return the favor.

Social animals like humans, bonobos and all primates, to an extent, have evolved to find pleasure in helping and pleasing each other. Even if we culturally and philosophically diverse human apes don't always have the same idea of what "helping and pleasing" really means (and all too often wind up hurting others even though we "mean well" and we're "only trying to help"), we tend to feel good when we sincerely believe we're doing good. Dr. de Waal calls this natural primate tendency "hedonic kindness."

You Can Have Your Sex & Eat It Too

Springing from our organic inclination to do good because it feels good is "ethical hedonism," a contemporary etiquette with pre-human roots for a global village whose doors are open to the World Wide Web in all its diverse, pansexual, empathetic, multi-dimensional glory. Ethical hedonism mixes the classical philosophies of Aristippus of Cyrene, Epicurus of Athens, and the Stoics with Zen/Tantric Buddhist compassion and the Tao of Bonobo.

And yes, all you skeptics and non-believers, Doubting Thomases and Cynical Cyndies, you can be an ethical hedonist, just as you can very easily be an unethical puritan. You can have your sex, and eat it too, at least sometimes. As the pendulum swings toward less superstitious moralizing and more science-friendly openness and alternative, non-traditional ways of relating and being sexual around the world, a form of ethical hedonism appears to be the emerging philosophy for much of our plugged-in, *Cosmos*-viewing, *Cosmo*-reading, Cosmo-sipping, spiritual yet skeptical society.

Despite popular misinterpretations, being an ethical hedonist doesn't mean "anything goes" or "if it feels good, screw it" or "damn the consequences, the kids and the neighbors." First and foremost, you must respect others' desires, or lack thereof. That's the "ethical" part. And no, you don't have to "do it all," and certainly not all at once.

Then again, you certainly *can* do it all (or at least have fun trying), if that's what you and your consenting partner(s) want. If you decide to swing, explore BDSM (pain is a pleasure, if you're a hedonic masochist), try cuckoldry or become polyamorous for real, enjoy the adventure! Though it's not for everybody, and some may criticize your "morals," rest assured you're normal, and very moral, here in Bonoboville.

Were America's Founding Fathers Ethical Hedonists?

Inscribed into one of America's most sacred documents, the Declaration of Independence, right there on the list of basic demands, along with "life" and "liberty," is a key component of ethical hedonism: the "pursuit of happiness."

This is not so surprising since the Declaration was penned by Thomas Jefferson and influenced by Benjamin Franklin, both of whom led colorful, controversial sex lives, according to most historians. Like many Enlightenment era "deists,"[89] including Max's illustrious ancestor on his mom's side, Pr. Gaetano Filangieri, an Italian jurist, author and reformist philosopher who corresponded with Benjamin Franklin, our founding fathers essentially spoke, wrote and behaved as ethical hedonists.

Of course, puritans of various faiths have long denounced hedonism, even the ethical kind, declaring that pleasure is the opposite of happiness, that the former is external and fleeting while the latter is internal and lasting. But all their anti-hedonic semantic gymnastics don't obscure the fact both pleasure and happiness *feel good* (and are maddeningly elusive), and people often use the terms interchangeably. Parents take great pleasure (or is that happiness?) in their children's accomplishments, and new lovers find great happiness (or is that pleasure?) in each other's arms.

Whatever term you prefer, just as important as the "pursuit" is the cultivation and appreciation of the happiness (or pleasure) that we already have. This sounds like fun, and it is! Yet we often take for granted the best of what we have, especially our loved ones. This normal human tendency might be nature's way of getting us to move along like good hunter-

---

[89] Deism, the belief that reason and science can coexist with the presence of a deliberately unspecified impersonal god/creator/watchmaker, was popular among progressive thinkers in the 18th century.

gatherers. But most of us like to settle in comfortably with people, places and things. Then, just when we're ready to savor and enjoy the fruits of our labors, down the sinkhole of jaded ennui we often go, even when surrounded by opulence, splendor and love.

One way to avert this human tendency to take the pleasures we have and people we love for granted is to employ a visualization exercise such as the kinds we practiced in Steps 2 and 7, creating a bonoboësque version of an old Stoic challenge.

The Power of Negative Thinking

Imagine that you are very poor, all alone, and you *don't* have the good things, health or people in your life that you do actually have.[90] Notice that this involves the power of *negative* thinking, quite a departure from the power of positivity that has ruled post-industrial human society with an iron smile. But if you do it right, it gets you in touch with your deepest positive feelings about those people and pleasures a lot more effectively than the "law of attraction (LOA)."[91]

There's nothing wrong with being optimistic, but "positive thinking" dogma is essentially unrealistic and marginalizes many people, not to mention the less "successful" species on this planet. It creates false attributions by encouraging folks to feel that their (all too often very real) troubles are their own fault or something they "attracted" because they don't "think positive" enough. It also assumes that if you've got it, you deserve it, even if you're a heinous criminal, a selfish billionaire or both. Moreover, constant positive thinking about all the stuff you want and don't have because you aren't thinking positive enough can be damn frustrating, even depressing. It's certainly not very hedonic.

So here's a lesson in the healing, hedonic, and sometimes darkly humorous powers of negative thinking: close your eyes and imagine that the lover with whom you are quarrelling or bored has just left you for someone else. *Ouch!* Or pretend that they are now on life support or dead (take your pick of disasters). Really allow your imagination to fill in the

---

[90] Dr. Albert Ellis, celebrated psychologist and founder of the Society for the Scientific Study of Sexuality (SSSS), suggests a variation on this Stoic exercise which he calls Rational Emotive Imagery (REI).
[91] LOA is one of the mantras of *The Secret*, a popular, positive-thinking book (and assorted branded merchandise) that also states "Everything in your life you have attracted." What does that say about victims of, earthquakes, floods, birth defects, child molestation, rape and mass shootings?

details of this negative fantasy and let it gel until your emotions sting more with loss than anger. *Ugh.* Now doesn't it feel better to see them still here with you? Don't you want to forget your minor differences and give them a big hug (or blowjob)?

It doesn't always work. For instance, not if you really wish your lover(s) were dead! But this nifty Stoic visualization, which I call "Things Could Be Worse," often shakes you out of your greedy snit, nitpicking funk or sex-averse blues and gives you the well-placed mental butt-kick you need to *go bonobos* with the pleasures and people you love—before it's too late, because one day, it will be. A nice side bonus is that it also helps you cope when you do lose those precious pleasures and irreplaceable people.

What Does "Ethical Hedonism" Mean to You?

What are these pleasures and people all about? For some, ethical hedonism involves being the kind of "ethical slut" that Dossie Easton and Janet Hardy (pioneer guests on my show back in 1998) so joyously describe in their classic book of that name about open relationships. For others, it means putting superstition, bigotry and tradition aside and using science, compassion and consideration for the rights and feelings of others to inform your values and guide your actions.

For many, the essence of ethical hedonism lies in the politics of pleasure. There are many hedonists among us, but most aren't very ethical, and a good many are sexual hypocrites. Not only do these double-dealing pleasure seekers refrain from practicing what they preach, they are usually the very people with a soapbox, pulpit or position that enables them to do their preaching publicly (often in literal sermons or speeches) as they endorse, vote, pay lip-service, and pass oppressive laws that are just the opposite of what they practice "behind closed doors." They allow their guilt and shame over their sexual desires to extinguish their ethics.

Overcompensating for what they see as a transgression (i.e., seeing an escort), they rail, lobby, campaign and vote against the very things they privately enjoy (anything—and sometimes everything—from prostitution to recreational drugs to supposedly deviant sexual practices). This is just what evangelical "Pastor Ted" Haggard did when he preached intolerance toward homosexuality and supported anti-gay legislation, even as he himself was engaging in drug-fueled sex with at least one male escort, making Pastor Ted the flamboyant poster boy for hedonistic hypocrisy, the political polar opposite of ethical hedonism.

So, if you consider yourself an *ethical* hedonist, and if you even fantasize about sex with someone of your gender, you really ought to support LGBTQ rights, or at least don't oppose them. If you utilize the services of sex workers, support sex workers' rights, and if you watch porn, support porn stars' and First Amendment rights! If you're a guy who likes the ladies, support women's rights, including the reproductive kind. Otherwise, you're a hypocritical hedonist, not an ethical one.

This is the sociopolitical side of ethical hedonism, that, for the warriors among us who are fearless—or crazy—enough to try to publicly practice what we preach, involves fighting (non-violently, of course) for sexual freedom, sometimes putting your body on the line, as Pr. Max did when he fought (and mostly won) against antiquated obscenity laws in the 1970s.

Moving from the political to the very personal, for some couples, ethical hedonism provides guidance and a "moral compass" for interacting erotically with others. You may or may not want to have full-on horn-honking sex with these others. You might or might not feel free and open enough to go all the way every day with various partners, sharing the adventure like bonobo best friends. You may prefer to stick with flirting, outercourse, simply watching, or maybe extracurricular phone sex, webcam sex, salsa dancing or a couple's massage. You could go to a strip club together, get a lap dance, then come back home to ravish each other, hot and high on all the sexual energy you pick up from these exploratory, slightly transgressive activities. Just fantasizing out loud about having wild bacchanalian group sex while you and your mate make love can be a very effective way to liberate your inner bonobo, even while you remain physically monogamous, or at least monogam*ish*. One key to being an ethical hedonist at any level of the swinger continuum is putting the needs and desires of your partner(s) above your own.

Ethical BDSM

Your physical exploration of ethical hedonism might have more to do with fetishes, domination and establishing rules for dangerous games. After all, freedom is the greatest aphrodisiac. But restraint is a close second.

I'm talking about consensual restraint, of course, which may be achieved with rope, cuffs, nylons, neckties and/or the psychological ties that bind the mind. It's kind of ironic, but some of the freest folks on Earth get off on giving up their freedom... in a controlled, circumscribed way. Many are turned on by being "forced" to experience things they really want but don't feel free to receive unless they're restrained, mentally and/or physically. They may become aroused by struggling against the restraints or by surrendering to them as they enter "sub space," a state of ecstasy resembling the transcendent rapture of religious mystics.

Because these altered states of sublime surrender may wander into various physical and psychological danger zones, standard rules of play include basic safety precautions like choosing a "safe word" (or, if you're into being gagged, a gesture), as the word "no" may not mean "no" in some fantasy scenarios you might like to play out (a home invasion fantasy roleplay won't get far if the first "no" brings play to a screeching halt). BDSM requires a great deal of trust between partners, since one is usually giving up control to the other. As for the Dom, Top, Mistress or Master, he or she takes on responsibility for the safety of the submissive, bottom or slave, but must also trust the sub's integrity. After all, a Dom risks accusations and potentially even criminal charges, since BDSM activities are often misperceived by the outside world, including law enforcement, as "abuse."

Consensual practitioners of the sadomasochistic arts often devise elaborate contracts that spell out what is allowed or expected in the context of their dynamic together, be it Mistress/slave, Master/servant, Dominant/submissive, etc., making it clear that their wild games are conscientiously considered forms of ethical hedonism. Such contracts don't hold up too well in modern court[92] since the law doesn't recognize that adults may consent to be "abused" via whipping, spanking, bondage, etc. However, these contracts are respected in the BDSM community, which helps to keep the signers of such documents safe and ethical.

Eco-Sexual Ethics

Being an ethical hedonist involves taking good care of your body, your partner(s)' bodies and the beautiful body of planet Earth. Trusting more in the Epicurean "clear evidence of the senses," a.k.a., science and experience, ethical hedonists don't put much faith in gods, pharmaceutically compromised doctors or politicians in bed with their corporate sponsors, when it comes to taking care of our health and the

---

[92] In Old Testament times, of course, with all the testifying on testicles, it would have been a different story.

health of the planet. Though the free, unfettered, consumer-baiting market that feeds materialistic compulsions might seem pretty hedonistic to the puritans among us, it goes directly against Epicurus' basic philosophy of (ethical) hedonism: "Not what we have, but what we *enjoy*, constitutes our abundance."

Ethical hedonists are "eco-sexual" and sex-positive while taking responsibility for how our pleasure might affect others, even indirectly. This means attempting to be conscious and up front about sex, despite our culture urging us to be "spontaneous," secretive and ashamed of our sexuality. It involves practicing risk-aware safer sex and birth control, as well as methods for disposing of our used-up sexual accessories. It can involve tough decisions and some tedious tasks that may seem pretty unhedonic on the surface. But it's worth the time and effort it takes to review the options (preferably while sober), and try to make the least toxic choices for ourselves, our partner(s) and the Earth.

"The earth is an organism, like your body," writes Stefanie Iris Weiss in *Eco-Sex: Go Green Between the Sheets and Make Your Love Life Sustainable,* "and it needs tender loving care at every level of its complex, intertwined system." Weiss' book is an eco-sexual Bible, and just like the old Bible, reading it might make you feel guilty. But there's bad, unconstructive guilt (like feeling ashamed of your sexual desires) and there's good, constructive guilt (like feeling bad about betraying your partner or using sex toys made or powered by toxic materials). *Eco-Sex* makes you feel the good guilt, helping you to take whatever steps you can to clean up your sex act... and clean up after it as well. "If you use condoms, don't flush them!" Weiss warns. "They wreak more havoc in our waterways than they do in our landfills." Ditto for tampons and packets of lube.

The Best Laid Plans May Not Get You Laid the Way You Planned

Communication is another key to pleasure and happiness in any kind of sex involving more than one person. Ethical hedonists emphasize the positive, but don't shove the negative under the rug to fester and breed. When conflicts arise, try to use the "clear evidence of (your) senses" to shine a clarifying light on your feelings. Exercise your empathic muscles by taking frequent "empathy breaks," as described in Step 7, even when you're not fighting. Stretch the boundaries of your imagination and think outside the box of your own ego. Think eco-sexual. Be an ethical hedonist.

It's not always easy, but it's well worth the effort because it really does feel good to do good.

Of course, some problems defy clarification, in which case, the best, most ironic, hedonic, bonoboësque solution might be to just laugh. After all, comedy and tragedy are soul mates, and much humor involves the power of negative thinking with a twist. We humans used to claim to be the only creatures to get jokes, but now we know that bonobos love to laugh too, grinning and gasping with joy (or sometimes nervousness), just like we do. Human or bonobo, laughter is a mental orgasm, so it's almost as good as sex… sometimes better (especially for hardcore sapiosexuals), making it among the most effective Weapons of Mass Seduction in an ethical hedonist's armory.

Step 9: Be Bonobo Friendly.

We've covered your lovers. Now how about going bonobos with friends? Being "bonobo-friendly" doesn't mean you have to have sex with your friends, though you could try it with one or two if there is mutual attraction. You might even find your "soulmate," like Max and I found each other after five years of platonic friendship.

A lot of people think they can't fall in love with a good friend because they know each other too well. But perhaps they are missing out on one of the most fulfilling relationships known to humankind. There they go for strangers who are distant, difficult, unfriendly and unavailable (people who string them along or treat them like baby wipes), while they brush off the caring, close, natural love of a friend.

"Oh Harry (or Sally)," they say, "He (or she) is just a friend." But "just a friend" could be just what you need.

For bonobos, sex and friendship go together like leaves and trees. They also like to do it with strangers, but most bonobo sex is among friends. Of course, it's not quite so simple for us humans thanks to all of our elaborately constructed social boundaries, sins, taboos and transgressions. For most of us, sex and friendship go together like Crisco and Perrier. Often, the thick wall of familiarity is a desire-dulling DMZ[93] of superstition, false incest taboos (i.e., you "feel" like siblings, even though you're not really related), repression and confusion. But if, by chance, that barrier is transgressed, you just may find yourself falling more deeply in love than you ever imagined possible.

All too often, trust kills lust, as we learned in Steps 4 and 7. Part of the reason for this is that we usually fall in lust with someone long before we can trust that person. As we get to know them, "warts and all," we gain trust, and we tend to lose lust. But first-time sex with a friend for whom you've always felt attraction injects a heady dose of lust into a relationship where trust has already been established. That is, suddenly, you find yourself brimming with newly discovered desire for someone you already know you can depend on. Jackpot!

---

[93] DMZ is a "Demilitarized Zone" or "neutral zone" in military-speak. In player talk, it's known as the dreaded "friend zone."

Falling in Love Makes You Go Bonobos Without Even Trying!

When people fall head-over-heels in love (usually fueled by high doses of lust), they are said to enter a state of momentary insanity that is really quite normal. In fact, you could say that falling in love releases your inner bonobo, at least temporarily, without even knowing what a bonobo is. The medieval troubadours sang songs of this feeling, calling *amor*, or romantic love, a force as great as the love of God and its opposite in some ways. Amor (Cupid) is the Roman counterpart of the Greek Eros. Spelled backwards, Amor is Roma, which some say signifies how romantic love is less in tune with Rome or the Vatican's marriage protocols, and more in harmony with the intense passion a lover succumbs to when pierced by the arrow of *amor*.

Psychologist Dr. Dorothy Tennov calls the feeling "limerence," describing a passion that is the greatest ecstasy, if reciprocated. But if it is unrequited or only partially returned, it can be yearning, burning agony. In his novel *Middlesex,* Jeffrey Eugenides dubs it "periphescence... the first fever of human pair bonding. It causes giddiness, elation, a tickling on the chest wall, the urge to climb a balcony on the rope of the beloved's hair. Periphescence denotes the initial drugged and happy bedtime where you sniff your lover like a scented poppy for hours running. (It) lasts... up to two years—tops." Polyamorists call this natural high of hot love that usually occurs in early romance "New Relationship Energy" (NRE).

Whether you call it amor or NRE, limerence or periphescence, it can happen anywhere with anyone. You can go bonobos and fall in love with a sexy stranger just as easily as you can with a friend... probably even more easily with the "perfect" stranger since his/her annoying faults are totally unknown to you. But going bonobos with a good friend might be one of the very few ways that you can have your lust and trust together, at least as long as that fickle limerence lasts. And many years after the NRE fades or grows and ripens into ORE (Old Relationship Energy), even if you can't quite—that spark (and I believe that with the help of the Bonobo Way, you can—you'll probably still be friends because that's how you started. Couples who stay married for a long time often say what keeps them together is that they're good, good friends.

So if you find yourself chasing after lovers who don't love you back, take another look at that special friend that's always been there for you and is actually very sexy. Let the Bonobo Way guide you toward turning a good friendship into something much better. You may be surprised at how exciting sex can be with a friend who gets your jokes, won't be fazed by your moods, and already feels you're worth spending time with for activities other than sex. Nothing is sexier than a friend who gets what's between your ears before they get what's between your legs.

When I first met Pr. Max, he had just married wife #2 and I was going strong with boyfriend #22 (approximately), so platonic friendship was our only acceptable option. But sparks flew between us and unfulfilled romance seethed beneath the surface of our sexless bond as we shared many special, seemingly platonic moments over the next five years. When Max announced he was separating from his wife, I happened to have had it with boyfriend #25 (or so), and suddenly, there it was: the sea of love swirling before us. We dove right in.[94] If we hadn't released our inner bonobos (even though we had no idea what bonobos were at the time), we might never have fallen in love. And it sounds like a corny old song that I personally wouldn't believe if I hadn't lived it for 24 years, but the passion and romance just get stronger every day. So, think about us the next time your best friend suggests being something more than a friend.

Then again, everybody's different, and there could be some excellent, human reasons why you shouldn't have sex with your friend(s). For instance, 1) you're not physically attracted to your friend or vice versa, or 2) your friend is married to your brother who is a jealous homicidal maniac. And that's just the beginning. Obviously, we shouldn't make like bonobos in all situations.

Nevertheless, you can usually render your friendships and acquaintanceships a bit more bonoboësque with a few more hugs, more play, more closeness, more openness, more intimacy, more empathy, more laughs and/or more bonobo love. Try it! Assuming your friends are not psychopaths, religious fundamentalists or touch-averse misanthropes who don't bathe, it can't hurt (unless everybody wants it to hurt, of course).

Maximize Your Erotic Capital

What if you don't have many friends? Or maybe you just don't have the right friends. If you're shy, let the bonobos inspire you to come out of your shell. Bonobos are really nice to each other partly because they really need each other to survive in the wild. Humans need other humans too, though many of us think we don't. Our amazing technology allows us to live apart

---

[94] Lots more about our truly amazing or super sickening (depending on how you feel about us) romance in our upcoming memoir.

in princely solitude, supported by our smartphones and single-serving pizzas. But continuously going at it alone goes against our intrinsic needy human nature, and our luxurious space can easily turn into devastating isolation, especially if you're shy.

Your BLC is to cultivate more warmth and playfulness in your relationships with friends, acquaintances, business colleagues, co-workers, cashiers, postal workers, tech support—everyone. But how much playfulness is too much? That's always hard to gauge and has been the subject of many a court case. Err on the side of caution and common sense, especially if you are male.

One of the sexiest, least aggressive, yet highly effective bonoboësque things you can do is make eye contact and smile. When bonobos smile, it looks to us kind of like they're gritting their teeth in fear, and sometimes they are. Smiling out of fear is actually a well-known trait among humans and other primates. But more often than not, a big toothy bonobo grin is a sign of pleasure, just like with humans. Pleasure is contagious, so keep smiling and look folks in the eye. Try not to stare, though. A quick but warm glance will do. Remember how quickly Lana glanced at me and looked away during our first flirtation? Use your EQ and SQ to make that subtle but strong "human" contact that is really very bonoboësque.

Whether or not it leads to sex, being bonobo-friendly will increase what Dr. Hakim calls your "erotic capital," i.e., your public sex appeal, which is worth just as much as academic degrees and social connections are in today's markets. It's not just "what you know" or "who you know," it's who knows you. The more erotic capital you exhibit, the more people want to know you. Of course, your natural good looks make up part of your erotic capital, but much more has to do with your warmth, confidence, humor, empathy, sexual intelligence and style. Don't neglect good grooming—look at the amount of time and effort that bonobos and other apes spend on grooming. They may not look like beauty queens to us, but popular bonobos "go to the hairdresser" every day.

Maximizing your erotic capital at work will help you to seduce new clients, co-workers, subordinates and even your grumpy boss. Everybody should get more hugs, more warmth, more empathy and more understanding. The gifts you give will come back to you even before you are done giving.

Jesus probably said it best: "Give, and it shall be given unto you" (Luke 6:38). But you don't have to be a believer to feel the pleasure of giving.

It's organic. It's hedonic. It's bonoboësque. And it inspires others to give as well. The power to give pleasure is the greatest power we have.

How About a Friendly Game of Stranger?

Good friends make the best lovers, but there's something undeniably appealing about sex with a sexy stranger. This is as true for bonobos, as shown in studies by Hare, Woods and Tan (discussed in Chapter 13), as it is for humans. Apparently, a lust for the unknown excitement that a stranger represents is deep within our hominid DNA. This is one reason it may feel like you've fallen out of love when your lover transitions from enchanting stranger to familiar friend, and all the warm cuddly trust snuffs out the spark of lust.

That's why I recommend that best friends who are committed lovers (i.e., couples) play the Stranger Game to spice up that friendly trust with a sense of wild lust every once in a while. Pr. Max and I do this quite often. It can be as elaborate as dressing up in disguises and driving in separate cars to a designated spot, such as a new bar across town where you are both unknown. One of you might enter a few minutes before the other arrives, perhaps getting hit on before the "stranger" enters and you spot each other, "meeting" as if for the first time, flirting with the line between fantasy and reality as you flirt with each other, using made up names, touching as if you've never touched before, seducing each other and then going to a motel for wild sex that might be as good as, or even better than, the first time, now that you've got your Stranger Game juices flowing. Or it can be as simple as one of you catching the other's eye and playfully posing a Stranger Game-inducing question, "Well hello there, I haven't seen you before. Are you new here?" or even just whistling, like an appreciative stranger might, as your naked partner walks by. Like all roleplay, the game requires "buy-in" or the "suspension of disbelief." Remember how seriously you took make believe as a child? Tap into that intensity of play.

The Stranger Game is an old fantasy roleplay scenario that has been recommended to monogamous couples (who know each other all too well) at least since the days of Ovid and his ancient Roman *Art of Love*. Maybe that's because, if you actually play the game, it really works! It's one of the hallmarks of the Bonobo Way for committed couples, blowing a breeze of lust through the bed sheets of trust.

Casual Hookups & Friends-with-Benefits

The friends-with-benefits relationship style, always gaining in popularity despite general social disapproval of such things, is very bonoboësque. Most bonobo sex involves friends with no particular ownership rights, pair-bonding or exclusive commitment... and the benefits are many. Problems among human friends-with-benefits may arise when one of you wants to get serious while the other prefers to remain just friends. Well, at least nobody's stuck in the "friend zone." Still, it can get complicated.

What about casual hookups? Complications vary. A standard "hookup" involves meeting for erotic activity without commitment, dating or even, necessarily, friendship. The erotic activity could be anything from a make-out session to anal sex. The media generally portrays "hookup culture" as a moral crisis among today's godless and horny college students, but hookups are part of a cultural revolution that has been going on at least since the 19th century, accompanying technological advancements such as the electric light, the car, the movies, the computer and the mobile phone. Essentially, this techno-cultural transformation has gotten multitudes of young people "off the farm" and away from the judgmental eyes of their families, into the cities and universities where they can more freely experiment and experience the kind of casual sex they desire.

Despite popular perception, hookups aren't just for college kids, as shown by Dr. Zhana Vrangalova's "Casual Sex Project," a website that solicits true stories of "one-night stands, friends-with-benefits, short flings, fuck buddies, booty calls, sex with an ex" and more, from adults of all ages and from around the world. With online dating sites galore and smartphone apps designed to bring the hot and horny together, hooking up is more efficient than ever. Casual sex is on the rise and so is not feeling bad about it, as evidenced by the positive tone of Dr. Vrangalova's project. There's even talk of "the transformative power of the hookup—from opening their minds and bodies to enjoying sex more freely to making it painfully clear to them that sex without love is not for them." Whether transformative or just a turn-on, consensual hookups are pretty bonobo-friendly, especially when they involve breakfast.

Social Media "Friends"

Various online communities have coopted the word "friend" so that it means little more than a random person, that person's assistant or even a bot who clicks "like" on your posts. This step is more about the friends you actually know and see occasionally.

However, you can certainly get bonobo-friendly with the folks you "meet" on the Internet. In a way, social media makes hunter-gatherers of us all, as the entire world has become our happy hunting grounds, as well as a place to gather support and spread our seed... and our memes.

If you're already a social media maven, you can get started by making your posts more bonoboësque, sex-positive and eco-sexual. Hashtag #bonobo, share information, photos and videos of the real bonobos, as well as you and your friends going bonobos (if you dare). Spread the message of peace through pleasure and erotic exploration.

Usually, it's fine to just go with the flow and not make waves, but sometimes you've got to rise against the tide. As bonobos get more famous, they also get more defamed. Therefore, Capt'n Max and I have formed the "Bonobo Anti-Defamation League," and it's only partly a joke. Bonobos need human protection from the lethal "bushmeat" threats to their lives (see Step 12) as well as "pro-bonobo" protection from the ignorance and slander of some in the media. We've already tackled *The New Yorker* (Chapter 10) and 20th Century Fox (Chapter 7) for misleading the public about bonobos. Assuming you've gotten this far in the book, you know more about our kissing cousins than most, so when you see people, publications or blockbuster films misrepresenting *Pan paniscus*, I hope you will set them straight... peacefully, of course.

A side benefit of being pro-bonobo in social media is that it will help you make more pro-bonobo social media friends. Of course, you can and should flirt with these "friends" when it feels right. A "like" or retweet can be the social media equivalent of making brief but meaningful eye-contact or blowing a quick bonobo air kiss. A volley of clever comments can take you to instant messaging, like flirtatious bar banter can take you to the backseat of a car. There you can get down and dirty... naked selfies, sexting, phone sex, webcam... and who knows where that might lead? Maybe a not-so-virtual "poke" if you get lucky.

What if you're in a real-life relationship? How bonobo-friendly can you be online without betraying or just annoying your partner(s)? That's a boundary you might need to set, or at least discuss. Online affairs can be as emotionally intense as in-the-flesh liaisons and virtual cheating can be as destructive to a monogamous relationship as actual "unsanctioned" PIV Intercourse. Then again, perhaps the two of you are looking for a third for a threesome or another couple for a foursome, in which case, social media is an excellent place to start or extend your search.

Whether or not you hookup in real life, it can be fun to express your erotic nature on the Interwebs. What an opportunity for global exhibitionism! The world is your voyeur. But keep in mind that if your posts are flagged as "too sexy" (which is always rather vaguely defined with phrases like "prevailing standards" even though it's usually more of a whim than a standard and prevails because of censorship, shaming, and bullying), some social media sites will penalize you and might even delete your whole profile or ban you. For the bonobo-friendliest community online, join us in Bonoboville… coming up in Step 10!

Whatever your approach, try not to take social media too seriously. Don't sit staring at your friends' walls filled with pictures and posts about all the fabulous things they're doing and sexy people they're seeing as you stew in toxic envy and enervating depression. Despite all the talk of "friends" and "sharing," remember that social media is, first and foremost, *media*, which means it's always at least a little full of crap.

"I Was Just Being Bonobo-Friendly, Your Honor"

Be careful to respect people's boundaries when taking this step, whether in real life or the virtual world. Boundaries are often trickiest with the people closest to you. A good rule of thumb is not to get too bonobo-friendly with your own nuclear family, for example, especially not the younger generation. Use your EQ/SQ to maintain the required limits and to keep yourself and your loved ones out of trouble. These boundaries are some of the most complicated to navigate, but respect and common sense make for a good map and compass.

It's also best to be cautious in most workplaces, lest you get accused of sexual harassment. Test those waters for sharks and take baby steps. No bonobo handshakes under the desk without full (sometimes even written) consent. "I was just being bonobo-friendly, Your Honor!" probably won't cut you any slack in court.

Ah, the twin stresses of work and family life… This is why it's so important to be able to escape the cages and go bonobos in bed with your lover(s), at least occasionally. Better yet, you could join or create your own Bonoboville.

Step 10: Create Your Own Bonoboville.

Like bonobos, chimps and most monkeys, we humans are intensely social. Whether we like, love or hate each other, we can't live without each other, at least not very well. Banishment was once considered a punishment worse than death. Now it's solitary confinement. We may resent and rebel against "society," but unless you're a master Stoic, being booted out of it can hurt worse than a kick in the family jewels. Many have testified to that harrowing, lonesome pain. *Oh, the shame!*

Shame puts us in mortal fear of being caught with our panties down around our ankles, our names in the scandal sheets, our intimate bits exposed, mocked and reviled, as we are abandoned by family and friends, fired by our employers and excluded from our primate group, perhaps even forsaken by God Himself[95], left to perish alone and unloved in the wilderness, condemned to an eternity of misery.

That's why excommunication, slut-shaming, name-calling, bullying, shunning and other forms of erotophobic humiliation are such effective ways to get us to toe the party line. Churches, temples, mosques, governments, schools, fraternities, armies and parents all take shameless advantage of our primal fear of being shamed to keep us compliant and conformist. Thanks to all that pressure, many of us keep our inner bonobos silently caged in a closet deep within us.

Time for a Different Party!

Locked up and lonely, our inner bonobos yearn for some kind of sociosexual release and acceptance, like a great group hug of deep friendship... with benefits. But we can't get that kind of acceptance from the usual groups, especially if our feelings and philosophies don't always toe that narrowly defined party line.

So... maybe it's time for a different party.

Welcome to Bonoboville. I've been using the term throughout this book with all the poetic license I can muster, but now that you're ready to create your own, or join one, I'll break it down. Like most words, "Bonoboville"

---

[95] Though it's politically correct to give equal billing to the Goddess here, I just can't imagine *Her* forsaking you over anything to do with sex.

can mean a few things. First, it's the wild bonobos' natural habitat in the Congolese rainforest. Second, it's any group of bonobos such as Lana's tribe at the San Diego Zoo. Third, I use the term "Bonoboville" as a more generalized concept to describe the bonobos' ongoing culture.

The fourth kind of Bonoboville is for adult *Homo sapiens* only, though it is inspired by *Pan paniscus*. Any place, group, village, household, society, gathering, salon, retreat, colony, club or community may qualify. You might live full-time in your human Bonoboville, or it could be a place to escape your everyday life and take a metaphorical hit off that bonoboësque peace pipe of collective ecstasy. That doesn't mean you all have to have group sex (although that can go a long way toward unleashing your inner bonobos) and sex should never be "required" of anyone. There are other ways to share pleasures: eating, dancing, celebrating, collaborating, grooming, nurturing, nesting, playing and creating a community together. In Bonoboville, many types of erotic expression that are forbidden in other groups are permitted and even encouraged and celebrated as forms of art and culture. Polly Whittaker, effervescent creator of San Francisco's renowned "Kinky Salons," calls this "sex culture."

Creating your own Bonoboville, or even just participating in one, is an art. Though it may not be as easy as creating, say, your own shopping mall, it seems to me to be far more essential to human community. As Frank Moore writes in *Frankly Speaking*, "We artists must not make cynical statements from our inner worlds about how fucked up the rest of society is. We must create alternative community realities in which people can be actively involved." That's what Bonobovilles are all about.

"Saturday Night Group Therapy"

With the help of our ever-evolving and revolving staff, Pr. Max, a.k.a. "Capt'n Max" (in his "chief-of-staff" capacity) and I run our own Bonoboville, online and on *terra firma*. At least, we attempt to run it, though more often than not, it runs us. It's like trying to ride a bucking bronco or keep up with a swinging bonobo. Most of the week is relatively quiet, with everyone working on online projects, editing, set building and conducting private sex therapy sessions. Then, on Saturday nights, holidays or other special occasions, we "go bonobos," and turn the Institute into the Speakeasy, inspired by the swinging gatherings of Aristippus of Cyrene in ancient Athens, the fetish salons of Dr. Magnus Hirschfeld in Weimar Berlin, the Roman Lupercalia (the original Valentine's Day),

1950s Fellini movies, Andy Warhol's Factory, and Max's old "counterculture" *Love* and *Finger Magazine* erotic art parties with Willem de Ridder and Annie Sprinkle.

The Bonoboville Speakeasy hosts eclectic shows with stimulating conversation, sex educational demonstrations and *Commedia Erotica* (unscripted, erotic performance art and spontaneous sex comedy in the tradition of *Commedia dell'Arte*). At midnight, the show may spin off into an afterparty that has some folks swinging like bonobos, from the chandeliers, around the stripper pole and with each other. All of this happens while voyeurs watch, sapiosexuals chat and others dance, romance, hula-hoop, play pool, ride the rickshaw, paddle playmates, flog friends on the bondage cross, engage in discreet or very public sex on one of the beds or couches (or even, in a pinch, the kitchen table), tickling each other or tickling the ivories of my great-grandmother's Steinway baby grand.

"This is my Saturday night group therapy," explains one Institute member after a good paddling over the loveseat by the Speakeasy bar. "I can be myself in this place," another declares from the middle of a pile of grinning, half-naked friends, one of whom is her husband. "I love to play here!" proclaims a porn star from the trapeze. Our Bonoboville helps everyone (from members to featured guests to the staff to Max and me) release our inner bonobos in a fun, erotic, creative, cathartic, often orgasmic, very organic, always interesting, semi-regularly-scheduled way. Though, sometimes our Bonoboville can't be scheduled. It becomes a single living, breathing, growing, changing organism, and we are all its body parts and brain waves, moving to the primal beat of our collective drums.

Another regular guest, renowned skeptic, award-winning TV mini-series producer and *What Do You Do with a Chocolate Jesus?* author Thomas Quinn, who has been a member since the 20th century, calls our Bonoboville "A Naughty Nirvana, a Horny Heaven, an Erotic Eden, a Permissive Paradise, a Voluptuous Valhalla—you got 'em all covered."

Alliterative adorations aside, our Bonoboville, like any community, has its ups and downs, its lovers and haters, its prodigal sons and daughters, as well as its grateful graduates and lifetime members. Some are refugees from various shaming societies all over the world, alienated by their governments, excommunicated from their churches, shunned by their temples, snubbed by their families, discharged from the Marines or laid off from Disney because of their sexual orientation or erotic flamboyance. For such folks, the nonjudgmental openness, freedom of artistic expression and cozy togetherness is as important as the sex. Others "play the game" in order to maintain membership in their own religious, familial or professional enclaves, and can keep their lives compartmentalized for multiple purposes. But they can only release their inner bonobos and "be themselves," sexually speaking, in Bonoboville.

No Couple is an Island

It's not for everybody, but Max and I thrive on our little Bonoboville. When left to our own devices, we tend to prefer each other's company over anyone else's to the extent that sex addictionologists would probably call us "codependent." Maybe it's because about seven years into our marriage, when so many other husbands and wives get that "Seven Year Itch,"[96] various unwanted barriers were forced between us, from oceans to prison bars (Lana isn't the only one I've kissed through a glass partition), and we had to fight with all our might and passion just to be together. Ironically, though it would make perfect sense to Bataille, some of the calamities that drove us painfully apart seem to have brought us together sexually, keeping things edgy and romantic.

Yet no couple is an island. Max and I need our Bonoboville as much as our Bonoboville needs us. Maybe more. Sometimes, I think our love depends on it. Certainly our lust does. After all, an overdose of trust kills lust and a little distance stimulates desire. Though Max and I still stick together like superglue, at least in our Bonoboville, we have plenty of opportunities to interact with others socially, sexually, creatively and otherwise. This prevents us from suffocating each other. Plus it keeps those sperm wars raging, especially on active Saturday nights.

When our Bonoboville is rocking, with other couples, trouples, singles and groups interacting erotically, it's like a big interdependent group wedding night. It's also an old-fashioned speakeasy, an ultra-modern theater troupe, an artist colony, a halfway house, a clinic, a gallery, a getaway hotel, a live radio show (since 1984), a TV show (since 1992), a "Garden of Earthly Delights," a fantasy and The Institute (since 1991). Maybe you'll come and see us sometime. You could stay in one of the

---

[96] With an upswoosh of my pleated white skirt to my middle-namesake, Marilyn Monroe, star of Billy Wilder's iconic 1955 film about the ups and downs of monogamy, *The Seven-Year Itch*.

fantasy guest rooms.

Whether or not a real-life stay ever comes to pass, you can always join us online, even anonymously, at our social media site, Bonoboville.com. You can also talk with us about your deepest feelings and fantasies, and receive private BLT with our therapists by phone. Via webcam, you can even enter our real world and see what some of us are doing... right now. We can also see you and help you to go bonobos in whatever way you'd like to explore. The Interwebs have greatly expanded connective possibilities for us and Bonobovilles everywhere, as it has for all human communities, including countless individuals who used to be imprisoned by their own sexual fear, shyness and shame.

Now even the most fearful, shy, shame-ridden, caged-up souls can visit our Bonoboville and many others through the relatively safe anonymity of cyberspace and explore how the other half swings.

Party Like a Bonobo

Which brings me to other Bonobovilles beyond ours, and there are multitudes throughout the human world today. For almost every type of kinkster, swinger, fetishist, polyamorist, ethical hedonist, empowered slut, free thinker or loving libertine, there's a group of like-minded people somewhere on Earth or, at least, on the web. Your Step #10 BLC is to seek out a few areas of your interest, and then join, participate in or help create your own Bonoboville. In the beginning, as a baby step, you can do it anonymously, crafting an online alter ego or even a "second life" for your erotic self.

Let's start with the most obvious type of real-life human Bonoboville: the swing club or Lifestyle party. Human swingers are, as we discussed in Chapter 14, "50 Shades of Bonobo," very bonoboësque, being highly sexual and remarkably peaceful, with the ladies often in power. Like bonobos, swingers are into sexual quantity *and* quality, multiple partners, interesting positions, group sex, exhibitionism, erotic activity with friends as well as strangers, and orgasms all around.

A good sex party is an honest-to-goodness human Bonoboville, with more goodness when women outnumber men and the rules favor female choice (assuming most of the females are bisexual, which Lifestyle ladies tend to be). Sorry single guys, but that's why so many sex clubs are only open to couples and single women. There are notable exceptions, such as gay male clubs, bi-guy parties, consensual gangbangs and cuckold nights.

Unless you're hosting one of those, you might want to keep the gender balance heavy on females when creating the guest list for your own swinging Bonoboville. Real bonobo communities are also better off when the females outnumber the males so the gals can join forces to gently dominate the dudes, for the peace and benefit of all. Without greater female numbers, the males become more competitive, and less cooperative. One of the reasons the real bonobos are so peaceful is that there's enough food for females to forage in large groups where they can then outnumber any males they might encounter. Then, the sex that unfolds tends to be on the ladies' terms.

Under similar conditions, human males tend to be on their best behavior at swing parties, unlike regular bars where attractive single ladies are liable to get a nonconsensual butt-groping, slipped a roofie, or even raped in the parking lot. Male Lifestylers tend to behave more like peaceful, young-at-heart bonobo boys that know they've got a good thing going and won't mess it up by doing anything that will get them thrown out of paradise.

Of course, you'll have many choices to make in your Bonoboville that you won't be able to adopt directly from wild bonobo behavior, such as safer sex requirements (condoms, Truvada[97] or both?), dress or undress code, what kinds of refreshments to serve, whether to offer alcohol or cannabis, whether to allow cameras or phones, what type of music to play and whether to charge and, if so, how much, and what percentage to give to organizations helping save the real bonobos from extinction in the wild.[98] To minimize potential issues and keep all guests on the same page, you might want to make up a list of rules or etiquette, the vital dos and don'ts, or 10 Commandments of Good Behavior for your Bonoboville. You also might want to make *The Bonobo Way* required reading for your regulars. Food for thought.

Revolutionary Bonobovilles from Iran to LA

Most sex parties are mainly about the sex. Others are more about the socializing, the music, the art or a cause. And some are revolutionary political events. Attending a sex party in the Islamic Republic of Iran, for instance, such as the ones documented by Iranian-American anthropologist

---

[97] Tenofovir/emtricitabine, trademark Truvada, available by prescription, is a fixed-dose combination of two antiretroviral drugs used for the treatment and prevention of HIV.

[98] More about that in Step 12: Save the Bonobos, Save the World.

Dr. Pardis Mahdavi in *Passionate Uprisings: Iran's Sexual Revolution*, is always a revolutionary political event with overtones of major personal risk.

Talk about transgressing! If you are caught simply drinking and dancing, you can be arrested by the *Komiteh*, Iran's notorious morality police, and given up to 70 lashes. Having sex outside marriage subjects you to more lashes and even possible execution by hanging or stoning, depending on your status and locale.

Despite, and partly because of, these draconian punishments, a sexual revolution is taking place in Iran, especially among the young. Bonobovilles are popping up in and around Tehran, featuring erotic parties where brave women toss off their hijabs (in a country where showing too much ankle can land you in the backseat of a Komiteh patrol car) and participate in group sex for the thrill of transgressive pleasure and in protest of the oppressive regime. "Iran gives new meaning to party like there's no tomorrow," exults one partier in Dr. Mahdavi's book. The ultimate Bonoboville revolution might be an orgy in Iran.

But Iran, with its sinister morality police, is just one exotic example. There are other revolutionary sex parties throughout the world, as there have been throughout history. Not every neighborhood watch is ready to bust down the door of your private domicile, arrest you and lash your bare buttocks with leather whips just for dancing a rumba. Yet, every human culture to date has had its ways of shaming, punishing and even eliminating people who express a sexuality that deviates from the standard model.

Though I've never been whipped by the *Komiteh*, my Bonoboville was "raided" (twice!) by the LAPD, and that's close enough. That's right, our very own home-grown Southern California "morality police," the Los Angeles Police Department, has long been notorious for shutting down swing clubs all over this supposedly liberal county. And we weren't even running a swing club! We were just doing our Saturday night show.

The first time, two detectives posing as a couple with relationship issues came to our Hollywood Hills studio during a live broadcast, when suddenly, 15 of their uniformed pals showed up like Keystone Kops in the wrong movie. Confronted by First Amendment attorney Jeffrey Douglas and a Channel 13/UPN-TV news crew that happened to be shooting a segment about the show that night, the officers quickly realized their goof was being broadcast and left without charging me or anyone else with anything.

Their second entrance was more dramatic—and dangerous. Yelling "SWAT!" and threatening to break down my door, 20 heavily armed police officers, backed up by a thunderous, clattering helicopter shining a blinding light through my windows, swarmed into my Downtown LA studio and art gallery without a warrant. Their excuse this time? An anonymous 911 caller allegedly said that four gunmen had just robbed and kidnapped someone, dragging the victim into my studio. Within 10 minutes, the officers could see there were neither kidnappers nor kidnappees anywhere on the premises, but they hung around for two-and-a-half very long hours, making themselves at home, poking through the refrigerator and my lingerie drawers (looking for kidnappers?), and calling in reinforcements. Several of "LA's finest" asked when the "action" started. One of the officers even whispered to me, "Sorry about this. I enjoy your show." He seemed sincere but helpless to stop the "investigation." Again, in the end, nobody was charged with anything.

But this time, we had had enough. Whether this was harassment or a bumbling mistake, we felt we needed our local police to know exactly who we were and that what we do is perfectly legal and well within our Constitutional rights. So we sued them. The tale of our lawsuit[99] against the LAPD for infringement of our fourth amendment rights would make an exciting sequel to *Legally Blonde*, and it was one of the greatest—and funniest—Bonobo Liberation Challenges of our lives.

We were up against bull-necked LAPD defense attorney Don W. Vincent, who claimed, with a straight face, that the looming presence of my giant furry pink penis-shaped pillow was grounds to search my studio. Aiding him was the notoriously reactionary Federal Judge Manuel Real, who was later publicly reprimanded for lying to the Ninth Circuit Judicial Council and abusing his power in a corruption scandal that revealed he was granting inappropriate favors to a certain young lady at the center of a Canter's Deli family lawsuit. But at the time, Judge Real was firmly ensconced in his power seat from which he squinted and waggled his puritanical finger at me as if I were Hester Prynne incarnate, advising me to be grateful I hadn't been arrested or shot on the spot.

I try always to be grateful, but Judge Real's "advice" made me mad, especially knowing how many innocent people do get shot by those sworn to protect and serve us. With the help of a few brilliant, behind-the-scenes lawyers,[99] Max and I put together a kick-ass appeal that hit the LAPD the same way their boots had hit our door. Within weeks, the City of L.A. was on the phone, offering us a very nice settlement (which, incidentally, helped to finance some much-needed renovations in Bonoboville), plus a public apology from then Mayor Richard Riordan. That was well over a decade ago, and we haven't been raided since, thank you very much. *Mwah!* Love you too, LAPD.

I really hope your local morality police don't harass you. I wouldn't wish this kind of challenge on anyone. But it happens to a lot of innocent people in one form or another, and if it happens to you, I hope you have the nerve, the means and the support to stand up for your Bonoboville's rights. Because your right to party is our right to party.

Witness & Be Witnessed

All modern human cultures have their versions of morality police who shame, shun, harass, perjure, plant "evidence" on, entrap and arrest people who take part in sexual activity outside of the most private spaces. Thus, engaging in any kind of public display of affection (PDA) is, by its very nature, transgressive, dangerous, "deliciously nasty"[101] and sometimes revolutionary. In that context, attending your first orgy may very well free your inner bonobo unlike anything else you've ever experienced, even if you do nothing but observe.

When couples are curious about the Lifestyle, I often suggest they go to a swing party together with the agreement that they will just watch. If they want to participate, they can do that on the second visit and many times thereafter. But it helps take the pressure off if they limit their first experience to observation.

But oh, what they observe! Viewing all that in-person erotic action, listening to the sounds and inhaling the potent smells of group sex is a sexual revelation for people who have always confined sex to darkened, private spaces. Very often, couples who go to swing parties have intense sex when they get home, stimulated by the bonoboësque scenes they have just observed "up close and personal." Both *The Lifestyle* and *Plays Well in Groups* include numerous accounts of this heart-warming phenomenon that

---

[99] You can check out my "briefs" on my blog "The Dildo Dialogues."
[100] Thank you Councilors Barry Fisher, John Burton and Steve Yagman.

stirs a little spicy lust into the warm marital soup of trust.

To observe and be observed extends far beyond acts of exhibitionism and voyeurism, though it certainly includes them. The real bonobos learn about sex (not to mention love, empathy, reciprocity, making peace through pleasure and all those other bonoboësque traits) by watching and *witnessing* their elders and peers.

We humans tend to learn about these things by literally fumbling around in the dark. For better and worse, but mostly for better, the Bonobo Way brings sex out of the closet and into the community (or at least, *a* community) where we can witness and be witnessed as our erotic personas. It's quite the learning experience… in a veritable Bonobo Sutra of ways.

"Mainstream sex education doesn't even usually include photographs, much less action-focused instruction," points out Dr. Katherine Frank in *Plays Well in Groups*. "Watching others have sex, however, is still a way of obtaining information."

Porn Star Bonobovilles

Not everybody has the nerve, means or opportunity to get involved with an in-the-flesh group sex experience for this sort of sex education. Nowadays, most people obtain sex education the way they get most information, from the Internet. Some go to actual sex educational sites with lots of text and diagrams or comedy sites with lots of silly sex jokes. The vast majority go to porn sites with lots of hardcore videos and images.

We call the people who populate these images and films "porn stars." Yes, even a first-time performer is a porn star, or maybe a starlet. And yes, most porn still features actual human beings, though cartoons and anime are gaining in popularity. In a very physical way, porn stars and erotic performers are on the front lines of society's battle for bonobo liberation, literally putting their bodies on the line, inside and out. On the other hand, most porn presents an unrealistic view of sex and keeps many of its viewers passive instead of actively engaging with others. Moreover, much as they may love their porn, not many porn fans are willing to fight for porn stars' rights or even for their own right to view porn. Shame still reigns over porn.

Thus the "cummunity" that calls itself the "porn industry," loosely

---

[101] My old friend, the actor Norman O. Alexander (one of the iconic Jive Brothers in the original *Airplane)*, uses this phrase to describe anything that turns him on, and with his slight Caribbean lilt, it sounds even deliciously nastier.

based in Los Angeles, but spread all over the world, is another kind of Bonoboville vital to those who lead very bonoboësque lives. The best adult performers regularly go bonobos, at least when they are on camera.

Some porn stars are exhibitionists who love being watched, not to mention recorded, for posterity. Some have postgraduate degrees from the world's finest universities (fellow Yalie Zak Smith Sabbath comes to mind). Others have virtually no formal education at all. Some could do anything they wanted in life. Others can't do anything but porn. Some are sex activists or revolutionary experiential artists who crave being witnessed as they perform their erotic art. Some will only "play for pay." But then again, some bonobos will only do oral for apples.

There are many reasons why people get into porn, especially when it's as easy as pointing your phone at your body parts. Who hasn't texted naked selfies to a special friend? Some just have more talent for it. Or more drive. Or more friends, special and otherwise. Some porn performers are refugees from sex-negative churches and families who shamed them for their intensity. Others continue to practice the religions with which they were raised, with the sincere belief that God loves porn stars as much as anybody else. A few are hardcore atheists. Many are ethical hedonists.

Some porn stars are just physically attractive, adventurous, high-libido individuals who enjoy sex and, in tough economic times, choose to exploit their own erotic capital and get paid for doing what they enjoy. Some porn stars are themselves exploited by unethical operators such as you find in any field, but the great majority practice their erotic craft with eyes as wide open as their legs.

Whatever their background and motivation, it's not easy to navigate the semi-underground world of porn. So most appreciate the sprawling Porn Star Bonoboville that has grown up around the Industry, with everything from STD clinics to karaoke clubs to glittering Oscar-like awards ceremonies (like AVN and Xbiz), the better to cushion them from the stigma they endure from PG society. That stigma, however, is dissolving. As human culture gets more wired and bonoboësque, most young people know at least one person who has dabbled in porn or other types of sex work, even if "accidentally" (Kim Kardashian anyone?).

Over the years, I've been lucky enough to have had hundreds of porn stars, a few that I count as friends, as guests on my show and at our parties. When I tell them about the bonobos, many recognize kindred spirits. One of the most prestigious DrSuzy.Tv awards that we bestow annually is

"Most Bonobo" for the most sensual, playful and giving guest that year. Usually that guest is a porn star.

On some level, all types of sex work involve releasing your inner bonobo so that you can help others release theirs, at least enough to enjoy momentary erotic pleasure. Sex work is some of the most valuable and least valued work on Earth.

If you're a sex worker, the Bonobo Way can give you the natural validation and strength you need to cope with your local version of the morality police. Whether your erotic community is for business, pleasure or a bonoboësque combination, a webcam house, brothel, bordello, strip club, massage parlor, sauna, Tantra center, swing club, soft swap party, burlesque troupe, Gaia festival, Jack and Jill-off club, Kinky Salon, Bawdy Storytelling circle, erotic cabaret, gangbang group, gay bathhouse, leather club, queer alliance, sex geek gathering, BDSM dungeon, lifestyle munch, nudist resort or an eco-sex conference, you can consider it a type of Bonoboville. You and your group just may find deep erotic inspiration in the "alternative great ape paradigm" of the real-life bonobos.

Beware of False Bonobovilles!

Not every group that incorporates sex into its communal life is a true Bonoboville. Not at all! When I was a grad student riding the bus home from a class at San Francisco State, a cute hippie-ish guy with a dazzling smile sat down next to me. He showed me some cool-looking comic books with drawings of happy people frolicking naked in what looked like a modern Garden of Eden and invited me to dinner at his commune. Always up for an adventure, I considered his offer until he mentioned that all this love and frolicking was based on accepting Jesus Christ as my Lord and Savior, at which point I said thanks but no thanks. Mercifully, the next stop was mine, and I was gone, avoiding the human sucker trap that then called itself the Children of God.

Any groups, and there are many, in which the elite members force others to engage in any kind of sex, often in the name of religion, such as the Children of God, which now calls itself Family International, the Moonies or the cults and "families" of violent, coercive "prophets" like David Koresh and Charles Manson, don't deserve the Bonoboville name. They give sex itself a very bad name. Beware of them.

Stealth, Science & Love Songs of Bonoboville

On the bright side, there are many types of "stealth Bonobovilles" that don't emphasize sex (though it's always lurking in the background, between the lines or in the restroom), but draw upon other vital *Pan paniscus* qualities. Examples include art galleries, ecovillages, skeptic societies, travel groups, cosplayers, musical ensembles, drum circles, sweat lodges, tribal celebrations, pagan congregations, circus communities, artists' collectives, theater troupes, geek gatherings, cuddle parties, Cacophony Society events, Burning Man decompressions, workers' cooperatives, cannabis dispensaries, ecstatic dance jamborees and even some sex-positive political campaigns.[102] Any group that sincerely tries to follow the Bonobo Way in any way could be a human Bonoboville. If the Mafia ever turn in their guns for vibrators, they might be better at making an "offer we can't refuse." We could call them the Bonobo Nostra!

How about your local dance club? Most clubgoers are often attired in clubwear skimpier than most lingerie, led by MCs exhorting you to shake your booty, get down and go down, singers moaning the throes of orgasm. The hottest clubs turn into simulated public orgies that stop just short of "indecent exposure," and that's in the public areas. Illicit sex sometimes occurs in semi-private areas or right on the dance floor, if it's crowded enough. Exuberant fans toss panties at the band, crawl onstage to give their favorite rappers blowjobs (sometimes while they're rapping[103]) or have pounding threesomes in the DJ booth. It's like a real Bonoboville at feeding time, but instead of munching bananas as they hoka-hoka, they're sipping champagne and twerking the night away.

From the clubs to the circus, political campaigns to gang bang parties, music is the soundtrack to life in human Bonobovilles. Many real bonobos are quite musical, as we learned in "Jamming with Kanzi" and, given the proper percussion instruments, they can really pound out a beat. And bonobos aren't alone. At a 2014 meeting of the American Association for the Advancement of Science, where Drs. Gray and Large gave a talk on their research into bonobo rhythmic ability, scientists presented studies of various animals "dancing" to human music, including a sea lion who nods

---

[102] Sex-negative political efforts can also involve illicit sex parties and secret trysts (former Republican Congressman Mark Foley's dalliances with Congressional pages come to mind), but that's extremely hypocritical and doesn't deserve the name "Bonoboville," even in private.

her head in time to her favorite songs.

Many more non-human animals, including an array of birds compose their own harmonies, make natural music out in the wild. This music is as pleasing to human ears as any symphony or rock anthem, as proven by the robust sales of albums that bring you sounds of the rainforest or, if you prefer, the sea or a lake. Max and I love to make love to the love songs of the seagulls calling to each other across the pacific roar of the ocean waves. The evolving field of biomusicology, a.k.a. zoomusicology, explores the deep desire to create and respond to the innate musicality that animals possess.

It seems to me that the human love of music, from classical to rock, rap and the complex electronica of "Bonobo,"[104] is far older than humanity itself. The primary purpose of these musical sounds, from humpback whales to nightingales, is to attract and communicate with mates, indicating that humanity's first forays into music were probably not war chants (one popular theory) but love songs composed to give their listeners mellifluous eargasms.[105]

In *The Descent of Man,* Darwin himself suggested as much: "When we treat of sexual selection we shall see that primeval man, or rather some early progenitor of man, probably first used his voice in producing true musical cadences, that is in singing, as do some of the gibbon-apes at the present day; and we may conclude from a widely-spread analogy, that this power would have been especially exerted during the courtship of the sexes, would have expressed various emotions, such as love, jealousy, triumph, and would have served as a challenge to rivals."

Though the war chants of chimps, baboons and the MIC may excite primal feelings, the love songs of bonobos, monkeys and troubadours are probably older in primate history. No wonder music is such an essential accompaniment to any seduction, from a pop star enchanting a packed stadium to a lover serenading (or cranking up just the right tune on the iPod for) one special someone.

---

[103] This happened to rapper Danny Brown who handled it like a champ, barely missing a beat.
[104] "Bonobo" is the stage moniker of the amazing band leader, musician and DJ Simon Green.
[105] "Eargasms," a kind of Autonomous Sensory Meridian Response (ASMR), are orgasmic sensations in the ear that can arise from having your ears rubbed (one of my own favorite forms of massage, especially after a couple hours of wearing a headset!), tongued or from hearing intensely erotic sounds.

Love the Earth You Make Love On

"We need to expand our concept of love to include entire communities and perhaps even the ecosystems that sustain us," writes Dorian Sagan in his introduction to *Gaia & the New Politics of Love* by Dr. Serena Anderlini-D'Onofrio. This is deeply sage advice but, tree-huggers aside, it's very difficult for most humans to "grok," let alone put into practice. Many, from Plato to Focus on the Family, have claimed that *eros* and *agape* are irreconcilable opposites.

Though the terms "eros" (the Greek word for ardent physical passion) and "agape" (Greek for spiritual, altruistic compassion) represent two very different types of love, they aren't actually opposite or adversarial. Indeed, the bonobos have a much easier time integrating *eros* and *agape* (passion and compassion) than we do, and this seems to me to be a lead we humans ought to follow. Without a real, practical, loving, caring commitment to your partner(s), your community, your world and all of nature, your Bonoboville is no more than a one-night-stand. No matter what your gender, be a good husband[106] to the Earth: support it.

More specifically, support the bonobos! If your Bonoboville is a commercial enterprise, donate a portion to help save the bonobos in the wild. There are several ways you can do this, and we'll get more into that in the all-important Step 12. But for now, just imagine if all types of Bonobovilles (erotic *and* stealth) gave a small percentage of their earnings to organizations working in the field to prevent the imminent extinction of *Pan paniscus*. We just might save the bonobos, and the whole rainforest, the "lungs" of the Earth. That's the power of the human Bonoboville… at least the potential power. It's up to each of us to make it actual.

Speaking of which, what about *your* human Bonoboville? Your final BLC for this step is to tell us about it! Bear (as bare as you dare) witness, brothers and sisters! Send us your stories, videos, photos and fantasies, and we'll feature the most interesting Bonobovilles on our site and in an upcoming book.

---

[106] One definition of "husband" (the verb) is to manage, care or take responsibility for something or someone.

Step 11: Swing through Life.

Swinging is an art. Watch how bonobos swing from branch to bough to vine to each other's outstretched arms for a rollicking round of grab-the-banana. Now you try it. Not literally, of course. Unless you're in Cirque du Soleil, you'll fall on your butt and possibly break your banana. Good thing you needn't be an aerialist to learn the art of swinging through life. In these uncertain times, however, it's a critical skill to develop.

Whether you're trying to cope with a pink slip or a police raid, rape or rejection, losing a house or a hard-on, it usually helps to take a deep breath and release your inner bonobo. This is the part of you that knows, as my old friend, the artist Jirayr Zorthian, used to say, "The purpose of life is to live."

Actually, Eleanor Roosevelt said, "The purpose of life is to live it, to taste experience to the utmost, to reach out eagerly and without fear for newer and richer experience." But I prefer Zorthian's brevity. In complicated times, simple answers are usually the best. It doesn't get much simpler than that.

I like to imagine that most humans once had this innate, swinging adaptability, but lost touch with it around the advent of agriculture, which literally kept us down on the farm. I say "imagine" because it's not like anyone has solid proof of such an ineffable aptitude. But we do know that before we humans started reaping and sowing, we were hunter-gatherers, akin to bonobos. We didn't exactly swing like a Paleo Tarzan through the trees, but we walked, ran, danced and crouched among them, picking fruits and catching game, synchronizing our movements with our environment, constantly on the move, going with the flow of the seasons. All that moving and flowing was probably mixed in with a lot of rest and recreation since, as long as the weather was good, there wasn't much "work" required to keep yourself and your small tribe fed and sheltered. At least, that's what certain evolutionists such as Drs. Ryan, Jethá and Diamond say.

The World is Our Real Estate

Our species seems to have done this sort of hunting, gathering, flowing and swinging for several tens of thousands of years, until some genius(es) figured out where babies come from. Then socially-controlled reproduction, fertilization, planting, harvesting and breeding (i.e., agriculture) appears to have followed as swiftly and hard as a jailhouse door slamming shut on a condemned man's freshly strip-searched buttocks. *Ouch!*

Suddenly, within a few thousand, or maybe even a few hundred years, human beings went from being relatively independent nomads (who owned nothing but what they could carry) to being farmers, builders and "owners" of land (now "property"), plants (now "crops"), animals (now "livestock") and other humans (now wives, children and slaves, a.k.a. "chattel").

All that ownership might make you rich, but it's a heavy burden, crushing your innate ape ability to swing through life. Besides, the great majority of people didn't (and still don't) get rich at all. They were (and still are) working a lot for very little on some rich dude's plantation, factory, or corporate cubicle. Rich or poor, owner or owned, with the advent of Big Agriculture, humanity's openly swinging days became numbered.

Now the world is our real estate. Beavers build dams, birds make nests, spiders weave webs, ants construct anthills and dogs scent-mark their territory. But *Homo sapiens* take building and owning things to extremes. We can be proud of our life-saving hospitals, exquisite art museums, beautiful theaters, impressive universities and great libraries filled with some of the wisdom of our species. But throw in a few war rooms, sacrificial altars, torture-filled prisons, munitions facilities, nuclear power plants and pollution-belching factories, and all that construction doesn't seem so benign.

Don't get me wrong. I wouldn't turn the clock back to prehistory, even if I could. I don't want to live in a nest, especially not in one I have to recreate every night, like bonobos do. In my twenties, I tried living in a teepee for a month with Jordy, a sexy Rocky Mountain man, in the pristine foothills outside Boulder, Colorado[107]. It was very romantic for about three weeks, making love under golden sunsets and starry nights, snuggling in close to nature. Then wigwam leaks and peeing in the bushes surrounded

---

[107] At the time, I was a student at Naropa Institute, on summer break from Yale, studying Tibetan Tantra with Chogyam Trungpa Rinpoche, Alan Ginsburg, William Burroughs… and Jordy. Needless to say, I missed a lot of classes at Naropa while living in the teepee with Jordy, but it seemed to fit in with the Tantric-Beatnik early eco-sex curriculum.

The Bonobo Way

by hungry coyotes and creepy park rangers (and Jordy) got to me. I like a good solid roof, indoor plumbing, high-speed Internet, my Sybian, Hitachi and gazillions of other modern gadgets and convenient geegaws.

But life has a habit of going one way, then turning an unexpected corner and suddenly changing. Whether it's a hurricane or a heartbreak, when something happens to wipe out much of the civilized world and all those unsustainable geegaws you've so carefully accrued for yourself, it helps to be able to swing through the jungles of death, destruction and disappointment until you can grab a branch from the next flowering tree of life and breathe normally again.

This kind of adaptability is partly physical. We human apes spend a huge amount of time sitting on our lovely, lazy asses. We bend ourselves into the standardized sitting position when we eat, drink, drive, fly, poop, work or play on our computers. No wonder we get backaches[108] that diminish our enjoyment of sex and the rest of life. All that sitting also puts us at greater risk for heart attacks, cancer, kidney disease and a host of obesity-related ills as well as a shorter life expectancy.

Your first BLC for swinging through life is to get out of your chair, stretch your spine, confront your fears and change your scenery. Walk, run, juggle, sail, swing, dance, swing-dance or climb something, as if your life depended on it. Because it does.

Hot Date: Bridge-Climbing with the Suicide Club

It helps to have a fun objective (besides just exercise) to your walking, swinging or climbing. Back in the enervating '80s, just before I discovered swinging, I loved climbing up, up and as far away from the dull daily horror of Reagonomics and the emergence of HIV as I could get. From the summer camps of the Adirondacks to the monkey temples of the Himalayas, I trekked, scrambled and skinned my knees. But being a city gal at heart, my favorite climb was the urban trek up to the top of the Golden Gate Bridge, which I scaled (several times) with a super-secret group of metropolitan daredevils called the Suicide Club.[109] Seven hundred and forty-six feet high, with the roiling San Francisco Bay to our left and the tempestuous Pacific to our right, with cars that rolled like marbles

---

[108] I'm getting a major backache sitting here writing this book... where's my masseuse?
[109] The now legendary Suicide Club dissolved in the late 1980s, and from its ashes rose the phoenix of the Cacophony Society which eventually spawned Burning Man, one of the world's biggest Bonobovilles.

across the shimmering suspension down the middle, we faced our fears and raced our hearts.

And what a hot date it was! With just one foot of solid space on either side of us and no railings or net, we slithered across the damp, dark, orange box beams, clinging to the slippery rivets for balance. Despite the name "Suicide Club," and the fact that the Golden Gate is the world's second-most used suicide site, we didn't climb bridges to jump or fall off, but to tease death with a zany, yet serious and mildly transgressive zest for life. The view from the top at dawn was untouchable, as starry and special as could be, the city sparkling and the bridge lights glittering like belly chains around the voluptuous bay.

Sex was almost inevitable after a climb up the bridge, even if I wasn't especially attracted to the guy with whom I had just dared death. In their classic psychological study, Drs. Donald Dutton and Arthur Aron showed that terror can be a tremendous aphrodisiac, particularly where bridges are concerned. The study involved two randomly selected groups of college men. The first set talked, one at a time, with an attractive woman on an old rickety bridge swinging in the wind overlooking a steep rocky canyon and the second group chatted with the same woman on a stable bridge overlooking a short drop. The first group was measurably more attracted to the woman than the second group, demonstrating that being in a fearful situation heightens sexual attraction. The moral of the study is: Take your date up the Golden Gate, but never trust lust on a swinging bridge!

Moral #2: Embrace your erotic fears! If you always shy away from the scary stuff, your sex life will slide down the sinkhole as if it were lubed and specially ribbed for your displeasure. Scary stuff happens to everyone anyway, whether you swing through life or not. So many natural and social disasters—divorce, disease, death of a loved one, job loss, foreclosure, betrayal, rape, robbery, assault, accidents, outsourcing, war, the Apocalypse (actual or imagined), climate change, a black swan event, a zombie invasion (real or simulated), "industrial growth society" collateral damage, the fall of an empire or other "acts of God" or "of Goddess"—can grind everything you've labored to create into stardust. The great tragedy is that much more can be destroyed than just material things, as your spirit can be crushed along with your property. Unless you can swing through life, that is.

Ironically, in collective disasters, it often helps to cling as you swing. "I look at the path we're on, to the future, as having a ditch on either side," eco-visionary empath Dr. Joanna Macy told *Truthout*'s Dahr Jamail. "We have to hold onto each other, not to fall into the ditch on the right or left, which are, on one side panic and hysteria, and on the other side is paralysis and shutting down." Bonobos help each other through tough times.

What about personal disasters? The ancient Stoics didn't know bonobos from bacchantes,[110] but their philosophy was all about swinging from plenty to poverty, and back to plenty and so on, enjoying life's pleasures to the fullest, but ready to take the pain with a shrug, should circumstances change, as they always do.

The silver lining of personal failure and adversity is that they build character. And that's not like building a house that can be destroyed, looted, foreclosed on or taken by your awful ex. Nobody can take your character away from you. Swinging through a good catastrophe can transform you from a sheltered, bored and boring creature to an interesting, experienced, wiser survivor who has seductive stories and luscious lessons to share.

Sex Heals a Billion Times More Than It Kills

What if the catastrophe is sexual? In our erotophobic world, so many seem to be. Sex is often portrayed as the ultimate evil, a deceitful seductress, a succubus and a killer. And it can be. But statistically speaking, sex heals a billion times more than it kills.

That doesn't mean that so-called "sexual liberation" is the cure for the many ills of existence. Of course it is not. Untethered sexual activity can be accompanied by despicable violence, misogyny, drug abuse, child abuse, lying, cheating, sexually transmitted diseases, bad art and enervating boredom. There's also the ever-increasing over-commercialization of sex, and I don't just mean porn. I mean car and perfume ads waving sexual "success" as enticement and panacea, turning sex itself into a repressive pressure to conform, perform, purchase and pollute our environment.

But, sex itself is not the cause of these ills. As Camille Paglia put it, "Sex is a comedy, not a tragedy." In general, the great tragedy of life is death, the opposite of sex. But that's just the logic talking, and sexual feelings do not love logic.

Sexual snafus can seem like the most tragic and catastrophic of all. What if the one you love doesn't love you back? What if you catch your

---

[110]Bacchantes are priestesses of Bacchus, god of wine and revelry.

lover cheating on you? What if you can't "give" your partner an orgasm? What if your spouse won't try the sexual kink you crave? What if she finds your secret stash of taboo porn? What if you catch him wearing your favorite lacy panties? What if you realize her Facebook friend is more than just a friend? What if injury, sickness or age changes your ability to function sexually? What if, like Nate, you lose your erection at a crucial moment? What if you can't properly fuck anymore?

Too many of us allow such disturbing but non-lethal events to virtually destroy our sexuality, self-image, relationships and even our passion for life itself. The irony is that if you can swing through a sexual crisis, something about it will teach you how to have sex and/or make love on a whole new, exciting level. Remember, if everything went your way all the time, you'd never learn much, in or out of the bedroom, and you'd be an insufferable unshaggable bore. In fact, sometimes an unexpected setback is just what you need to enjoy a better, more bonoboësque life.

My NDE & the Blowjob from Hell

I remember when my own sex life and whole world almost came to a skidding halt in a matter of seconds. There I was, blogging along to the delightful music from that Saturday night's Whim 'n' Rhythm[111] show, when suddenly, without warning, a ferocious pain, like a herd of raging buffalo, charged up from my feet to my thighs and into my pelvis, stampeded across my chest, galloped into my throat and kicked me hard in the head again and again and again... until I passed out.

Just before losing consciousness, I managed to tell Max to call 911 and paramedics were soon packing me up like a suitcase and whisking me off to USC Medical Center where my completely comatose body fought severe septic shock poisoning for ten days. Every year, severe sepsis strikes about 750,000 Americans, according to National Institute of General Medical Sciences, with 28 to 50 percent dying from the illness. With my vital signs failing fast, my inner bonobo struggled to stay out of that statistical sinkhole, clinging to a thin, rapidly fraying vine of life. I'll save the full story of my harrowing near-death experience (NDE) for another book. For now, let's just cut to the chase: I woke up.

You'd think I'd have been happy to wake up. But thanks to my gradually dawning awareness of the presence of a long, thick, hard, phallic

---

[111] Whim 'n' Rhythm is Yale's oldest all-gal *a cappella* singing group.

object deep inside my windpipe, I was not happy at all. And no, this was not a scene from *The Fine Art of Fellatio*.[112] This was extreme throat-rape torture worthy of the most diabolical Inquisition. Talk about the Blowjob from Hell! I felt like I'd swallowed a car axle[113] that just wouldn't go down.

Medically speaking, I was on a breathing tube, a.k.a. an orotracheal intubation. In order to keep my weakened, anesthetized throat muscles from collapsing in on my air passages, a plastic tube had been forced through my mouth, down my larynx, and into my trachea. Otherwise, I'd have been dead within a few short gasps.

But I didn't know any of this at the time. The high-dose morphine-ketamine cocktails they were feeding me calmed the pain, but they also turned the theater of my mind into Dr. Caligari's cabinet[114] of "ICU psychosis[115]" horrors. I couldn't mentally grasp that I was in a hospital. I simply assumed I was being tortured, possibly for political reasons[116], by a bunch of evil, white-coated, blue-scrubbed sadists.

And I am not much of a masochist. I do enjoy a little light spanking now and again, but, partly because I've been a victim of real-life nonconsensual bondage,[117] I don't relish being tied down except in fantasy. And here I was, bound, hand and foot, mainly so I wouldn't rip the damn breathing tube out of my gullet. I also don't love being gagged, especially ball-gagged. Intubation is the world's worst ball gag.

For three days, I lay there, muzzled, immobilized and soon agonizingly awake, my inner bonobo swinging like a tired and drunk Philippe Petit[118] tightrope-walking over an endless black abyss in freezing rain. Everything around me blurred in this turbulent blizzard of misery, but when I looked

---

[112] This is the title of my sex-educational video on the subject of giving oral pleasure to men. The sister video is *Luscious Cunnilingus*.
[113] The amazing Murrugan the Mystic has actually swallowed a real car axle on my show (twice!) *while* the lovely Cici LaRue swallowed his penis.
[114] One of my favorite silent horror films is the German expressionist masterpiece *The Cabinet of Dr. Caligari*.
[115] ICU psychosis is a disorder experienced by patients in an intensive care unit (ICU) who hallucinate and suffer severe anxiety, paranoia and delirium.
[116] Shortly before my NDE, I had received a couple dozen death threats regarding a few of my articles in *Counterpunch* that criticized the Anglo-American invasion and occupation of Iraq, including a piece entitled "Rape of Iraq."
[117] The full story of how this insanely jealous cuckold hogtied me with UPS plastic packing ties and almost killed Max and me will be explained in gory detail in the upcoming memoir.
[118] The amazing French high-wire aerialist, Philippe Petit, walked, and even danced, on a wire between the World Trade Center Twin Towers in 1974... much crazier and far more impressive than climbing a bridge!

down, I saw clear, peaceful darkness, like an enormous pile of soft, black pillow-clouds. I felt keenly aware of how effortless and natural it would be to quit all that strenuous swinging through the storm and just let go of that pathetic, fraying vine. Then I would simply and gracefully fall down, down, down into the dark, invitingly restful Valley of Death, never to resurface again. Oh, how easy it would be to just fall... My inner bonobo trembled and shook, but somehow, weak as she was, she kept on swinging.

Meanwhile, in the outside world, against all odds, my condition was improving, so the doctors began lowering my morphine-ketamine dosage. As the drugs decreased, the memories rushed back, including a recollection of suddenly taking ill, which explained what I was doing in the hospital. I was still awfully uncomfortable and utterly immobile, unsure if I would ever walk, speak or even breathe on my own again, but I was alive, and something in me was determined to stay alive even though my life seemed almost as bleak as (and a lot less restful than) death. That damned rubber fire hose down my throat didn't help either.

Then suddenly, one fine morning, I felt my inner bonobo bouncing up, up and out of the darkness like a girl on a trampoline, toward radiant, heavenly gates that swung open to greet me. Was I finally dying and witnessing the famous NDE "flash of light" at the end of life's tunnel? No, it was just the quivering fluorescent beams from the ICU ceiling and the feeling of pure, sweet air filling my poor, violated throat as my latex-gloved, masked master (a.k.a. my nurse) removed the hellish breathing tube. Heaven or hell on Earth, as bad as all that guttural agony had been, that's how good my newly freed esophagus felt, bursting with joy greater than a thousand *Deep Throat*[119] orgasms... except this profound pleasure was in evacuation, not penetration. But who cares? I was swinging—and breathing—free. I was also well on my way to what my excellent team of USC doctors (with special kudos to the wonderful Dr. John Klutke) would call a "miraculous" and complete recovery.

"Do Not Put Anything in Your Vagina"

Release from the evil tracheal intubation was a major step back into the land of the living, but there was another month of excruciating recuperation before the hospital would release me. I was just starting to

---

[119] In the original *Deep Throat* film, the main character, played by Linda Lovelace, is said to have her clitoris in her throat, which is why the only way she can climax is through giving oral sex to well-endowed men.

feel "human" and looking forward to a little hardcore conjugal reunion when my doctor informed me that for the next eight weeks I was to have "no sex." Most patients might nod and leave it at that (whether or not they would follow doctors' orders is another story), but I insisted on clarification. You should too, if and when you find yourself in a similar situation. Due to a woeful lack of sex education in most medical schools, many doctors are not comfortable bringing up sexual issues. But if you ask questions, they will usually answer them. Of course, they may not give you the answers you want to hear, as I discovered that hot summer day of my release.

"Do not," he specified, "put anything in your vagina."

This was unfortunate, because I love to put things in my vagina, and at that point, it was actually one of the few parts of my body that felt okay. It seemed ironic and unfair that my throat had been so violated with a large phallic object, and now the orifice that would welcome one was being shut down like a Detroit automotive plant during a recession. But these doctors had just saved my life as surely as my inner bonobo had, so I was not about to disobey them in my infirm state. That didn't stop me, however, from panicking that I might never have sex again.

After a festive Bonoboville homecoming, the hubby and I retired to our private quarters, at which point tears started drenching my pillow as I "mourned" my now-officially-dead sex life. Poor Pr. Max didn't know what to do. He had stayed by my side virtually every minute of this crazy, harrowing NDE, tirelessly helping me and the nurses, leaving the hospital only to take showers. And now here I was, back home, on the mend and in our bed. He was ready to celebrate! And I couldn't stop crying. "What can I do to help you feel better?" he asked gamely.

I was tempted to retort "nothing" so I could continue stewing in self-pity, but he looked so adorable, sitting on the edge of the bed in his boxers, I had to smile. Then I remembered the "doctor's orders" of "no sex," and started bawling again.

Of course, Max took this personally. He sighed, got up off the bed and went for the door. I started to run after him before I realized I couldn't walk. "Wait!" I gasped, taking a deep healing breath and doing the Stoic exercise of putting myself in his shoes (or, in this case, shorts), realizing how lousy I'd feel if he'd been the one blubbering as I offered to help him feel better while wearing nothing but a pair of panties. My inner bonobo decided to make amends.

"You could take off the shorts," I suggested, in answer to his earlier question. That made him turn around. It also made him take off the shorts. It also made me happy, though I still wasn't quite sure where I was going with this. I left that up to my hands and mouth, which pretty much took over as soon as he crawled into bed with me.

Thus, I made a very personal discovery of something the ancients had long known: Deprivation is the wicked but very effective stepmother of invention. With my own genitalia in medical lock-down, my hands and mouth became orgasmic. I was happy to make my befuddled husband the beneficiary of this sexual revelation as long as he maneuvered himself into position (strategically placed pillows and a *Liberator Shape*[120] wedge helped here) since I was about as mobile as a mushroom.

It wasn't the best blowjob I've given, but it was among the most meaningful. Part of the fun was sharing a transgressive thrill. Even though we weren't putting anything in my vagina, we were, in a sense, flaunting the doctors' orders of "no sex." Plus it helped get the bad taste of that awful intubator out of my mouth. Mainly, I was just happy to be physically sexual again. It may not have helped me survive, but it helped bring me back to life. I felt my inner bonobo's favorite swinging vines growing strong and lush again within me.

In an interview with Psychotherapy.net, Dr. Esther Perel talks about growing up in a community of Holocaust survivors where "there were two groups: those who didn't die, and those who came back to life. And those who didn't die were people who lived tethered to the ground, afraid, untrusting. The world was dangerous, and pleasure was not an option... Those who came back to life were those who understood eroticism as an antidote to death."

In the throes of sepsis, and even in convalescence, dying often seemed a lot more appealing than simply "not dying." What I needed was to come back to life. Eroticism (and sloppy blowjobs) was the lifeline that kept my inner bonobo swinging.

Bonobo Yoga Gets You Ready to Swing

Now that my yoni is back in the sack again, I've returned to my preference for good old vaginal intercourse (with many side dishes), but those initial nights of sex after my illness were all about oral. This being

---

[120] *Liberator Shapes* are special hard pillows used for sexual positions, great for erotic athletics as well as folks with disabilities.

the first time in over a month that Max had a hand, let alone a mouth, to help him along, it wasn't surprising that he enjoyed himself, but what it did for me was a revelation. Not that I don't normally like giving head, but this time, my mouth, tongue and hands really went bonobos. I could feel his pleasure. Moreover, it totally killed my own pain, at least for a little while. I already knew that sex was a natural painkiller, but I thought it was mainly about having orgasms and receiving pleasure. On a very personal level, I discovered that giving sexual pleasure is as effective as morphine, or at least half a Vicodin. Erotic touch releases painkilling chemicals (oxytocin instead of Oxycontin), whether you're the toucher or the touchee. In a sense, giving *is* receiving. It's the Bonobo Way.

Any kind of orgasmic activity, playful outercourse or eroplay floods your body with nourishing endorphins and enlivening hormones that heal pain, reduce stress, boost your immune system, improve cardiac health, combat depression, induce deep relaxation, lower the risk of many cancers, improve your mood, *and* make you smarter. All in all, erotic, affectionate touch is a rejuvenation treatment. This is one of the "secrets" of the bonobo Fountain of Youth. Lots of good sex, erotic play and intensive cuddling helps make older bonobos look and act much younger longer than their chimpanzee counterparts who seem to grow grumpier with the passing years. Which way will you choose?

Whether or not regular sex and eroplay actually reduce your wrinkles, they certainly help to keep you young-at-heart and in shape to spring (or swing) into action when the time comes. And it will come... often when you least expect it, like when you're just blogging along to one of your favorite songs. Then suddenly, the music changes, and a strong gust blows you right off your high bridge. Will you be able to grab a vine and swing with it?

If you've never released your inner bonobo before, it may not be so easy to swing into action at crisis time. Constricted old habits can ossify into stagnant inertia. BLT can help you to release and reboot and regain your momentum. So can many other therapies and programs (bonobos aren't the only swingers), as well as simple experience, the mother of maturity.

One way to stay youthful and swing-ready is to do your daily dose of bonobo yoga. That is, the more you practice these 12 Steps on a regular basis, the easier it will be for your inner bonobo to swing into action at a moment's notice... when it might literally save your life.

Step 12: Save the Bonobos, Save the World.

Saving your life is important, to say the least. So is saving other human lives whenever possible. Every human life is precious beyond measure, especially when it's someone you love. But numbers-wise, there are more than enough humans inhabiting planet Earth right now, and we keep multiplying. In contrast, there are very few bonobos, and their numbers keep dwindling. The tragic irony is that just as many of us are discovering our kissing cousins, we are coming very close to losing them forever. Your BLC, the most ecologically important, immediate, critical challenge facing all of us right now, is to keep *Pan paniscus* from going extinct.

This is no easy challenge to meet. The current risk of extinction for bonobos is extremely high according to the International Union for Conservation of Nature (IUCN) Red List and the lists of every other conservation organization. The estimates on how many bonobos are left waver considerably, but at most, there are less than 10,000-50,000 bonobos in their natural habitat in the Congolese jungle (as opposed to 170,000-300,000 common chimpanzees in the wild), plus the few hundred scattered around zoos, sanctuaries and primate centers throughout the world (compared with several thousand captive chimps). Talk about precious.

"Heart of Darkness"

Bonobos are native only to the Democratic Republic of Congo (DRC), a country that rarely makes headline news, though for over a decade it has suffered some of the bloodiest wars on Earth since World War II. Over five million people have died as a direct result of massacres, mass starvation and disease in the DRC, and many millions more have been displaced.

Called Zaire under the corrupt 32-year reign of that infamous old leopard-capped dictator, Mobutu Sese Seko, the current DRC is the formerly enslaved nation of the Congo that was essentially a fiefdom of King Leopold of Belgium. The Belgian monarch turned the Congo into his own private, personally aggrandizing "Heart of Darkness,"[121] the

---

[121] Joseph Conrad's classic novel of this name details some of the destruction wrought by colonialism.

devastating effects of which still handicap this vast, resource-rich country today. The awful, complicated wars in and around the DRC must be understood in the context of its history of ruthless exploitation by Europe, the United States and, more recently, China. In other words, this is not just an "African problem," but an international crisis. We are all responsible.

The fallout from wars in neighboring countries, notably Rwanda, contributes to the devastation of the bonobos' natural habitat in the world's second largest rainforest. So does the logging industry and the mining of diamonds, gold, granite and many other minerals, some of which can only be found in this highly exploited region. Coltan, short for "columbite-tantalite," is one of the most sought-after minerals in the DRC since it is a vital component in the capacitors that control flow in our smart phone circuit boards and other cherished pieces of cellular equipment.

But the worst, most immediate, lethal danger to wild bonobos is poaching. Not only is human commerce destroying their natural habitat, but human hunters are literally killing bonobos one by one, sometimes slaughtering a whole tribe in one bloodbath. Though it's against Congolese law, the criminal massacre of bonobos and other endangered species continues. Some of these hunters and their families are starving and just trying to feed themselves in a land where livestock is scarce and expensive. Or they may sell the "bushmeat" for a premium on the black market where restaurants feature grilled bonobo on a special secret menu, as described in deeply disturbing detail in Dale Peterson and Karl Ammann's *Eating Apes*. Rebels sometimes force local people into the forest to kill bonobos, holding their families ransom unless the reluctant hunters come home with fresh bushmeat.

BCI & the Bonobo Peace Forest

Despite the grim situation, hope is on the rainforest horizon in the form of some hard-working, visionary conservationists. One group, the Bonobo Conservation Initiative (BCI), under the direction of my old friend, the luminous and indefatigable Sally Jewell Coxe, a.k.a. "Mama Bonobo," is making remarkable strides in sustainable conservation and education in the Congo, much of it lovingly detailed in Béchard's *Empty Hands, Open Arms*.

I've watched BCI grow from a gleam in Sally's green eyes (when she was first on my show in 1997) to an active, award-winning, international organization that's making a real difference in the future of bonobos, as well as other wildlife and human life in the region, and becoming a model for a new kind of inclusive, very bonoboësque conservation. With grassroots support and help from DRC President Joseph Kabila, BCI is expanding a constellation of linked community-based reserves called the "Bonobo Peace Forest" to over 12,000 square miles including Kanō's original research station at Wamba where many bonobos were lost during the wars.

Unlike a park where no humans are supposed to live except the park rangers (though poachers can and do still break in illegally), a reserve contains people, even whole villages. This way, nobody gets evicted when the conservationists move in. Hunting bonobos is prohibited and policed with a lot more personal vigor on the reserve than it is in a park. The idea is for the villagers to protect "their" wild bonobos in the forests surrounding their village. Some are paid administrative staff and trackers with BCI or its local partner, *Vie Sauvage*, while the rest of the villagers benefit in other ways.

Sally and her partner Michael Hurley modeled BCI on actual bonobo society, putting a strong focus on taking care of each individual staff member and volunteer, regardless of their roles. Even a staff member's relatives can receive help and care. This way, by helping the bonobos, the villagers can directly *witness* the bonobos through BCI, reciprocally helping them by providing much-needed food, medicine and education, in addition to paying the salaries of the local people who work in the clinics and schools as well as BCI offices and outposts.

It's important to note that the education flows both ways. Sally speaks fluent Lingala and works closely with tribal chiefs and village mamas, as well as with dynamic Congolese conservationists like Albert Lokasola of Kokolopori and André Tusumba of Sankuru. She learns at least as much from the Bongandu people and other Congolese about bonobos and the rainforest as she's learned from the many prominent scientists with whom she's also worked.

It's the bonobos, however, that taught her the most. "I learned more about my own nature reading about great apes than in years of psychology courses," she tells Deni Béchard in *Empty Hands, Open Arms*. "In bonobos, I saw a creature so much like us, one that has learned to cooperate—the closest thing to us on the planet, mirroring a side of ourselves that we often ignore."

In one of Sally's favorite Bongandu folktales, a Mongandu[122] villager finds himself stuck at the top of a tall tree after he accidentally drops his rope. Along swings a bonobo, almost scaring the man out of the tree. Before he falls, the bonobo catches the man and carries him on his back carefully down to safety on the ground where the two part company. Time passes and some of the Mongandu's fellow villagers come upon a troop of bonobos feasting on their sugarcane crop just before harvest. The furious villagers catch the bonobos in a net and are just about to kill them when the man who the bonobo rescued from the tree picks up the edge of the net and lets all the bonobos escape into the forest. The villagers become livid! But the Mongandu man calms them down, telling them the story of how his life was saved by a bonobo. The Bongandu villagers are so impressed, they promise never to harm a bonobo again.

That promise must never be broken. Retelling ancient folktales like this is as at least as effective as scientific reports and endangered species lists in inspiring people to protect their bonobos especially when you add in financial incentives and respect for local traditions like in BCI scenarios. BCI is a small but powerful conservation organization, fostering the very bonoboësque quality of positive reciprocity, so all can benefit from working together to protect bonobos from poaching and other hazards.

Unfortunately, the wheels of NGO[123] funding turn very slowly and all too often in adverse directions. Though BCI works wonders with its tiny budget, the poaching continues, and each bonobo killed is a tragedy, especially since, despite all that sex, bonobos don't reproduce very quickly. Like humans, bonobos have rather large brains, the development of which requires slow growth, capping their reproduction rates.[124] This is yet another reason why every bonobo life is so valuable.

Claudine André: Saint Joan of the Bonobos

Besides shooting mature bonobos for their bushmeat, poachers also capture baby bonobos, usually the sons and daughters of the adults that they've killed. Since these babies don't have much meat on their tiny

---

[122] "Mongandu" is the singular term for an individual member of a Bongandu tribe.
[123] An NGO is a Non-Governmental Organization, typically a non-profit.
[124] Like bonobos, prehistoric humans reproduced at a much lower rate than many people do today. Thanks to the "benefits" of agriculture and the pressures of certain social groups, we live in an age of "Octomoms" that we are not anatomically or emotionally equipped to handle.

bones, the hunters try to sell them as pets to wildlife traffickers, disreputable zoos[125] or ignorant animal lovers who toss them after the age of five. The United Nations Environment Program (UNEP) *Stolen Apes* report tells the story of a couple caught on an Air France flight trying to smuggle an infant bonobo in a handbag into Russia. Hunters without buyers or smuggling prospects often just leave the babies to die by the side of the road. It's a dire situation reminiscent of a Charles Dickens novel.

But thank goodness, within this *Bleak House*[126] there is another angelic heroine, a true savior of orphans I call Saint Joan of the Bonobos. Claudine André is a French-Belgian native who spent most of her life in the Congo where she raised a family of five before she discovered her extended family of fellow apes. Like Joan of Arc, Claudine is a born leader, combining tough masculine assertiveness with deep feminine warmth and irresistible charisma. But unlike the martyred Saint Joan, Claudine is a survivor. She's been through wars, lootings and massacres. She saw her house ransacked by rebels who, moments before, had slaughtered her next-door neighbors, but left Claudine and her family alive when she and her husband Victor graciously invited them to take everything, even stripping the pipes from the walls. Through it all, nothing has stopped Claudine's flow as she swings like an alpha mama bonobo from one crisis to another, sheltering the weak and commandeering the strong, a halo of sunset-red hair framing her pretty but purposeful face.

Like me, Claudine didn't know bonobos from bamboo until 1993[127] when she volunteered at the Kinshasa Zoo, and someone handed her a sick baby bonobo orphan named Mikeno. Claudine noticed that Mikeno needed much more constant care than the common chimps, but whatever warmth and affection she gave him, he returned and more, his scrawny little arms embracing her body as his big brown eyes engulfed her soul. So began Claudine's love affair with *Pan paniscus* and her focused effort on saving them, one orphaned baby at a time.

For a while, she didn't even have space for them. At one point,

---

[125] No reputable zoos get their bonobos directly from Africa anymore. Instead, they trade with each other with an attempt to reflect natural migration practices.
[126] A tip of my bowler hat to Dickens, renowned champion of orphans.
[127] Careful readers may note that this is the same year I discovered bonobos on PBS, though Claudine's story of saving Mikeno is much more impressive than my tale of being enlightened by my boob tube.

Claudine was keeping as many as eleven bonobos in her garage.[128] Somehow, with a mix of diplomacy, ingenuity and miraculous luck, she acquired a 90-acre piece of primary forest just outside Kinshasa, the capitol of the DRC. Ironically, the very same woodland property was once Mobutu's favorite weekend getaway. Claudine called her leafy green sanctuary *Lola Ya Bonobo*, which means "Bonobo Paradise" in Lingala. She transformed the land into an oasis for orphaned bonobos (including that baby in the handbag that was almost smuggled into Russia), and since that time she has been expertly nurturing these little refugees until they are strong enough to be released back into the wild.

It's no easy task. Most of the orphans aren't just sick, starving and scared, but also deeply traumatized by having witnessed their mothers' murders. Can you imagine how they feel? Go back to Step 2: Be a Bonobo, and try to visualize what they have been through. Rumor has it that sometimes when an adult bonobo sees a hunter aim his rifle, she claps her hands together, then holds out one palm, wiggling her fingers in a begging motion, as if pleading for her life. Of course, this poignant last request is rarely granted.

Envision your mother begging to be spared, while you cling to her breast or ride on her big strong back, just before a bushmeat poacher shoots her dead. Or imagine you're the mom, swinging through life with hedonic simian *savoire faire,* when boom—in one terrible flash, you're gone, leaving your children alone to starve or be further victimized.

Take on this BLC with care. It can be a very disturbing exercise, if you're doing it right, as I learned when I related the scene to an audience of sexologists at an SSSS conference. There I was, clapping and reaching out to the room like a wild bonobo in a tree, begging for my life from the poacher's gun, when suddenly I choked up as if I really had been shot. How embarrassing! At least I wasn't actually being blasted out of my tree, and my voice returned within seconds, but still. Thankfully, my audience forgave me. At least I think they did. Who can't relate to the awful pathos of being shot, or seeing your beloved mama struck dead for the sake of someone else's barbaric notion of gourmet cuisine?

If We Lose the Bonobos, We Lose Part of Ourselves

But this is just one among many traumatic scenarios that bonobo

---

[128] Fortunately for the bonobos, Victor is a wonderfully indulgent husband, half-Italian (like my Max) and half-Tutsi.

orphans endure before arriving at Lola Ya Bonobo. Interestingly, while common chimp babies who go through similar ordeals almost always survive if they make it to a chimp sanctuary, bonobo refugees tend to be more fragile. Sometimes, despite the best of care, they simply fail to rally. Perhaps one painful consequence of being sensitive and "spoiled" by a gentle, peaceful, loving community within an abundant environment is greater difficulty coping with the cold-blooded murder of loved ones and the harsh aftermath of separation.

After all, high levels of sensitivity are as much a part of what it means to be bonobo as sexuality. This has its distinct downside in our often-brutal civilization that bonobos are forced to experience as they are increasingly exposed to us. Toward the end of World War II, when the Allies were bombing Dresden, there were chimps and bonobos in a zoo nearby. Though the bombs didn't hit the zoo, the deafening sounds of explosions thundered through the whole area. After the attack, zookeepers found that the chimps were okay, but that all the bonobos had died of heart attacks, presumably from sheer fright.

Not that bonobo sensitivity, empathy or sexuality has much to do with their Red List status as a highly endangered species, and don't let any bonobo-bashers tell you it does. Bonobos survived and thrived as a species for almost a million years undisturbed in their native, food-rich habitat deep within the rainforest. But in just the last few decades, human civilization has severely encroached upon bonobo life, coming dangerously close to snuffing it out. If I had to sum up bonobo problems with one slogan, it would be:

It's the humans, stupid![129]

Digging for treasure and waging war, humans cut roads into previously pristine jungles, devastating wildlife along the way. If it weren't for these highways of hominid ingenuity, *Homo sapiens* may never have discovered *Pan paniscus*, which would be a shame for you and me and our partners. But in discovering them, we have invaded their territory in a manner that is destroying them. Can we stop this speeding train? We have to try. You might say that we owe it to our kissing cousins—and to ourselves—to save them from extinction.

---

[129] A variation of "(it's) the economy, stupid!" the phrase made famous by James Carville, campaign strategist for Bill Clinton's 1992 run for the Oval Office.

Of course, dolphins, Asian buffalo, cheetahs, spotted owls and all other endangered species deserve our efforts too. But bonobos are so close to humans. They are a living piece of our own heritage, and they hold such a vital key to unlocking the better parts of human nature. If we lose them, we lose a very precious part of ourselves that we can never ever get back.

As with these 12 Steps, it's all about release. The culmination of Claudine's plan for the rescued bonobo orphans is releasing them back into the wild. She does this in a forest area three times the size of Manhattan that is inhabited by the Ilonga Pô tribe. The Pô seem to be the ideal guardians for the newly released bonobo "graduates" of Claudine's school for survival. Unlike many other tribes, the Pô aren't much for hunting, as they are primarily fishermen along the Maringa and Lopori Rivers. Like all *Pan paniscus* relationships and the work of BCI, Lola's association with the Pô is one of reciprocal benefit. In the Pô village of Basankusu, someone has painted these words in blue across the side of a building:

Nous Protegeons Bonobos et Bonobos Nous Sauvera
We Protect Bonobos and Bonobos Will Save Us

In this case, the ideal and the real almost match up. The Pô underwent terrible poverty and collateral damage as soldiers and rebels occupied their capital and proceeded to massacre each other and anyone who got in their way. But as of this writing, the Pô are living in peace, soldier-free, rebel-free and practically gun-free. In appreciation for their guardianship of the newly released bonobos in the forest that surrounds their villages, Lola supporters around the world provide medicine for the Pô clinic, supplies for their schools and support for their soccer team, the "Bonobos of Basankusu," which won a provincial championship in 2009.

In a sense, the bonobos are teaching the Pô the Bonobo Way. As Vanessa Woods reports in *Bonobo Handshake*, "Schoolchildren learn that when bonobos get angry, they hug. Women hear that together, bonobo females are strong. Men understand that it is possible to live a life without war."

Imagine how the world might evolve if we all took the Pô approach, protecting the bonobos and practicing the Bonobo Way? We can do it. We humans have successfully rallied around saving the whales, the whooping crane, the American crocodile and many other endangered species. Why not rally in a big, viral way around our closest genetic cousins, who have so much to teach us and may even hold the key to peace on Earth?

A Cause That's Right and Sexy

Your BLC is to step up to the plate and do whatever you can to help save our frisky family members from extinction. Yes, some folks are squeamish about bonobo sexuality, and many of the richest charities, NGOs and even some of the big conservation groups are controlled (politically and monetarily) by the most puritanical of individuals and corporations. Therefore, I call upon my brothers and sisters in the erotic arts and sexual sciences—from university sexology departments to sexy superstars to mom 'n' pop swinger shops to silent souls self-pleasuring in the dark—to pick up the slack. Take the bonobo as your personal totem or spirit animal, your symbol of peace through pleasure, empathy under pressure, girl power forever or whatever peels your banana, and pitch in now to help save them from extinction.

"Why should I?" you may ask yourself, wallowing in the depressed but reassuringly familiar discomfort of your personal sinkhole. "What does saving an obscure ape have to do with my lousy love life?" If you can't answer that question, you'd better read this book all over again. Or just consider these simple words that Sally shared with Deni Béchard when he asked her how she tolerates the insanely tough conditions of the DRC and the challenge of saving bonobos: "I remember hearing people say that if you're depressed, help someone else and it will make you feel better on the simplest level."

"As we work to heal the Earth," writes eco-philosopher Dr. Joanna Macy in *World as Lover, World as Self*, "the Earth heals us."

Help the bonobos and your love life will improve, if for no other reason than you'll get that erotic "glow" from knowing you did something good, supporting a cause that's both right and sexy. This step involves releasing your inner bonobo to perform the kind of compassionate generosity that really makes a difference in the world. That means grabbing that nice, big, thick wallet of yours or clicking into your PayPal account and giving freely.

There are various ways you can help. Support the Bonobo Peace Forest. Adopt a bonobo orphan or a whole orphanage. Iconic French actress and animal activist Brigitte Bardot built a playground at Lola for the babies to swing and frolic. Even if you can't afford a swing set, give what you can. If you don't have the cash, donate your time. Volunteer with bonobo conservation groups. It's a great way to get outside of yourself and your problems and gain the perspective you need to deal with them. You can also meet other cool volunteers who practice the Bonobo Way in their own unique ways. Educate yourself on environmental issues and vote for politicians who support conservation policies and ask them specifically to help the bonobos. Help spread #bonobo in your real and virtual lives. Get everyone you know in your Bonoboville to do what they can to save our kissing cousins from extinction. Be creative. Give away the Bonobo Way in any way you can.

This is the last step of the program. But in many ways, it's number one. Unlike most 12-step programs, you needn't follow all 12 steps, and you don't have to go in order. In fact, if you only have time in your busy life for one step, this is the one to take before the others, preferably right now, before it's too late. If enough of us meet this BLC, we can do it. We can stop the poaching. We can turn this tide of human destruction. We can save the bonobos.

Help the Bonobos & They Will Reciprocate

I was deeply touched by *Bonobo Handshake* author Vanessa Woods' story of how she, Claudine André and the Lola Ya Bonobo "Mamas," the local women who take care of orphaned bonobos as if they were their own babies, worked together day and night to save one particular little baby bonobo girl named Kata. Little Kata did so well she was soon helping other newcomer bonobos. I wanted to do my part to support her, so I visited friendsofbonobos.com and adopted Kata. Considering that she was still up for "adoption" a year later, I figure she must have at least a few hundred adoptive parents by now. I hope she gets a few million. If it takes a village to raise a child, it might take the whole world to save the bonobos.

Whatever it takes, they are worth it! After all, their reciprocity will help us save ourselves.

Epilogue: Go Forth and Go Bonobos

That's it, brothers and sisters, lovers and sinners! That's the Bonobo Way. Written for humans, it is inspired by the amazing bonobo apes, our kissing cousins who swing through the trees as well as with each other, and who often seem more human—and humane—than many people.

May these stories, studies, steps, images, fantasies and ideas arouse, invigorate, tickle and challenge you to release your inner bonobo, go bonobos in bed and beyond, explore the erotic theater of the mind, practice anger management bonobo-style, love the Earth you make love on, swing through the jungles of life with panache, make sperm wars not real wars, help save the real bonobos from imminent extinction and maybe even help save humanity from insanity. If a bunch of baboons can go bonobos, we can too.

Thank you for taking this journey with me, from the lush depths of the rainforest to the satin sheets of our bedrooms. I hope you've enjoyed exploring the secrets of the bonobos, their remarkable eco-sexuality, deep empathy, fountain of youth, healing reciprocity, their erotic, playful, gender-egalitarian lifestyle and their extraordinary ability to make peace through pleasure. I imagine you've liberated (or at least fantasized about liberating) your inner bonobo in some of the ways suggested in this book. Or perhaps you have some ways of your own you'd like to share. If so, I'd love to hear about them.

And if the bonoboësque spirit moves you, come join us in Bonoboville as we wake up and shake up the world to a new way of doing business that's really a very old way to play. This is the Bonobo Way, the way of love, not war, the way of peace through pleasure. This is the way of the future, if there is to be a future, for all of us.

Appendix A:

Where You Can Help

Here are some places where you can donate to help save the real bonobos in the rainforest:

Lola Ya Bonobo
http://www.friendsofbonobos.org/

Bonobo Conservation Initiative
http://bonobo.org

Bonobo Hope
http://www.bonobohope.org

Bonobo Species Survival Plan
http://www.zoosociety.org/Conservation/Bonobo/

African Wildlife Foundation (AWF)
http://www.awf.org/projects/lomako-conservation-science-center

Lomako Forest Bonobo Project
http://blogs.uoregon.edu/fwhite/bonobo-research/sample-page-2/

City of Joy: Power to Women and Girls of the Democratic Republic of Congo
http://drc.vday.org/city-of-joy

World Wildlife Fund (WWF)
http://worldwildlife.org/species/bonobo

Block Bonobo Foundation
http://blockbonobofoundation.org

The Dr. Susan Block Institute and Block Bonobo Foundation are dedicated to protecting, promoting and researching bonobo chimpanzees, as well as educating people in the Bonobo Way: that is, how these great apes use pleasure to maintain peace and gender balance in their societies, and how we can learn something from them about sex, love and peace on Earth.

To find out more about the Block Institute and Block Bonobo Foundation, call us anytime at 310.568.0066

Join us in Bonoboville, our new online community of ethical hedonists, friends and lovers:
http://bonoboville.com

Appendix B:

Where You Can See Bonobos around the World

United Kingdom:
Twycross Zoo: World Primate Centre

North America:
Columbus, OH
The Columbus Zoo

San Diego, CA
San Diego Zoo (See Lana and her mates here!)

Cincinnati, OH
Cincinnati Zoo

Jacksonville, FL
Jacksonville Zoo

Des Moines, IA
Bonobo Hope Sanctuary

Fort Worth, TX
Fort Worth Zoo

Memphis, TN
Memphis Zoo

Milwaukee, WI
Bonobo Conservation

Mexico:
Parque Zoologico Benito Juarez

Europe:

Planckendael/Antwerp, Netherlands
Netherlands Zoo

Europe Collaborative
European Association of Zoos and Aquarium

Berlin, Germany
Zoo Berlin

Cologne, Germany
Kolner Zoo

Belgium
Apen Heul

Frankfurt, Germany
Zoo Frankfurt

Leipzig, Germany
Zoo Leipzig

Stuttgart, Germany
Wilhelma Zoo

Democratic Republic of Congo:

Kokolopori
Kokolopori Reserve
Les Petites Chutes de la Lukaya
Lola Ya Bonobo

Kinshasa
Bonobo Congo and Biodiversity Initiative

Acronyms & Abbreviations

AASECT	American Association of Sexuality Educators, Counselors and Therapists
AOL	America Online, Chapter 2
ASMR	Autonomous Sensory Meridian Response, Step 10
BCI	Bonobo Conservation Initiative, Step 12
BDSM	Bondage & Discipline (BD), Dominance & Submission (DS), Sadism & Masochism (SM), Chapter 14
BJ	Blowjob, Chapter 5
BLC	Bonobo Liberation Challenge, Chapter 15
BLT	Bonobo Liberation Therapy, Chapter 1
BLZ	Bonobo Liberation Zone, Step 3
CEO	Chief Executive Officer, Step 6
DMZ	Demilitarized Zone, Step 9
DNA	Deoxyribonucleic acid, Chapter 3
DRC	Democratic Republic of Congo, Chapter 3
EI	Emotional Intelligence, Chapter 3
EQ	Emotional Quotient, Chapter 3
E.T.	Extra-Terrestrial, also the name of a 1982 Steven Spielberg film, Chapter 12
GG	Genito-Genital, Chapter 10
G-spot	Gräfenberg Spot or Goddess Spot, Step 2
HBO	Home Box Office, Chapter 1
HR	Human Resources, Step 9
ICU	Intensive Care Unit, Step 11
IQ	Intelligence Quotient, Chapter 3
IUCN	International Union for Conservation of Nature, Step 12
LAPD	Los Angeles Police Department, Step 10
LGBTQ	Lesbian, Gay, Bi-Sexual, Transgender, Queer, Chapter 14

LOA	Law Of Attraction, Step 8
MFM	Male, Female, Male threesome, Chapter 11
MIC	Military Industrial Complex, Part II
MILF	Mother I'd Like to Fuck, Chapter 9
NDE	Near Death Experience, Step 11
NGO	Non-Governmental Organization, Step 12
NRE	New Relationship Energy, Step 9
OM	Orgasmic Meditation, Step 2
ORE	Old Relationship Energy, Step 9
PBS	Public Broadcasting Service, Chapter 1
PC	Pubococcygeus muscles, Step 3
PDA	Public Display of Affection, Step 10
PIC	Prison Industrial Complex, Chapter 13
PIE	Profound Interspecies Event, Chapter 12
PIV	Penis-In-Vagina intercourse, Chapter 4
Pr.	Prince, Chapter 1
P-spot	Prostate, a.k.a. "the male G-spot." Chapter 14
PTSD	Post-Traumatic Stress Disorder, Chapter 13
REI	Rational Emotive Imagery, Step 8
SQ	Sexual Intelligence, Step 7
SSRI	Selective Serotonin Re-Uptake Inhibitor, Step 5
SSSS	Society for the Scientific Study of Sexuality, Step 12
STD	Sexually Transmitted Disease, Step 4
SUV	Sport Utility Vehicle, Step 7
T3	Triiodothyronine, Chapter 9
TED	Technology, Entertainment, Design lecture series, Chapter 9
TS	Transsexual, Photos Part 3
UNEP	United Nations Environment Program, Step 12
USC	University of Southern California, Step 11
WWF	World Wildlife Fund, Appendix I

Bibliography

Books, Periodicals & Websites

Abramson, P. (2010). *Sex Appeal: Six Ethical Principles for the 21st Century*. New York, NY: Oxford University Press.

Alston, C. (2012). *Hotwifing: Whether to Try It, Ways to Go About It, How to Handle It*. Austin, TX: Bold Type Press.

Anapol, Dr. D. M. (1997). *Polyamory: The New Love Without Limits: Secrets of Sustainable Intimate Relationships*. San Rafael, CA: Io Resource Center.

Anderlini-D'Onofrio, S. (2009). *Gaia and the New Politics of Love: Notes for a Poly Planet*. Berkeley, CA: North Atlantic Books.

André, C. (2006). *Une Tendresse Sauvage*. Paris: Calmann-Levy.

Angier, N. (1997, April 22). Bonobo society: Amicable, amorous and run by females. *The New York Times*. Retrieved from http://www.nytimes.com/1997/04/22/science/bonobo-society-amicable-amorous-and-run-by-females.html

Baker, N. (2011). *House of Holes: A Book of Raunch*. New York, NY: Simon & Schuster.

Baker, R. (2006). *Sperm Wars: Infidelity, Sexual Conflict, and Other Bedroom Battles* (Revised Edition). New York, NY: Basic Books.

Barbach, L. G. (Editor). (1985). *Pleasures: Women Write Erotica*. New York, NY: William Morrow Paperbacks.

Bataille, G. (1962). *Eroticism, Death and Sensuality*. New York, NY: Walker and Company.

Béchard, D. (2013). *Empty Hands, Open Arms: The Race to Save Bonobos in the Congo and Make Conservation Go Viral*. Minneapolis, MN: Milkweed Editions.

Bell, D. (2007, March 8). Ape returns fingertip to keeper. U-T San Diego. Retrieved from http://legacy.utsandiego.com/news/metro/bell/20070308-9999-1m8bell.html

Benjamin, M. & Evans, J. (Editors). (2005). *Stop the Next War Now: Effective Responses to Violence and Terrorism*. Maui, HI: New World Library.

Bergner, D. (2013). *What Do Women Want? Adventures in the Science of Female Desire*. New York, NY: Harper Collins.

Block, I. (1914). *Handbuch der gesamten Sexualwissenschaft in Einzeldarstellungen* (Handbook of Sexuality in Its Entirety). Berlin: Louis Marcus Verlagsbuchhandlung.

Block, J. (2008). *Open: Love, Sex and Life in an Open Marriage*. Berkeley, CA. Seal Press.

Block, S. (1996). *The 10 Commandments of Pleasure: Erotic Keys to a Healthy Sexual Life*. New York, NY: St. Martin's Press.

Block, S. (2007, July 25). *Bonobo bashing in the New Yorker*. CounterPunch.org Retrieved from http://www.counterpunch.org/2007/07/25/bonobo-bashing-in-the-new-yorker/

Block, S. (2014, July 29). *Dawn of the Planet of the Apes Defames Bonobos*. CounterPunch.org. Retrieved from http://www.counterpunch.org/2014/07/14/dawn-of-the-planet-of-the-apes-defames-bonobos/

Blue, V. (2011). *Fetish Sex: A Complete Guide to Sexual Fetishes*. San Francisco, CA: Digita Publications.

Borenstein, S. (2012, June 13). 'Hippie chimp' genome may shed light on our dark side. *The Associated Press*. Retrieved from http://www.nbcnews.com/id/47800795/ns/technology_and_science-science/t/hippie-chimp-genome-may-shed-light-our-dark-side/ - .U41d8flkTsa

Boteach, S. (2000). *Kosher Sex: A Recipe for Passion and Intimacy*. New York, NY: Harmony.

Boteach, S. (2002). *Kosher Adultery: Seduce and Sin with Your Spouse*. New York, NY: Adams Media Corporation.

Boteach, S. (2010). *The Kosher Sutra: Eight Sacred Secrets for Reigniting Desire and Restoring Passion for Life*. New York: HarperOne.

Bright, S. (1997). *The Sexual State of the Union*. New York, NY: Touchstone Publishing.

Broderick, R. (2013, January 13). *Our very own settler problem: America's Culture-of-Gun-Deaths*. Ground Zero, Daily Planet. Retrieved from http://www.tcdailyplanet.net/blog/rich-broderick/our-very-own-settler-problem-america-s-culture-death

Bussell, R. K. (Editor). (2013). *Best Sex Writing 2013: The State of Today's Sexual Culture*. Berkeley, CA: Cleiss Press.

Byrne, R. (2006). *The Secret*. Hillsboro, Oregon: Atria Books/Beyond Words Publishing.

Cabot, T. (1985). *How to Make a Man Fall in Love with You*. New York, NY: Dell Publishing.

Carrellas, B. (2012). *Ecstasy is Necessary: A Practical Guide*. Carlsbad, CA: Hay House.

Cavalieri, P. & Singer, P. (Editors). (1994). *The Great Ape Project: Equality Beyond Humanity*. New York, NY: St. Martin's Griffin.

CBS News. (2012, June 27). Adult chimpanzee kills baby chimp in front of shocked Los Angeles Zoo visitors. *CBS News*. Retrieved from http://www.cbsnews.com/news/adult-chimpanzee-kills-baby-chimp-in-front-of-shocked-los-angeles-zoo-visitors/

Chomsky, N. & Schoeffel, J. (Editor), & Mitchell, P. R. (Editor). (2002). *Understanding Power: The Indispensable Chomsky*. New York, NY: The New Press.

Clay, Z. & de Waal, F. (2014). *Sex and strife: post-conflict sexual contacts in bonobos*. Brill Online Books and Journals.

Clinton, H. (1996). *It Takes A Village*. New York, NY: Simon & Schuster.

Conrad, J. (1990). *Heart of Darkness*. New York, NY: Dover Publications.

Daedone, N. (2012). *Slow Sex: The Art and Craft of the Female Orgasm*. New York, NY: Grand Central Life & Style.

Darwin, C. (2003). *150th Anniversary Edition. The Origin of Species*. New York, NY: Signet Classics.

Darwin, C. (2004). *The Descent of Man*. London: Penguin Classics.

Dasgupta, S. (2014, August 12). *Are Apes as Empathic as Humans?* The-Scientist. Retrieved from http://www.the-scientist.com/?articles.view/articleNo/40741/title/Are-Apes-as-Empathetic-as-Humans-/

Davenporte, B. (2012, March 14). Study: Female Bonobos Use Sex to Boost Social Standing. *LAWeekly.com*. Retrieved from http://www.laweekly.com/afterdark/2012/03/14/study-female-bonobos-use-sex-to-boost-social-standing

De Sade, M. (1990). *Justine, Philosophy in the Bedroom and Other Writings*. New York, NY: Grove Press.

De Waal, F. . (1982). *Chimpanzee Politics: Power and Sex among Apes*. New York, NY: Harper & Row.

De Waal, F. (1990). *Peacemaking among Primates*. Cambridge, MA: Harvard University Press.

De Waal, F. (2001). *The Ape and the Sushi Master: Cultural Reflections of a Primatologist*. New York, NY: Basic Books.

De Waal, F. (2006). *Our Inner Ape: A Leading Primatologist Explains Why We Are Who We Are*. New York, NY: Riverhead Trade.

De Waal, F. (2011). *The Age of Empathy: Nature's Lessons for a Kinder Society*. New York, NY: Souvenir Press.

De Waal, F. (2013). *The Bonobo and the Atheist: In Search of Humanism among the Primates*. New York, NY: W. W. Norton & Co.

De Waal, F. & Lanting, F. (1998). *Bonobo: The Forgotten Ape*. Berkeley, CA: University of California Press.

Debusmann Jr., B. (2011, July 20). Police bust prostitution ring catering to Wall Street. *Reuters*. Retrieved from http://www.reuters.com/article/2011/07/20/us-crime-prostitution-idUSTRE76J73N20110720

Diamond, J. (1999, May 1). The Worst Mistake in the History of the Human Race. *Discover Magazine*. Retrieved from http://discovermagazine.com/1987/may/02-the-worst-mistake-in-the-history-of-the-human-race#.Uve-i_lkTsY

Diamond, J. (1993). *The Third Chimpanzee: The Evolution and Future of the Human Animal*. New York, NY: Harper Perennial.

Dicker, R. (2013, January 15). Gina, Seville zoo chimp, addicted to porn, scientist Pablo Herreros says. *The Huffington Post*. Retrieved from http://www.huffingtonpost.com/2013/01/15/gina-seville-zoo-chimp-addicted-porn_n_2477806.html

Dixson, A. (2009). *Sexual Selection and the Origins of Human Mating Systems*. New York, NY: Oxford University Press.

Dodson, B. (1987). *Sex for One: The Joy of Selfloving*. New York, NY: Harmony House.

Easton, D. & Hardy, J. (1997). *The Ethical Slut: A Practical Guide to Polyamory, Open Relationships & Other Adventures*. Berkeley, CA: Ten Speed Press.

Ehrenreich, B. (2007). *Dancing in the Streets: A History of Collective Joy*. New York, NY: Henry Holt and Company.

Ellis, A. (1994). *Reason and Emotion in Psychotherapy: Comprehensive Method of Treating Human Disturbances: Revised and Updated*. New York, NY: Citadel Press.

Ensler, E. (2000). *The Vagina Monologues*. New York, NY: Dramatists Play Service.

Eugenides, J. (2002). *Middlesex*. New York, NY: Picador.

Firefox, L. (2010). *Sexy Witch*. Woodbury, MN: Llewellyn Publications.

Fisher, H. (1992). *Anatomy of Love: A Natural History of Mating, Marriage, and Why We Stray*. New York, NY: Ballantine Books.

Fisher, H. & Thomson, A. J. (2008, March 20). Prozac and Sexual Desire. *The New York Review of Books*. Retrieved from http://www.nybooks.com/articles/archives/2008/mar/20/prozac-and-sexual-desire/

Fossey, D. (2000). *Gorillas in the Mist*. Boston, MA: Mariner Books.

Frank, K. (2013). *Plays Well in Groups: A Journey through the World of Group Sex*. New York, NY: Rowman & Littlefield.

Friedan, B. (1977). *The Feminine Mystique*. New York, NY: Dell Publishing.

Friedersdorf, C. (2013, May 16). The Ethics of Extreme Porn: Is Some Sex Wrong Even Among Consenting Adults? *The Atlantic Online*. Retrieved from http://www.theatlantic.com/sexes/archive/2013/05/the-ethics-of-extreme-porn-is-some-sex-wrong-even-among-consenting-adults/275898/?google_editors_picks=true

Friedman, T. L. (2005). *The World Is Flat*. New York, NY: Farrar, Straus, and Giroux.

Furuichi, T. & Thompson, J.M. (Editors). (2010). *The Bonobos: Behavior, Ecology and Conservation*. New York, NY: Springer Publishing.

Gardner, H. (2011). *Frames of Mind: The Theory of Multiple Intelligences*. New York, NY: Basic Books.

Glickman, C. & Emirzian, A. (2013). *The Ultimate Guide to Prostate Pleasure: Erotic Exploration for Men and Their Partners*. San Francisco, CA: Cleis Press.

Goleman, D. (2006). *Emotional Intelligence: 10th Anniversary Edition: Why It Can Matter More Than IQ*. New York, NY: Bantam Books.

Goodall, J. (1986). *The Chimpanzees of Gombe: Patterns of Behavior*. Cambridge, MA: Harvard University Press.

Gordon, M. (2006). *Voluptuous Panic: The Erotic World of Weimar Berlin*. Los Angeles, CA: Feral House.

Gould, T. (1999). *The Lifestyle: A Look at the Erotic Rites of Swingers*. Toronto: Vintage Canada.

Gray, P. (2011). How Hunter-Gatherers Mainted Their Egalitarian Ways. *Psychology Today.* Retrieved from http://www.psychologytoday.com/blog/freedom-learn/201105/how-hunter-gatherers-maintained-their-egalitarian-ways

Greene, R. (2000). *The 48 Laws of Power.* London: Profile Books Ltd.

Greene, R. (2004). *The Art of Seduction.* London: Profile Books Ltd.

Griffith, J. (2009*). Freedom.* Sydney: The World Transformation Movement.

Gruen, S. (2010). *Ape House.* New York, NY: Spiegel & Grau.

Gurdjieff, G I. & Orage, A.R. (Translator). (1963). *Meetings with Remarkable Men.* London: Routledge.

Guthrie, D. (2000, May 18). *The Erin Brockovich of the bonobo.* Salon. Retrieved from http://www.salon.com/2000/05/18/drblock/

Hakim, C. (2011). *Erotic Capital: The Power of Attraction in the Boardroom and the Bedroom.* New York, NY: Basic Books.

Hanh, T. N., Kohn, S. C. (Translator) (2004). *True Love: A Practice for Awakening the Heart.* Boston, MA: Shambhala.

Hare, B. & Woods, V. (2014, July 26). *Bonobos Invade 'Planet of the Apes.'* Livescience.com. Retrieved from http://www.livescience.com/47029-can-bonobos-bring-peace-to-planet-of-the-apes.html

Harris, M. (1990). *Our Kind: Who We Are, Where We Came from, Where We Are Going.* New York, NY: Harper Perennial.

Hartley, N. & Levine, I. S. (2006). *Nina Hartley's Guide to Total Sex.* New York, NY: Avery.

Heinlein, R. (1961). *Stranger in a Strange Land.* New York, NY: G.P. Putnam's Sons.

Hess, E. (2008). *Nim Chimpsky: The Chimp Who Would Be Human.* New York, NY: Bantam Books.

Hesse, H. (1929). *The Steppenwolf.* New York, NY: Henry Holt and Company.

Hochschild, A. (1998). *King Leopold's Ghost, A Story of Greed, Terrorism and Heroism in Colonial Africa.* New York, NY: Houghton Mifflin.

Hoff, B. (1982). *The Tao of Pooh.* New York, NY: Penguin Books.

Hollander, X. (1972). *The Happy Hooker.* New York, NY: Buccaneer Books.

Horgan, J. (2012). *The End of War.* San Francisco, CA: McSweeney's.

Hrdy, S. B. (1999). *The Woman That Never Evolved.* Cambridge, MA: Harvard University Press.

Ince, J. (2005). *The Politics of Lust.* Amherst, NY: Prometheus Books.

Irvine, W. B. (2009). *A Guide to the Good Life: The Ancient Art of Stoic Joy.* New York, NY: Oxford University Press.

IUCN 2013. (2013). *The IUCN Red List of Threatened Species.* (Vers. 2013.2). Retrieved from http://www.iucnredlist.org

Izquierdo, I. B. (2011). *Evolution's Gift of Play, from Bonobo Apes to Humans*. TED. Retrieved from http://www.ted.com/talks/isabel_behncke_evolution_s_gift_of_play_from_bonobo_apes_to_humans?language=en

Jacobson, D. (2013). *Of Virgins and Martyrs: Women and Sexuality in Global Conflict*. Baltimore, MD: Johns Hopkins University Press.

Jaiya. (2013). *Blow Each Other Away: A Couples' Guide to Sensational Oral Sex*. New York, NY: Three Rivers Press.

Jaiya & Hanauer, J. (2013). *Red Hot Touch*. New York, NY: Three Rivers Press.

Jamail, D. (2014, June 3). *On Staying Sane in a Suicidal Culture*. Truthout. Retrieved from http://www.truth-out.org/news/item/24083-on-staying-sane-in-a-suicidal-culture

James, E. L. (2011). *50 Shades of Grey*. New York, NY: Random House.

Joannides, P. (2009). *Guide to Getting It On*. Waldport, Oregon: Goofy Foot Press.

Jung, C. G. (1956-1966). *The Collected Works of Dr. C. G. Jung*. London: Routledge.

Kanō, T. (1992). *The Last Ape: Pygmy Chimpanzee Behavior and Ecology*. Palo Alto, CA: Stanford University Press.

Kaufman, W. (Editor). (1989). *Existentialism from Dostoyevsky to Sartre*. Cleveland, OH: Meridian Publishing Company.

Keim, B. (2012, August 21). *Video: Tool-Making Bonobos Give Glimpse of Human Origins*. Wired.com. Retrieved from http://www.wired.com/2012/08/bonobo-tools/.

Kerner, I. (2004). *She Comes First: The Thinking Man's Guide to Pleasuring a Woman*. New York, NY: ReganBooks.

Koerth-Baker, M. (25 June 2013). Want to Understand Mortality? Look to the Chimps. *The New York Times*. Retrieved from http://www.nytimes.com/2013/06/30/magazine/want-to-understand-mortality-look-to-the-chimps.html?_r=2&

Kinsey, A. & Pomeroy, W. & Martin, C. (1948). *Sexual Behavior in the Human Male*. Philadelphia, PA: W.B. Saunders Company.

Kinsey, A. & Pomeroy, W. & Martin, C. (1953). *Sexual Behavior in the Human Female*. Philadelphia, PA: W.B. Saunders Company.

Klein, F. (1993). *The Bisexual Option, Second Edition (Haworth Gay and Lesbian Studies series)*. Binghamton, NY: The Haworth Press.

Klein, M. (2006). *America's War on Sex: The Attack on Law, Lust, and Liberty (Sex, Love, and Psychology)*. Westport, CT: Praeger Publishers.

Klein, M. (2013). *Sexual Intelligence: What We Really Want from Sex –and How to Get It*. New York, NY: HarperOne.

Kleinplatz, P. J. (Editor). (2012). *New Directions in Sex Therapy: Innovations and Alternatives*. New York, NY: Routledge.

Krassner, P. (2005). *One Hand Jerking: Reports from an Investigative Journalist*. New York,

NY: Seven Stories Press.

Krassner, P. (2009). *In Praise of Indecency: The Leading Investigative Satirist Sounds Off on Hypocrisy, Censorship and Free Expression*. San Francisco, CA: Cleis Press.

Kundera, M. (1991). *Immortality*. New York, NY: Grove Press.

Leonard, T. (2014, June 6). He can cook, play music, use a computer - and make sarcastic jokes chatting with his 3,000-word vocabulary: My lunch with the world's cleverest chimp (who Skyped me later for another chat). *Daily Mail*. Retrieved from: http://www.dailymail.co.uk/news/article-2651004/He-cook-play-music-use-computer-make-sarcastic-jokes-chatting-3-000-word-vocabulary-My-lunch-worlds-cleverest-chimp.html#ixzz33w2AlSCy

Ley, D. J. (2012). *The Myth of Sex Addiction*. Lanham, MD: Rowman & Littlefield Publishers.

Le Blanc, S. & Register, K. E. (2003). *Constant Battles: The Myth of the Peaceful, Noble Savage*. New York, NY: St. Martin's Griffin.

Lichtenberg, J. (2007). *Sensuality and Sexuality across the Divide of Shame*. (Psychoanalytic Inquiry Book series). New York, NY: The Analytic Press.

Love, B. (1994). *The Encyclopedia of Unusual Sex Practices*. New York, NY: Barricade Books.

Lynch, D. (2014, June 02). Researchers Say Bonobos Have An Innate Ability To Keep A Musical Beat. *International Business Times*. Retrieved from http://www.ibtimes.com/researchers-say-bonobos-have-innate-ability-keep-musical-beat-1556190

Lyons, G. & Conason, J. (2001). *The Hunting of the President: The Ten-Year Campaign to Destroy Bill and Hillary Clinton*. New York, NY: St. Martin's Press.

Macrae, F. (2014, February 16). "Animals that can match us on the dancefloor: Study attempts to find whether creatures actually have rhythm. *Daily Mail*. Retrieved from http://www.dailymail.co.uk/sciencetech/article-2560976/Animals-match-dancefloor-Study-attempts-creatures-actually-rhythm.html#ixzz2tiyXHfbG

Macy, J. (2007). *World as Lover, World as Self: Courage for Global Justice and Ecological Renewal*. Berkeley, CA: Parallax Press.

Madsen, P. (2011). *Shameless: How I Ditched the Diet, Got Naked, Found True Pleasure and Somehow Got Home in Time To Cook Dinner*. New York, NY: Rodale Books.

Mahdavi, P. (2009). *Passionate Uprisings: Iran's Sexual Revolution*. Stanford, CA: Stanford University Press.

Margulis, Dr. L. & Sagan, D. (1990). *Origins of Sex: Three Billion Years of Genetic Recombination*. New Haven, CT: Yale University Press.

Maslow, A. (1954). *Motivation and Personality*. New York, NY: Pearson PLC.

Michaels, M. A. & Johnson, P. (2014). *Partners in Passion: A Guide to Great Sex, Emotional Intimacy and Long-term Love*. Berkeley, CA: Cleis Press, Inc.

Moore, F. (1998). *Nothing is hidden at Suzy Block's*. Retrieved from http://www.eroplay.com/Cave/Writings/drsuzyraid.html

Moore, . (2003). *Expanding sex*. Retrieved from http://www.eroplay.com/Cave/Writings/expandingsex.htm.

Moore, F. (2013). *Frank Moore's web of all possibilities*. Retrieved from http://www.eroplay.com.

Moore, F. (2014) *Frankly Speaking: A Collection of Essays, Writings and Rants*. Berkeley, CA: CreateSpace Independent Publishing Platform.

Morgan, E. (1972). *The Descent of Woman: The Classic Study of Evolution*. London: Souvenir Press.

Morin, J. (1995). *The Erotic Mind: Unlocking the Inner Source of Passion and Fulfillment*. New York, NY: Harper Collins.

Ness, E. (1999, October1). Sex sells, but can it save the planet? *Grist Magazine*. Retrieved from http://grist.org/article/ness-sin/

Nin, A. (1977). *Delta of Venus*. New York, NY: Harcourt Brace Jovanovich.

Ogden, G. (2007). *Women Who Love Sex: Ordinary Women Describe Their Paths to Pleasure, Intimacy, and Fantasy*. Boston, MA: Trumpeter Books.

O'Rourke, P. J. (2000, August 7). Democrats are the bad guys. *The Weekly Standard*. Retrieved from http://www.weeklystandard.com/Content/Protected/Articles/000/000/010/879ekald.asp.

Orwell, G. (1949). *Nineteen Eighty-Four*. London: Secker and Warburg.

Owen, J. (2014, June 10). Endangered Bonobos Reveal Evolution of Human Kindness: Experiments show the great apes share with strangers and empathize. *National Geographic*. Retrieved from http://news.nationalgeographic.com/news/2014/06/140610-bonobos-great-apes-animals-science-evolution/

Paget, L. (2004). *Orgasms: How to Have Them, Give Them, and Keep Them Coming*. New York, NY: Broadway Books.

Paglia, C. (1991). *Sexual Personae: Art and Decadence from Nefertiti to Emily Dickinson*. New York, NY: Vintage.

Paglia, C. (1992). *Sex, Art, and American Culture: Essays*. New York, NY: Vintage.

Paglia, C. (1994). *Vamps and Tramps: New Essays*. New York, NY: Vintage.

Parker, I. (2007, July 30 Swingers. *The New Yorker*. Retrieved from http://www.newyorker.com/reporting/2007/07/30/070730fa_fact_parker?currentPage=all

Parker-Pope, T. (2010). *For Better: How the Surprising Science of Happy Couples Can Help Your Marriage Succeed*. New York, NY: Dutton.

Partridge, B. (2002). *A History of Orgies*. New York, NY: Chicago, IL: Prion Publishing.

Patrick, T. & Borzillo, C. (2010). *Sinner Takes All: A Memoir of Love and Porn*. New York, NY: Gotham Books.

Perel, E. (2006). *Mating in Captivity: Unlocking Erotic Intelligence*. New York, NY: Harper

Perennial.

Peterson, D. & Amman, K. (2003). *Eating Apes*. Berkeley, CA: University of California Press.

Petersen, J. R. & Hefner, H. (1999). *The Century of Sex: Playboy's History of the Sexual Revolution, 1900-1999*. (Hugh Hefner, Editor). New York, NY: Grove Press.

Pinker, S. (2007). *The Stuff of Thought: Language as a Window into Human Nature*. New York: Penguin Books.

Pinker, S. (2012). *The Better Angels Of Our Nature: Why Violence Has Declined*. New York: Penguin Books.

Plath, S. (1971). *The Bell Jar*. New York, NY: Harper & Row.

Plotkin, M. J. (1994). *Tales of a Shaman's Apprentice: An Ethnobotanist Searches for New Medicines in the Amazon Rain Forest*. London: Penguin Books.

Prescott, J. (Nov 1975). *Body Pleasure and the Origins of Violence*. Retrieved from http://www.whale.to/a/prescott3.html

Prescott, J. W. (July/August 1989). Genital Pain Vs. Genital Pleasure: Why the One and Not the Other? *The Truth Seeker*, 14-21. Retrieved from http://www.violence.de/prescott/truthseeker/genpl.html

Queen, C. (1999). *Exhibitionism for the Shy: Show Off, Dress Up and Talk Hot!* San Francisco, CA: Down There Press.

Quinn, T. (2010). *What Do You Do with a Chocolate Jesus? An Irreverent History of Christianity*. Charleston, SC: BookSurge Publishing.

Radakovich, A. (2014). *The Wild Girls Club, Part 2: Tales from New York to Hollywood*. New York, NY: Skytower Publishing.

Raushenbush, P.B. (2014, August 28). ISIS and the Crisis of Meaning. *The Huffington Post*. Retrieved from http://www.huffingtonpost.com/paul-raushenbush/isis-and-the-crisis-of-meaning_b_5730284.html?utm_hp_ref=college&ir=College

Ray, D. (2012). *Sex & God: How Religion Distorts Sexuality*. Bonner Springs, KS: IPC Press.

Réage, P. (1965). *Story of O*. First English Edition. Paris: Olympia Press.

Reich, W. (1974). *The Sexual Revolution*. New York, NY: Farrar, Straus and Giroux.

Reuters. (2011, August 10). Bonobo crowned 'cleverest ape in the world'. *3 News*. Retrieved from http://www.3news.co.nz/Bonobo-crowned-cleverest-ape-in-the-world/tabid/1160/articleID/221728/Default.aspx

Rose, A. & Tobias, M. (Editor) & Solisti, K. (Editor) (1998). *On Tortoises, Monkeys and Men*. (Kinship with the Animals series,). Hillsboro, OR: BeyondWords Pub.

Rosenberg, M. B. (2003). *Nonviolent Communication: A Language of Life*. Encinitas, CA: Puddle Dancer Press.

Ryan, C. & Jethá, C. (2010). *Sex at Dawn: The Prehistoric Origins of Modern Sexuality*. New York, NY: HarperCollins.

Ryan, C. (2014, September 10). The Mysterious Case of Primate Peacefulness. *Psychology

Today. Retrieved from http://www.psychologytoday.com/blog/sex-dawn/201409/the-mysterious-case-primate-peacefulness

Sagan, D. & Volk, T. (2009). *Death and Sex*. White River Junction, VT: Chelsea Green Publishers.

Sapolsky, R.M. (2002). *A Primate's Memoir: A Neuroscientist's Unconventional Life Among the Baboons*. New York, NY: Scribner.

Sapolsky, R. M. (2011, April 8). Warrior Baboons Give Peace a Chance. *Yes!*. Retrieved from http://www.yesmagazine.org/issues/can-animals-save-us/warrior-baboons-give-peace-a-chance?b_start:int=1

Sartre, J. & Paul Bowles (Editor) (1958). *No Exit*. New York, NY: Samuel French.

Savage, D. (1998). *Savage Love: Straight Answers from America's Most Popular Sex Columnist*. New York, NY: Plume.

Savage-Rumbaugh, S. (2004). *The gentle genius of bonobos*. TED. Retrieved from http://www.ted.com/talks/susan_savage_rumbaugh_on_apes_that_write?language=en

Savage-Rumbaugh, S. & Lewin, R. (1994). *Kanzi: The Ape at the Brink of the Human Mind*. Hoboken, NJ: John Wiley & Sons.

Schwanbeck, L. (2012). Esther Perel on Mating in Captivity. *Pyschotherapy*. Retrieved from http://www.psychotherapy.net/interview/esther-perel-mating-captivity#top

Schwartz, J. (2008). *The Vision Board: The Secret to an Extraordinary Life*. New York, NY: Collins Design.

Seidman, B. F. & Dowret, A. (2011, February 27). Speaking of Sex: An Interview with Psychologist Christopher Ryan. *The Humanist*. Retrieved from http://thehumanist.com/magazine/march-april-2011/features/speaking-of-sex

Shelley, M. (1818). *Frankenstein; Or, The Modern Prometheus*. London: Lackington, Hughes, Harding, Mavor & Jones.

Sherfey, M. J. (1972). *The Nature and Evolution of Female Sexuality*. New York, NY: Random House.

Siegel, S. (January 2011). *Your Brain on Sex: How Smarter Sex Can Change Your Life*. Naperville, IL: Sourcebooks Casablanca.

Siegel, S. (2014, January). When It Comes To Sex There is No Difference between Male and Female Desire. *Psychology Tomorrow*. Retrieved from http://www.psychologytomorrowmagazine.com/comes-sex-difference-male-female-desire/

Sprinkle, A. (1998). *Annie Sprinkle: Post-Porn Modernist*. San Francisco, CA: Cleis Press.

Strachey, J. & Freud, S. (1957-1962). *The Standard Edition of the Complete Psychological Works of Dr. Sigmund Freud*. London: The Hogarth Press and the Institute of Psychoanalysis.

Sundahl, D. (2013). *Female Ejaculation and the G-Spot: Not Your Mother's Orgasm Book!* Newark, NJ: Audible Inc.

Talese, G. (1980). *Thy Neighbor's Wife*. Garden City, NY: Doubleday.

Taormino, T. (2008). *Opening Up: A Guide to Creating and Sustaining Open Relationships*. San Francisco, CA: Cleis Press, Inc.

Tennov, D. (1979). *Love and Limerence*. Maryland: Scarborough House Publishers.

Todd, B. (2006, March 15). Congo, Coltan, Conflict. Heinz College Review.

Toor, A. (2014, October 14). Monkey see, monkey feel: why we should care about ape emotion. *TheVerge.com*. Retrieved from http://www.theverge.com/2013/10/14/4834330/bonobos-and-humans-emotional-expression

Tufnell, N. (2013, October 18). Isabel Behncke on bonobos, play, trust and sex. *Wired*. Retrieved from http://www.wired.co.uk/news/archive/2013-10/18/isabel-behncke.

UNEP News Centre. (2013, March 4). Illegal Trade Robs Wild of Almost 3,000 Great Apes Annually, Threatening Populations. United Nations Environment Programme. *UNEP*. Retrieved from http://www.unep.org/newscentre/default.aspx?DocumentID=2704&ArticleID=9435&l=en

University of California, Santa Cruz. (2014, February 15). Beat-keeping sea lion shows surprising rhythmic ability. *Phys.org*. Retrieved from http://phys.org/news/2014-02-beat-keeping-sea-lion-rhythmic-ability.html.

Vaillant, G. E. (2012). *Triumphs of Experience: The Men of the Harvard Grant Study*. Cambridge, MA. Harvard University Press.

Vallis, M. (2010, May 6) Bonobos shake their heads no, just like humans: video. *National Post*. Retrieved from http://news.nationalpost.com/2010/05/06/bonobos-shake-their-heads-no-just-like-humans-video/

Wagstaff, K. (2014, July 10). Chimps Don't Cry: Behind the Science of 'Dawn of the Planet of the Apes.' *NBC News*. Retrieved from http://www.nbcnews.com/science/weird-science/chimps-dont-cry-behind-science-dawn-planet-apes-n151986

Weiss, S. I. (2010). *Eco-Sex: Go Green between the Sheets and Make Your Love Life Sustainable*. New York, NY: Ten Speed Press.

Whittaker, P. (2014). *Polly: Sex Culture Revolutionary*. San Francisco, CA: Moral Minority, Inc.

Wilde, O. (1996). *A Woman of No Importance*. New York, NY: Penguin Books.

Wilson, E. O. (1978). *On Human Nature*. Cambridge, MA: Harvard University Press.

Wilson, K. (2005). *Primal Tears*. Berkeley, CA: Frog Books.

Woods, V. (2010). *Bonobo Handshake: A Memoir of Love and Adventure in the Congo*. New York, NY: Gotham.

Wrangham, R. & Peterson, D. (1997). *Demonic Males: Apes and the Origins of Human Violence*. New York, NY: Houghton Mifflin Co.

Wright, K. (Editor). (2013). *Bedded Bliss: A Couple's Guide to Lust Ever After*. Berkeley, CA: Cleiss Press.

Yerkes, R. M. (1925). *Almost Human*. New York, NY: The Century Company.

Scientific Papers

Alexander, M. G. & Fisher, T.D. (2003). Truth and consequences: using the bogus pipeline to examine sex differences in self-reported sexuality. *Journal of Sex Research, 40*(1), 27-35.

Behringer, V. & Deschner, T. & Murtagh, R. & Stevens, J. M. G. & Hohmann, G. (2014). Age-related changes in thyroid hormone levels of bonobos and chimpanzees indicate heterochrony in development. *Journal of Human Evolution, 66*, 83-88. Retrieved from DOI: 10.1016/j.jhevol.2013.09.008

Behringer, V. & Deschner, T. & Deimel, C. & Stevens, J.M.G. & Hohmann, G. (2014, July 30). Age-related changes in urinary testosterone levels suggest differences in puberty onset and divergent life history strategies in bonobos and chimpanzees Hormones and Behavior. *Pub Med*. Retrieved from DOI: 10.1016/j.yhbeh.2014.07.011

Benuto, L. & Meana, M. (2008). Acculturation and sexuality: Investigating gender differences in erotic plasticity. *Journal of Sex Research, 45*(3), 217-224.

Bivona, J. & Critelli, J. (2009). The nature of women's rape fantasies: an analysis of prevalence, frequency, and contents. *The Journal of Sex Research, 46*(1), 33-45. Retrieved from DOI: 10.1080/00224490802624406.

Buss, D. M. & Haselton, M. (2005). The evolution of jealousy. *Trends in Cognitive Sciences, 9*(11), 506-507. Retrieved from http://www.sscnet.ucla.edu/comm/haselton/papers/downloads/busshaselton2005.pdf

Chivers, M. L. & Timmers, A.D. (2012). The effects of gender and relationship context cues in audio narratives on heterosexual women's and men's genital and subjective sexual response. *Archives of Sexual Behavior, 41*, 185-197.

Chivers, M. L. & Seto, M. C. & Lalumiere, M. L. & Laan, E. & Grimbos, T. (2010). Agreement of genital and subjective measures of sexual arousal in men and women: a meta-analysis. *Archives of Sexual Behavior, 39*, 5-56. Retrieved from DOI: 10.1007/s10508-009-9556-9

Clay, Z. & Zuberbühler, K. (2012, Feburary 1). Communication during sex among female bonobos: effects of dominance, solicitation and audience. *Nature*. Retrieved from http://www.nature.com/srep/2012/120301/srep00291/full/srep00291.html.

Clay, Z., Pika S. & Gruber, T. & Zuberbühler, K. (2011, February 16). Female bonobos use copulation calls as social signals. *Biology Letters*. Retrieved from rsbl.2010.1227v2.

Demuru, E. & Palagi, E. (2012, November 14). In Bonobos Yawn Contagion Is Higher among Kin and Friends. *PLOS One*. Retrieved from http://www.plosone.org/article/info%3Adoi%2F10.1371%2Fjournal.pone.0049613.

Dutton, D. G. & Aron, A. P. (1974). Some evidence for heightened sexual attraction under conditions of high anxiety. *Journal of Personality and Social Psychology, 30*(4), 510–517.

Gallup, G. G., et al. (2003). The human penis as a semen displacement device. *Evolution and Human Behavior, 24*(4), 277-289.

Glasper, E. R. & Gould, E. (2013). Sexual experience restores age-related decline in adult neurogenesis and hippocampal function. *Hippocampus, 23*(4), 303-312.

Goetz, A. T. & Shackelford, T. K. & Platek, S. M. & Starratt, V. G. & McKibbin, W. F. (2007). Sperm competition in humans: Implications for male sexual psychology, physiology, anatomy, and behavior. *Annual Review of Sex Research, 18*(1), 1-22.

Hare, B. & Herrmann, E. & Woods, V. & Wrangham, R. [Ongoing Research]. Comparisons of bonobo and chimpanzees in a cooperative problem solving task. *Max Planck Institute for Evolutionary Anthropology: Hominoid Psychology Research Group.*

Hare, B. & Wobber, V. & Wrangham, R. (2012). The self-domestication hypothesis: evolution of bonobo psychology is due to selection against aggression. *Animal Behaviour, 83*(3), 573-585.

Haslam, K. R. (2005-2013). Collection on Polyamory. *The Kinnsey Institute.* Retrieved from http://www.kinseyinstitute.org/library/Pdf/HaslamFindingAid_web.pdf

Hare, B. & Herrmann, E. & Woods, V. & Wrangham, R. [Ongoing Research]. Temperament comparisons in bonobos, chimpanzees and human children. *Max Planck Institute for Evolutionary Anthropology: Hominoid Psychology Research Group.*

Hare, B., Wobber, V. & Wrangham, R. (2012). The self-domestication hypothesis: evolution of bonobo psychology is due to selection against aggression. *Animal Behavior, 83*(3), 573-585.

Harris, C. R. (2004). The evolution of jealousy. *American Scientist, 92,* 62-71.

Kendrick, K. M. & Haupt, M. A. & Hinton, M. R. & Broad, K. D. & Skinner, J. D. (2001). Sex differences in the influence of mothers on the sociosexual preferences of their offspring. *Hormones and Behavior, 40*(2), 322-338.

Kilgallon, S. J. & Simmons, L. W. (2005). Image content influences men's semen quality. *Biology Letters, 1*(3), 253-255.

Kim, J. L., et al. (2013). Sexual activity counteracts the suppressive effects of chronic stress on adult hippocampal neurogenesis and recognition memory. *Brain Research, 1538,* 26-40.

Mayer, J. D. & Salovey, P. & Caruso, D. R. (2006). Measuring Emotional Intelligence with the Mayer-Salovey-Caruso Emotional Intelligence Test (MSCEIT). *Psicothema, 18*(suppl. 1), 34-41.

Mitani, J. C. & Watts, D. P. & Amsler, S. J. (2010). Lethal intergroup aggression leads to territorial expansion in wild chimpanzees. *Current Biology, 20*(12), R507-R508.

Nevo, Eviatar. (2012, July 30). Stone tool production and utilization by bonobo-chimpanzees (Pan paniscus). *PNAS.* Retrieved from http://www.pnas.org/content/early/2012/08/21/1212855109.abstract

Parish, A. (2011, April 14). Bonobo sisterhood: Lessons on sex, bonding, and dominance from our closest living relatives. *Darwin Evolving: Distinguished Naturalists.* Lecture conducted from UCLA Neuroscience Research Building Auditorium, Los Angeles.

Parker, G. A. (1970). Sperm competition and its evolutionary consequences in the insects. *Biological Reviews, 45*(4), 525-567.

Prüfer K., et al. The bonobo genome compared with the chimpanzee and human genomes. (2012, June 13). *Nature*. Retrieved from DOI: 10.1038/nature11128.

Rilling, J. K., et al. (2012) Differences between chimpanzees and bonobos in neural systems supporting social cognition. *Social Cognitive and Affective Neuroscience*, 7(4), 369-379.

Sapolsky, R. M. (1990, January). Stress in the Wild. *Scientific American*. Retrieved from http://academic.reed.edu/biology/professors/srenn/pages/teaching/2008_syllabus/2008_readings/9_Sapolsky_1990.pdf

Shea, B. T. (1983). Paedomorphosis and neoteny in the pygmy chimpanzee. *Science*, 222(4623), 521-522.

Springer. (2010, January 4). Women's bodies and minds agree less than men's on what's sexy. *Springer's Archives of Sexual Behavior*. Retrieved from http://www.springer.com/about+springer/media/springer+select?SGWID=0-11001-6-805634-0

Stiles, D. & Redmond, I. & Cress, D. & Nellemann, C. & Formo, R.K. (Editors). (2013). *Stolen Apes – The Illicit Trade in Chimpanzees, Gorillas, Bonobos and Orangutans. A Rapid Response Assessment*. United Nations Environment Programme & GRID-Arendal. Retrieved from http://hetq.am/static/content/pdf/Trade_in_Apes.pdf

White, F. J. & Chapman, C. A. (1994). Contrasting chimpanzees and pygmy chimpanzees: nearest neighbor distances and choices. *Folia Primatologica*, 63: 181-191.

White, F. J & Wood, K. D. & Merrill, M. Y. (1998). Comment on C. Stanford: The social behavior of Chimpanzees and Bonobos. *Current Anthropology*, 39: 414-415.

Zamma, K. & Fujita, S. (2004). Genito-genital rubbing among the chimpanzees of Mahale and Bossou. *Pan Africa News*, 11(2). Retrieved from http://mahale.main.jp/PAN/index.html

TV, Films & Recordings

Anderson, Paul Thomas (Director & Writer). (1997). *Boogie Nights*. [Motion Picture]. United States: New Line Cinema.

Astaire, Fred & Gershwin, Ira (Writer) & Gershwin, George (Composer). (1937). "Nice work if you can get it." *A Damsel in Distress*. [Motion Picture Soundtrack]. United States: RKO Pictures

Berrod, Thierry & Amouroux, Vincent (Directors). (2007). *Humanimal, the Animal Mind*. France: [Television]. United States: Mona Lisa Films.

Bloodhound Gang & Pop, Jimmy (Writer, Producer). (1999). "The bad touch." Hooray for Boobies. [Sound Recording]. United States: Geffen.

Bonham, John & Jones, John Paul & Page, Jimmy & Plant, Robert & Dixon, Willie (Writers). (1969). Led Zeppelin. "Whole Lotta Love." Led Zeppelin II. [Sound Recording]. United States: Atlantic.

Bruyère, Christian (Director). (2000). "Bonobos." *Champions of the Wild*. [Television]. Animal Planet.

Caron, Glenn Gordon (Creator). (1985-1989). *Moonlighting*. [Television Series]. United States: ABC.

Cooper, Merian C. & Schoedsack, Ernest B. (Directors). (1933). *King Kong*. [Motion Picture]. United States: RKO Radio Pictures.

Cowden, Jack & Browning, Ricou (Creators). (1964-1967). *Flipper*. [Television Series]. United States: NBC Television.

Cukor, George (Director). (1949). *Adam's Rib*. [Motion Picture]. United States: MGM.

Demme, Jonathan (Director). (1991). *The Silence of the Lambs*. [Motion Picture]. United States: Orion Pictures Corporation.

The Doors, The (1967). "Break on through (to the other side)." The Doors. [Sound Recording]. United States: Elektra.

Fitzgerald, Ella, & Armstrong, Louis & Gershwin, George (Writer) & Gershwin, Ira (Writer). (1957). "Let's call the whole thing off." Ella and Louis Again. [Sound Recording]. United States: Verve.

Franklin, Aretha & Otis Redding (Writer) & Jerry Wexler (Producer). (1967). "Respect." I Never Loved A Man the Way I Love You. [Sound Recording]. United States: Atlantic.

Godeanu, Ronnie (Producer). (1993). "The Nature of Sex." *Nature*. [Television]. United States: PBS.

Greene, Ernest (Director). (2007). *Nina Hartley's Guide to the Perfect Orgy*. [Video Recording]. United States: Adam & Eve Productions.

Kakogiannis, Mihalis (Director). (1964). *Zorba the Greek*. [Motion Picture]. United States/Greece: Twentieth Century Fox Film Corporation.

Kubrick, Stanley (Director). (1968). *2001: A Space Odyssey*. [Motion Picture]. United States: MGM,

Kubrick, Stanley (Director, Writer). (1999). *Eyes Wide Shut*. [Motion Picture]. United States: Warner Bros.

Lee, Ang (Director). (1997). *The Ice Storm*. [Motion Picture]. United States: Fox Searchlight Pictures.

Magafan, Irene (Director). (2012). *The Bonobo Connection*. [Motion Picture]. United States: Irene Magafan.

Rednour, Shar & Strano, Jackie (Directors). (1998). *Bend Over Boyfriend*. [Video Recording]. United States: Sir Video.

Reeves, Matt (Director). (2014). *Dawn of the Planet of the Apes*. [Motion Picture]. United States: Twentieth Century Fox.

Spielberg, Steven (Director). (1982). *E.T. the Extra-Terrestrial*. [Motion Picture]. United States: Universal Pictures.

Stagliano, John (Director). (1989-2013). *Buttman* [Series]. United States: Evil Angel Productions.

Stevens, Kirdy (Director). (1980). *Taboo*. [Motion Picture]. United Stats: Dart Enterprises.

Streisand, Barbara & Syne, Jule (Composter) & Merrill, Bob (Lyricist). (1964) "People." Funny Girl Original Broadway Cast Recording. [Sound Recording]. United States: CBS Records.

Troop of chimpanzees approach, kill, and eat chimpanzee from another group. [Video Recording]. Wildscreen Arkive. Retrieved from http://www.arkive.org/chimpanzee/pan-troglodytes/video-03a.html

Acknowledgements

It takes a Bonoboville to make a book, and this book owes a whole lot of gratitude to a whole tribe of apes, human and bonobo. But there is one special "one," and first and biggest thanks and longest-lasting kisses go to my charming Prince Maximillian Rudolph Leblovic di Lobkowicz di Filangieri, a.k.a. Mickey, a.k.a. Xam Paris, a.k.a. my prime mate, my witness, my big *bambalone,* my collaborator, captain and husband of more than 22 years, for literally living this book with me.

More kisses, deep thanks and hoots of love to Lana, matriarch bonobo at the San Diego Zoo, who may not be able to read *The Bonobo Way*, but I'm sure she would understand it. Even more hoots and hugs of appreciation and admiration for all the other bonobos of the world, in the wild and captivity, for cultivating such an inspirational society that lives in peace through pleasure.

As for my editors… Though I've stayed with one husband over two decades, I can't claim the same track record with book editors. One editor ran away from Bonoboville with our IT guy in the middle of the night. Another tried to incite a Bonoboville rebellion. Still another had a panic attack mid-book, and simply disappeared, only to reappear months later, issuing eloquent apologies, do a round of edits and then vanish in a puff of cyber-smoke once again. Looking back, I realize that my editorial break-ups have been as numerous and drama-filled as my pre-marital relationship break-ups. Regardless, I am grateful to each of them for doing their part to whip my naughty prose into shape, and I would like to thank (in no particular order related to the above descriptions): Nick Morning, S. Patrick Cunningham, Hailey Justine Ryan, Vyns Watkins and Jade Song. Special thanks to my current editor, Keerthi Chandrashekar, for riding in on an editorial white horse to save *The Bonobo Way* from unsavory semicolons, pagination dilemmas and much worse with just a few weeks to go before publication.

Infinite gratitude to the amazing Vanessa Woods for her wonderful photos of bonobos at Lola ya Bonobo (friendsofbonobos.org) and much appreciation for all the important work she and her husband Dr. Brian Hare have done to help save *Pan Paniscus* from extinction.

For their wondrous photos of human apes in action, I must thank Jux Lii, Alex Saglimbeni, L'Erotique, Ajay Johnson, Mikee LaBash, Irwin J., Lydel Lydia and my brother Steve Block. For the photos of me and Lana, thank you Theron Marks and Vincent Amoreux. If you're now reading a print edition without photos, you'll just have check them out on Kindle or in the upcoming photo edition.

Extra special thanks to Dr. Christopher Ryan, whose landmark book *Sex at Dawn* so inspired me to turn a series of articles and stories into this book. After an early manuscript reading, Dr. Ryan told me the amazing tale of Sapolsky's baboons, making the idea of human culture getting increasingly bonoboësque even more plausible. If a bunch of baboons can go bonobos, why can't we?

For superlative public relations, marketing, enthusiasm and deliciously nasty memes, I must thank the indefatigable and (almost) always agreeable Nikki Knight. More hugs and hoots of love to citizens of Bonoboville, including Abraham Perez (lead web developer), Gonzo Bonobo (design), Mars FX (video), Maya Goddess, Chelsea Demoiselle, Luzer Twerksy, Casey K, Dark Phoenix, Ana and Miguel, Brian Redfern, Catherine Imperio and Samantha Fairley, Amor "Baby Block" Hilton and so many more, including Tom Quinn, Michael Donnelly and Dr. Tracy Cabot who looked at the manuscript in the early and middle stages and gave me much appreciated feedback that improved the book.

Special gratitude to Jeffrey St. Claire and the late great Alexander Cockburn for posting parts of *The Bonobo Way* over the years on *Counterpunch*, "America's Best Political Newsletter," and to Sheila Nevins, HBO's great programming empress, for encouraging my interest in bonobos when it was new and sending me my first copy of Dr. Frans de Waal's *Bonobo: The Forgotten Ape*. Speaking of forgetting, if I accidentally left someone out, sorry! Let me know, and I'll owe you a round of Bonoboville Communion at the Speakeasy bar.

Cheers and applause to all the people and bonobos mentioned in this book as well as the bibliography, some of whom I've had the pleasure of meeting personally. Others have inspired me from afar. Extra special gratitude to the wild bonobos' best human friends, Claudine André, Sally Coxe and others mentioned in this book (as well as some I may have accidentally left out) who have devoted much of their lives to saving our kissing cousins from extinction. You are my heroes.

Finally, to all the citizens of Bonoboville, past, present, future and in parallel dimensions in time, thanks for the love, the hate and everything in between. I couldn't have done any of it without you.

About the Author

Susan M. Block, Ph.D., a.k.a. "Dr. Suzy," is a world-renowned sexologist and director of The Dr. Susan Block Institute for the Erotic Arts & Sciences based in Los Angeles. An award-winning filmmaker and talk show host best known for her HBO specials, she is the author of numerous articles, essays, short stories and books, as well as a sex therapist in private practice with a global clientele. A leading champion in the causes of sexual freedom and saving the inspirational but highly endangered bonobos, Dr. Block practices and promotes peace through pleasure: The Bonobo Way. She is also the founder of the sex-positive, bonobo-supportive social media site, Bonoboville.com, and host of *The Dr. Susan Block Show* which can be seen and heard live every Saturday night from 10:30pm to midnight (Pacific Time) on DrSuzy.tv. Married over 22 years, Dr. Block collaborates on all her projects with her husband and prime mate, Pr. Maximillian R. Lobkowicz. She also loves bananas, though not as much as bonobos... or Max.

Photo by Jux Lii

The 10 Commandments of Pleasure by Dr. Susan Block

The power to give pleasure is the greatestpower you have. This is the book that gives you that power. With penetrating wisdom, engaging wit, fantastic advice and seductive sensuality, Dr. Susan Block's internationally acclaimed best-selling book, *The 10 Commandments of Pleasure*, shows you the way to a healthy yet deliciously naughty, thrilling but relatively stable sex life. A Literary Guild Alternate Selection, Doubleday Book Club Selection and Doubleday Health Book Club Selection. Available on Amazon and directly from the publisher.

Kindle Edition
First Print Edition: Hardcover
Second Print Edition (Paperback): British
Third Print Edition (Softback): featuring new chapters on female ejaculation and sperm wars
Translated into 11 languages!

Advertising for Love by Susan Block

Dr. Suzy's first book (published before she was Dr. Suzy!) is now a classic in its field. ***Advertising for Love*** predicted the online personal advertising revolution and is still the very best guide to finding love and lust through advertising anywhere. Dr. Suzy's humor, insight, experience, examples, advice and hilarious Bloom County cartoons make ***Advertising for Love*** the indispensable literary companion to anyone interested in posting, answering or just checking out the many different types of personals and dating sites on the Internet. Get hooked up now! Get ***Advertising for Love***.

Limited softcover copies available.

Dr. Susan Block

The Institute

THERAPISTS WITHOUT BORDERS

The Dr. Susan Block Institute for the Erotic Arts & Sciences is an internationally renowned center for sex education, exploration, expression, research and therapy. Our mission is to help individuals, couples, groups and communities to unlock and explore the secrets to their sexualities and to support them in finding ways, both conventional and creative, to meet their needs and desires in a safe yet exciting and fulfilling manner.

We provide private telephone sex therapy as well as webcam and in-person sex therapy, relationship counseling, fantasy roleplay, fetish exploration, life coaching and bonobo liberation therapy (BLT) at our headquarters in West Los Angeles. We also conduct seminars, events and produce *The Dr. Susan Block Show* live every Saturday night.

We serve a diverse array of men, women, couples, "trouples," tribes and communities of all types, orientations, cultures and lifestyles, helping people with a wide range of sexual pleasures and problems, from impotence to exhibitionism, sex addiction to orgasmic fulfillment, transgender issues to relationship problems, erotic fantasies to challenging realities, fears to desires, fetishes to marriages.

No matter where you are in the world, we're just a phone call away. Call 310.568.0066

The Show

RADIO WITHOUT BOUNDARIES

Enter the Erotic Theater of the Mind
Abandon All Preconceptions Ye Who Enter Here.

Listen Free or Watch Live Saturday Nights 10:30 pm – Midnight PST

A portion of all proceeds goes to help save the highly endangered wild bonobos from extinction.

Bonoboville

SURROUND YOURSELF WITH GOOD

Bonoboville is a small, beautiful village in cyberspace with a sexy mothership centrally located around a lovely, palm tree-filled garden on Mother Earth in West Los Angeles. Founded by bonobo advocate and sex educator Dr. Susan Block, Pr. Max and a team of fun-loving apes, we follow the "Peace through Pleasure" philosophy inspired by the wild bonobos.

We built Bonoboville to create a different kind of social media site for like-minded adults interested in a positive approach to sexuality, personal revolution and global change. Our mission is to raise millions of dollars for these amazing creatures that roam the Earth with us. The bonobos will become extinct without all of us helping, working and playing together. So what are you waiting for? Join us in Bonoboville!

Go Bonobos with Bonobo Way Gear!

Visit **The Bonobo Way** online

http://thebonoboway.com

MORE LOVE for THE BONOBO WAY

"First things first: this book is really good... something I rarely say these days! *The Bonobo Way* is a very unusual book: whimsical yet serious, easy to read yet thoroughly researched, challenging yet ultimately deeply comforting. Dr. Susan Block is living proof that bonobos aren't just sexy and fun—some of them are damned smart, too."
Christopher Ryan, Ph.D., international best-selling author of *Sex at Dawn*

"Bravo to Dr. Block for paving the way for a hopefully more bonobo future. *The Bonobo Way* is a playful but insightful glimpse into our own sexuality and what we can learn from our closest, perhaps superior, relatives."
Vanessa Woods, *New York Times* best-selling author of *Bonobo Handshake*

"I just finished reading *The Bonobo Way*. I love, love, love it. It is a fresh way to look at sexuality. The writing is light, informative and accurate. I made the mistake of starting to read it on Tuesday and now it's Thursday and I haven't been able to do anything else. I really appreciate how it uses the science without getting too 'scientific.' I also like these '12 steps'--they're certainly a big departure from all others!"
Darrel Ray, Ed.D., author of *Sex and God* and *The God Virus*

"*The Bonobo Way* is marvelous--a happy book for a happy life and a happier world."
Xaviera Hollander, best-selling author of *The Happy Hooker*

"As the 21st century begins, with more violence and war than began what became the ultra-violent 20th century, Dr. Susan Block's latest book is a welcome tonic. She illuminates a primeval, peace-sustaining, complex community--that of the bonobos--with lessons for humans that transcend the sexual. Only humans can, however, protect the bonobos from the threat of extinction they face in their Congo habitat, and Dr. Block demonstrates that such protection is essential as study of, and learning from, the Bonobo Way continues."
Barry A. Fisher, First Amendment/ International Human Rights Attorney & Lead Counsel in numerous U.S. Supreme Court Cases

"*The Bonobo Way* is a delightful, insightful look at how our closest genetic cousins embrace all aspects of sexual pleasure, showing us how masturbation, bisexuality, gender equality, sexual diversity and all other forms of sexual expression are not only natural, but vital to keeping the peace. Like we said back in the sixties, "Make love, not war!"
Betty Dodson, Ph.D., author of the classic best-seller *Sex for One* and feminist icon

"Brilliant book. Enjoyed it thoroughly."
Sherry Rehman, Pakistani Ambassador to the United States (2011-2013)

"Amazing! Super impressive. *The Bonobo Way* is a fun packed, clever, super creative, unique book. What a brilliant concept-- to look to the non-humans for answers to our human problems, and to show us the way to the future. Dr. Block is an eco-sex visionary."
Annie Sprinkle, Ph.D., Eco-Sex Artist

"I love every page of *The Bonobo Way*. The book is a real page turner and turn on. Susan Block's vivid descriptions of bonobo sex and peaceful living through mutual sexual gratification should be mandatory reading for everyone struggling to maintain joy in their lives and live life to its fullest."
Christian Bruyère, award-winning TV producer of *Champions of the Wild*

"Susan Block has brilliantly presented just what we can learn in a way that is first-hand and scientific, yet far from stuffy. Indeed, *The Bonobo Way* is a rambunctious, shrewd, serious, yet humorous look at Bonobo society; comparing its successful egalitarian intimacy with so many standard human missteps. Block also provides extensive info on how we can help protect Bonobo habitat; and, a pleasurable 12 Steps to ways we can adopt a more Bonoboesque cultural understanding and social scheme --- how we Clever Apes can move towards a more peaceful, life-affirming society by following our cousins' lead and switching dance partners from Thanatos and matrimonial lawyers to Eros and Gaia."
Michael Donnelly, *Counterpunch* environmental essayist & Silverback of the Monkey Clan

"I love your writing! It's really cool reading this!"
John Klutke, M.D., Associate Professor, Dept. of OB/GYN, USC

"Dr. Suzy educates, entertains and lectures us humans in a narrative that is personal, easy to read and captivating. Her prose gently asking that we examine our attitudes about sex through her observations such as we encounter early in her book: *"... they were engaging in sex for recreation and interpersonal communication, very much like humans, but without the pretense, hypocrisy and shame."* She goes on to tell us of the amazing Bonobos, of which very few of us likely even know of their existence, let alone of their culture. Her *12 Steps to Releasing Your Inner Bonobo* are a guide to a new understanding of how to enhance our personal sexual life and intimate relationships. Prior to reading her book I was of the opinion that I was fairly knowledgeable about human sexuality. Dr. Suzy's knowledge and ability to teach, as seen in this book, taught me that I was mistaken. I learned – and enjoyed it in the process."
Robert L. McGinley, Ph.D., President of The Lifestyles Organization

"Block provides us with a fascinating take on the world of a unique type of ape, the bonobo, whose lives are full of vigorous, lusty, hedonistic sex, and blissfully free of violence and war. She writes in a style that is light on its feet, funny and engaging, allowing her to give us a considerable amount of valuable science and information in a way that makes it effortless to take in. She also provides us with a great deal of practical insight into how we can bring the bonobos' guilt-free enjoyment of sexual pleasure into our own psyches and relationships. We have a lot to learn from our bonobo brothers and sisters, and this is a great place to discover just what that is."
Jason Martin, author of *Voluptua: a novel*

"The Bonobo Way is a wonderful, witty and engaging read that takes an holistic approach to human sexuality. The book brings together Block's belief in the potential lessons of bonobo harmony and freedom with her broad knowledge of sexuality. She recognizes that sex is much more than how body parts fit together, and her suggestions here for improving one's sex life include practicing meditation, visualization, working with memory, eating well, and living well. Block has created her own Bonoboville based on principles of ethical hedonism, which she shares with her readers and listeners, and her imaginative new work encourages us to do the same... I loved the book and will be recommending it."
Katherine Frank, Ph.D., cultural anthropologist & author of *Plays Well in Groups*

"With her trademark wit, wisdom and saucy irreverence, Dr. Susan Block explores the animal passions of the bonobo apes and finds insights into our own sexuality through an understanding of our most sensual relatives. The bonobos use sex and erotic play as the currency of their realm for everything from social bonding to conflict resolution. By examining these gentle and intelligent creatures, Dr. Suzy lays bare the primate passions common to both our species, and discovers the primal role sex and sensuality play in social cohesion, peaceful coexistence, gender equality and even environmental preservation. Think of it as Jane Goodall After Dark. A fun and fascinating read."
Thomas Quinn, Discovery TV producer & author of *What Do You Do With a Chocolate Jesus?*

"*The Bonobo Way* is a great and timely book that has provided an invaluable survey of the science of the bonobo, the most peaceful, loving primate on this planet in contrast to the human primate, which is the most violent, destructive primate on this planet. Infanticide and warfare are absent in the bonobo culture but prominent in human primate cultures. Sexual pluralism and high maternal-infant/child boding are the keys to preventing individual and cultural violence. Violent human primate cultures are predominately sexual monogamous that control women and are punitive to children. Building on the Bonobo Way, Dr. Susan Block provides a way to human harmony, peace and egalitarian relationships. All those interested in human happiness should read this book.
James W. Prescott, Ph.D., neuropsychologist & author of *Body Pleasure and the Origins of Violence*

"It works!"
Max, Dr. Block's husband

Dr. Susan Block

The Bonobo Way

Printed in Great Britain
by Amazon